WHICH? WAY TO REPAIR AND RESTORE FURNITURE

WHICH? WAY TO REPAIR AND RESTORE FURNITURE

Published by Consumers' Association and Hodder & Stoughton

Which? way to repair and restore furniture is published by Consumers' Association, 14 Buckingham Street, London WC2N 6DS and Hodder & Stoughton, 47 Bedford Square, London WC1B 3DP

Compiled by David Mason
Drawings by Diagram Visual Information Ltd
Cover photograph by Christopher Killip

First edition, revised reprint
© Consumers' Association 1983

ISBN 0 340 25050 X and 0 85202 193 3

Typesetting, printing and binding in Great Britain by Jolly & Barber Ltd, Rugby, Warwickshire

Measurements

The metric system of measuring has been adopted through most of this text. The main exception is in tools which are still described by their Imperial measurements, as in a 12-inch plane or 4-inch cramps.

Many of the measurements, especially in upholstery, are approximations, and the nearest convenient metric equivalent is given: for example: 40mm, for 'an inch-and-a-half'.

The following table gives the main metric equivalents of Imperial measurements. Readers would be advised to make a similar table to display on a workshop wall for reference.

$\frac{1}{4}$-inch	6mm
$\frac{1}{3}$-inch	8mm
$\frac{3}{8}$-inch	10mm
$\frac{1}{2}$-inch	13mm
$\frac{5}{8}$-inch	15mm
$\frac{3}{4}$-inch	20mm
1-inch	25mm
$1\frac{1}{2}$-inches	40mm
2-inches	50mm
$2\frac{1}{2}$-inches	60mm
6-inches	150mm
8-inches	200mm
12-inches	300mm

CONTENTS

INTRODUCTION

This book is aimed mainly at meeting the needs of the home owner who takes an active interest in his (or her) furniture, and is prepared to invest time and effort in preserving that furniture in fine condition.

It is not a manual of instant easy renovations. There may be ways of fixing up temporary repairs for furniture that is starting to fall apart. But this book adopts the working principle that there is a right way of carrying out a repair, and good cabinet-making practice applies to ordinary household furniture as well as to precious antiques. If the owner-restorer is prepared to invest a reasonable amount of time and effort in learning the skills involved, he will quickly find that it takes little more trouble to dismantle a faulty piece of furniture and reassemble it correctly, than it does to carry out a botch job on it. Properly carried out, the repair will be more durable and will give infinitely greater satisfaction than any temporarily effective short-cut.

At the same time the book is not intended as an encyclopedia for the professional craftsman. No book could cover all aspects of the work that a professional restorer is likely to encounter, nor can any replace the knowledge that a craftsman will acquire during a few years of restoring furniture every working day.

To accumulate all the skills the essentials of which are described here, at a comprehensive professional level, a workman would have to serve a five-to-seven year apprenticeship in at least three trades – cabinet making, polishing, and upholstery – and have some training in several subsidiary branches of those trades.

So this book is neither for the quick botcher nor for the professional, but for the home restorer. His needs are quite different from those of the professional, who will see many jobs passing through his workshop which he will have taken on frequently before.

The householder will by contrast normally expect to work on only the few examples of each kind of furniture that he owns. He will encounter a wide range of jobs, but each one perhaps only once or twice in several years. His need is therefore for guidance over a wide area.

He needs the aptitude to carry out several different operations, although he need never be so quick at any of them as the professional who must turn a profit. The home craftsman has on his side the inestimable advantage of time.

Fortunately, providing he has the aptitude, patience, and common sense, almost anybody can master the modest skills of basic carpentry and polishing that are needed for work on tables, chairs and cabinets.

Even for major renovations, involving stripping down, dismantling, reassembly, and complete refinishing, the techniques are only those required for the average range of do-it-yourself household operations.

And in the most advanced area, full antique furniture restoration, the handyman with average manual skills can work confidently, providing he has started modestly.

This book does not recommend that the home furniture restorer with a few hours experience should start dismantling fine quality antiques. But large numbers of people buy or inherit old furniture of a commoner sort which they could not afford to have restored at professional prices. For such owners, the techniques described in this book are exactly those that the professional restorer would employ. The only difference lies in experience, and it is therefore a recommendation throughout the book that any reader coming new to the work should start on simple household furniture on which mistakes will not be critical, or on pieces of junk furniture bought especially for practice. If you handle it, study it, take it apart, mend it, and re-polish it, you will soon build up the necessary confidence and experience to carry out a wide range of repairs.

The furniture may still have no great inherent value, but with what you have learnt you can progress to more expensive furniture, confident that you can take the right steps to achieve the restoration that the article deserves.

Very often the problem today is finding good furniture in need of restoration. For many people, the best source is close to home. Relations, retiring parents, close acquaintances, often own furniture in need of repair, without having the skill or the interest to restore it themselves. If you are lucky you may find something standing neglected in a corner, or hear of old furniture lying in pieces in an attic. Your practised eye will soon tell you the type of wood, the quality of the original workmanship, the finish it will have when restored.

The other main sources of furniture ripe for restoration are the auction room and the junk shop.

In the auction room, you will have one great advantage over the dozens of local antique dealers who will be bidding in competition with you. They know that when they have bought the piece, they will have to pay a restorer to bring it to showroom condition, and add a substantial mark-up, to make the profit that will give them their living.

You have none of these problems. Once you have paid for the piece, you can restore it in your own time, at a cost in materials that is almost negligible. You can enjoy owning an article of furniture that might have cost you twice as much in a shop, and, as a bonus, can be certain of the quality of the restoration.

Junk shops are less predictable. In fact many of them have disappeared, to re-emerge as antique shops with some pretensions to quality. The time when you could walk in and pick up a fine if delapidated chair or table for a few shillings are gone. Too many people are active in the antique and second-hand furniture trades to leave quality goods lying around with a low price mark waiting for the informed amateur to recognise their potential and scoop them up.

You may be lucky. At least some knowledge of restoration will mean that you are well informed, and able to form a reliable opinion about the faults, and the type and extent of restoration a piece needs.

In buying furniture knowledge is your most valuable asset, and the best way to acquire it is through your own hands.

Working on furniture, handling it, taking it apart, rebuilding it, and refinishing it, will give you knowledge that you could never glean from books or museums.

But knowledge is not achieved overnight. Furniture restoration needs a steady, painstaking approach, and you will absorb many an evening before a worthwhile job is completed. Almost inevitably, what starts out as an attempt to rescue a deteriorating article becomes, in the search for structural soundness and quality of finish, an absorbing and time-consuming occupation.

And when you have learned something about the woodworking side of furniture restoration, you will have to learn an entirely new set of skills, in upholstery. Most professionals concentrate on one or the other, but the householder will have to master both.

If you work on one without the other, you will end up with either a set of chairs on which the wood looks perfect, but the padding a disgrace. Or you may find you have a set of beautifully upholstered seats, on which the legs and other show-wood parts let down your achievements.

Fortunately upholstery, at least in the early stages, is not at all difficult, and it is possible for the beginner, working on simple seats, to carry out complete operations to a high standard without needing any special skills or aptitude.

The middle stages of upholstery, involving springing and sewing hard edges, appear to be intricate and complicated. In fact they also involve no special skills. In this area, unlike cabinet work, the beginner can do no harm, as the results of his work are hidden inside the finished chair. The only requirement for successful upholstery is to gather the materials and tools together and start work, following the steps described in this book one by one. The manual skills consist mainly of knocking in nails, tying knots, and basic sewing with large needles.

In the advanced stages of upholstery complications may arise, but by that time you should have built up enough expertise to deal with them, and be able to take pleasure in choosing from the vast range of materials, styles, and trim that are available to design your own finishes.

But upholstery also is time-consuming, and needs a steady build-up of experience. You should not expect to be building deep-buttoned Chesterfields after a few evenings' practice.

People work at different paces, of course, but as a rough guide allow some ten hours of work to complete a drop-in seat, two or three times as long to upholster a stuffed-over seat, and the equivalent of a good week of full-time work to build a small armchair.

When you start work yourself you will begin to appreciate why professional upholstery is so expensive.

In the long run, the great reward of this activity is a home full of well kept furniture. Clean furniture, looking much as it did when it left its maker's workshop, but matured by time, is infinitely more attractive than a dark dirty piece in which years of grime conceal the grain and character of the wood. And a polish lovingly and skilfully applied by hand has infinitely more appeal than a manufacturer's sprayed-on cellulose finish, or the quick brush over with button polish that some antique dealers apply to turn a quick profit. And a well stuffed, well trimmed armchair, in fresh, clean fabric, is smarter to look at and more pleasant to use than a worn, grimy seat with its stuffing hanging out.

Beyond that, there is the further satisfaction of knowing that you have produced and maintained these beautiful items of furniture through your own effort and skill, without having to rely on the help of professionals.

The pride that comes from personal achievement of that kind, from being independent of other people's skills, is a reward that cannot be measured in money.

1. STARTING

The first problem in almost all furniture repair is often the most difficult: identifying the piece, and assessing what needs to be done.

Before you begin work, you will have to answer a whole series of questions about what attention the piece of furniture needs. You have to be able to tell what has gone wrong with it. You must judge how far it needs to be dismantled. You have to determine how much of the piece needs replacing, and how much you can preserve. If you do too much work you will have carried out not a restoration but a replacement; too little, and the faults you are trying to correct will show up again when the furniture has been in use for a short time.

If you are working on antique furniture, you have to be capable of restoring the piece in sympathy with the style and spirit of the original. If it is modern furniture – and some almost new pieces can be dramatically improved by the methods described in this book – you must be able to assess the details of its construction and finish, and determine which factory techniques could be improved by your own hand-work.

Many of these questions can only be answered in the light of experience and practice. There are no ground rules.

The only reliable way to gain the kind of familiarity with furniture that gives confidence in assessing what work it needs, and in carrying out the restoration, is to handle furniture yourself. Get to know your pieces of furniture, both as individuals and as types.

If you watch how a craftsman restorer approaches a job, you will find that he first spends several minutes thoughtfully examining the piece. If you do the same, you will come to valuable conclusions that allow you to plan and complete a restoration effectively.

Feel the piece. Press your hands on it and move it about to test for firmness. Move the legs to see if the joints are sound. Run the drawers in and out to test for fit. If the piece is small, turn it over to look underneath. What sort of condition is it in? Can you see any woodworm holes? Are there signs of previous restoration? If

so, how neatly was it done? If the furniture is large, kneel or lie down to look under it. If it is heavy and bulky, lean it back against a wall, protected by a duster or pad. Take out the drawers, turn them over and make the same kind of investigation. Look inside the drawer recesses. If the runners are worn, will you have to replace them? Or can you just add a small piece of new wood?

This kind of investigation will give you a clear idea of the true condition of the piece, something often disguised by surface appearances. A few simple operations will enable you to assess a job. In addition, your understanding of all furniture will grow rapidly.

Your knowledge of how furniture is made, gained from dismantling, reassembling, and refinishing your first few pieces, will serve as an increasingly reliable guide in assessing the value of other pieces. And your experience in doing simple restoration work will not only give you the confidence to carry out more complex restoration, but will also improve your judgement when buying further pieces. If you are interested in going to the lengths of repairing and restoring your own furniture, you will soon find that your interest extends to collecting better, more attractive, and no doubt more valuable pieces.

There is no more reliable way to become a knowledgeable and astute collector of antiques than through developing a knowledge of furniture by carrying out your own repairs with your own hands.

There are no special difficulties. Anybody who can achieve average competence with tools can repair furniture. Manual skill is important, but even more vital is the right attitude. This kind of work requires monumental patience. If you cannot control your impetuosity, or cannot bear the frustration of seeing a job stretch into the indefinite future, it would be wise not to embark on furniture restoration. Otherwise, it is simply a question of deciding where to start.

You will not choose a fine quality antique to begin learning about furniture repair: much fine furniture has, alas, been ruined by an excess of ambition over ability.

The right place to start is on an ordinary piece of household furniture. Follow through the basic processes involved in repairing an ordinary chair, table, or chest of drawers, and you will soon know whether you have the patience and ability to work on more valued and valuable possessions.

You will also discover that no two jobs are alike. No book can specify exactly how to repair any individual piece of furniture. Materials, construction and finish are peculiar to each item, and much of the satisfaction of restoration work lies in making decisions about how to deal with each case, and in knowing, from the appearance and serviceability of the restored article, that your decisions were right. As you begin to work on unusual and complicated furniture, you will find you have to devise your own techniques for restoration and repair.

But before you reach that stage, there are a number of typical processes to master. This book describes them. In each of the two main aspects of furniture work – woodwork repairs, and upholstery – there are straightforward jobs that need doing in almost every home.

We recommend that anybody starting furniture restoration first carries out these simple projects, which will give them the confidence to move easily to the next stage. Often, each new process is only a small step in advance of what you have done before; sometimes, especially in upholstery, the work is the same, and the scale alone makes it more complicated. Even advanced work that would be formidable for a beginner appears simple if you have worked up to it by stages. Set yourself an informal 'course' on the lines which this book follows, and you will rapidly accumulate skill and knowledge.

The rewards of furniture restoration are enormous. In financial terms you will save, with a few evenings of work, the hundreds of pounds you would have to pay to a professional restorer or upholsterer. Often you can carry out work which would be too expensive to contemplate giving to a professional, and thereby save furniture you might otherwise have to scrap.

Once you have mastered the techniques of repairing the furniture, there is no reason why you should not go on confidently to make your own. The cost of quality hand-made furniture puts it out of reach of all but the wealthy, while the cost of materials is, by comparison, modest. If you can construct your own frames, or buy frames and upholster them yourself, you can acquire furniture to your own specifications which would be beyond your means if bought through orthodox retail outlets.

But the greatest rewards are the most intangible. A home full of well kept furniture is a beautiful, relaxing, refreshing environment. Clean furniture, looking much as it did when it left its maker's workshop, but with the additional beauty that comes with years of maturing in considerate hands, is infinitely more attractive than dark dirty pieces in which years of grime conceal the grain and character of the wood. And a polish lovingly and skilfully applied by hand has infinitely more attraction than a manufacturer's sprayed-on cellulose finish or the quick brush over with button polish that some antique dealers apply to turn a quick profit.

Beyond that, there is the satisfaction of knowing that you have produced and maintained beautiful furniture through your own effort and skill, without having to rely on the help of professionals.

The pride that comes from personal achievement of that kind, from being independent of other people's skills, is a reward that cannot be measured in money.

TOOLS

Furniture restorers need few special tools. Some expert restorers prefer to work with smaller, lighter tools than are used in the average run of carpentry work, but ordinary household tools, if you already have them, are perfectly adequate for virtually all the jobs you are likely to encounter.

However, if you are buying new tools, you should consider your buying policy carefully. Tools are expensive, but providing you are going to use them on a regular basis over a fairly long period, they represent an investment. People starting furniture restoration are inclined to make the mistake of buying too many tools, and spending too much money, then find that they rarely need most of them. The thing not to do is go out and buy a big comprehensive tool chest. Inevitably, some of the tools in it are not quite what the restorer really wants – sometimes more expensive than he needs, and sometimes not good enough for the job.

The best policy is to start with the smallest possible number of tools but of the highest quality you can afford. Add a new tool to your collection when you need it, again buying the best you can afford. Before long you will find you have a comprehensive collection; the satisfaction of building up a tool kit sometimes seems to match the satisfaction of building the furniture itself.

Details of some essential tools are given in this book as their applications arise, but in general the tools most restorers would use are as follows:

Mallet. The cabinet maker's model is smaller than the standard carpentry model, but either will do. Use it with softwood pads, in dismantling and reassembling.

Cramps. Essential for control of any work. Wedges and tourniquets can provide a substitute (see page 28) but the pleasure you get from working with correct cramps will prove that there are no real substitutes. Buy two sash cramps at least 36-inches long (you can make your own bars, as described on page 27, and two G-cramps, at least 4-inch size.

Screwdrivers. Cabinet maker's screwdrivers differ from engineer's in having no bevelled or wedge-shaped end. They are square ended and rather thick, and are produced in various sizes. The aim is to get maximum torque with the least chance of slipping, which can seriously damage surrounding wood. The better British toolmakers supply screwdrivers with boxwood and beechwood handles, which seem more appropriate for furniture work than plastic-handled screwdrivers, and are a delight to use.

Start collecting them, so that you can work with one which fits exactly the screw you are turning. That produces the best torque, and avoids stripping the metal from the screw. A medium (say 12-inch) screwdriver is a good start, followed by smaller and larger versions as you need and can afford them.

Cruciform head screwdrivers are not yet generally accepted in quality cabinet work.

Saws. You will be able to make most of the straight cuts in restoration work with a tenon saw. Again, a smaller than average version will be more suitable for this kind of work. If you want to extend your range, a dovetail saw is an excellent supplement, and makes a finer cut.

A panel saw is used for rough cuts, and can be used for cutting along planks, though restorers normally buy wood cut roughly to size. Amateur restorers have no need of the full range of saws a professional carpenter or cabinet maker would carry.

Planes. Absolutely vital. Today's planes are almost universally of steel, and will give greater accuracy than old wooden planes, however desirable the latter may look. A No. 4 plane will serve most needs. In strong hands a larger plane will do all the same jobs, and can be steadier because of the extra weight and length. However it is more tiring to use.

Small planes are useful for working with one hand in awkward locations on assembled furniture. The block plane is an example. Buy it when you need it.

Good tool shops also sell a variety of elaborate planes for highly sophisticated work – plough planes, rebating planes, planes to cut mouldings. Generally, they are more useful in making new furniture from scratch than in restoration work. But if you are an enthusiast, you will soon find applications for them, and they make ideal presents. Study the catalogue to decide exactly which version you would find suitable.

Spokeshave. Closely related to the plane, it is invaluable for smoothing wood on curves.

Try Square. Will be vital before you have done much

restoration work. Bigger ones give greater accuracy, but are more difficult to handle. Buy the best quality from a reliable manufacturer.

Mortice gauge. Gauges have one scribing point: mortices gauges have two, but can be used perfectly easily with only one. The largest version of this handsome brass-and-wood tool produces the best work.

Rulers. A flexible steel ruler is useful in hundreds of applications, but do not use it for closely accurate cabinet work. It is floppy and tricky to handle. Instead use either a wooden rule (folding varieties are useful) or a 12-inch steel rule. This also provides an accurate and firm guide edge for making cuts.

Knives. Since surgeon's scalpels with disposable blades became generally available, they have found innumerable uses in art studios, hobby work, and a great deal of furniture work. They are extremely sharp but flexible. You will find them useful.

Also have available a 'craft' knife. It has a more sturdy handle and a stiffer blade. A disposable blade variety like the Stanley knife is advisable.

Hammers. Rarely used in fine furniture work. Its main use is for hammering veneer pins, and for this a lightweight hammer is best.

Other tools include pliers and pincers, to be bought as needed, a fret-saw for some veneer work, a drill and a brace, both with bits of various sizes. A screwdriver-shaped bit is also useful, used in a brace for moving stubborn screws. Various bradawls, rasps and files may prove handy for particular jobs.

Power tools. Do not neglect them. They can save a great deal of work. The main ones are a power drill, which in inexperienced hands can give a more accurate hole than a hand drill, and various types of power saw. A circular saw, used by hand or on a bench, can make short work of long cuts. The more modern development, which some carpenters are finding indispensable, is the hand-held jig-saw. A supply of fresh sharp blades is relatively inexpensive, and they are made in various grades to cope with different kinds of work. Bench jig-saws and band-saws give excellent results, but are for the woodwork enthusiast who is seriously interested in building up his workshop facilities.

Lathes also come into this category. If you are at the level where you want to contemplate using a lathe, you will know enough about woodworking generally to be able to choose and use the one you want.

Chisels. Rather than spend extravagantly on elaborate power tools, most amateurs would benefit by stocking their workshops with a good range of chisels, possibly the woodworker's and restorer's most important tools. A large proportion of restoration work consists of cutting away wood, replacing it, then paring that wood down to blend with other surfaces. Much of the rest consists of wood carving. Every article of furniture includes some joints, and most of them need to be cut or at least cleaned with a chisel.

As the text shows, there are different kinds of chisels for different jobs, and different widths of chisel within each different type. You can get away with a limited number of chisels, but work is far easier if you can pick up the right one for the job in hand. This is one place where buying individual items may not pay, and it can be good policy to buy them in boxed sets.

However, the skill with which you use them is far more important than the type of chisel you buy. Given a choice, most restorers would opt for boxwood-handled chisels. As with screwdrivers, wood seems to come more comfortably to hand when you are working on fine and cherished articles of furniture. The only drawback is that when you are using the chisel in any application that requires it to be struck, you will have to use a mallet. On a black or yellow 'plastic' handle you can use a hammer without damaging the chisel handle.

The main chisels used today for cutting joints are bevel-edged chisels. In amateur hands, these blades hold a sharp corner more easily than the older square ended type. Quarter-inch, half-inch, and one-inch are probably the least you can get away with if you are intending to do serious restoration work of any kind.

On many joints a sash mortice-chisel is useful. Its blade is thicker from front-to-back than from side-to-side. This gives it greater rigidity and strength for cutting across the grain in mortices. Again a small collection will prove invaluable.

Looking after most tools is a matter of common sense. They must be kept clean, and wiped over occasionally with a lightly oiled rag to keep them free of rust. And they should be kept in places where they will neither be damaged nor cause damage.

Chisels, screwdrivers, hammers, and other small tools should be kept in racks. The simplest rack is a shelf with holes drilled into it of the appropriate size, and channels cut from the edge to the hole so that you can slip the tool through. It is surprising how little space tools take up if stacked in this way.

Larger tools like planes should be laid carefully aside, on their sides, to protect the blade.

SHARPENING CHISELS

Chisels require more elaborate attention. You cannot work successfully with a chisel unless it has a super-sharp edge. Paring wood soon dulls that edge, especially if you subject the chisel to the shock of hitting it with a mallet. On average woods, an hour of working will be enough to destroy an edge. So you must be capable of sharpening it yourself. It is simply no use having to take it to a hardwear shop or ironmonger each time you need to hone up the edge. The time wasted through being unable to work when you want to, let alone the time and money spent in getting this simple job done, make it worthwhile learning to sharpen your own chisels. It is easy, but if you cannot do it freehand, then a chisel-honing guide can be a great help, although good craftsmen tend to look down on their use.

Make a habit of sharpening the tool before you start to use it, rather than waiting until you find it will not do the job you are asking of it.

To sharpen a chisel, you will need at least one oilstone, preferably two, a medium grade and a fine grade. If you can afford a coarse grinding stone also, it can be useful, but grinding the chisel is a job that needs to be done only rarely, and you could reasonably leave that to a professional. Most woodworkers make up small boxes to hold their oil stones. The box keeps the bench and stone tidy, and with the top on, stops the surface accumulating dust and grit.

You will also need a small can of household oil.

First secure the medium grade oilstone on your bench and squirt it liberally with oil. Lay the chisel on it, pointing away from you, with its bevel edge down. Raise and lower the chisel handle until you can feel the bevel lying flat on the stone. If you rock it slightly you should feel a soft clunk as one end of the bevel then the other strikes the stone in turn.

When you can feel it lying flat, press the fingers of your left hand down to hold the bevel in that position, and hold the chisel in your right hand. (Vice versa for left-handed people.) Holding your right hand palm up with the handle cradled in it may help if you are not fully experienced.

Now rock your body back and forth gently, so that your elbows start to swing. The chisel will start to move forwards and back on the oilstone, and all the time your left hand will be holding the bevel flat against the stone.

Do this for a few seconds, then lift the chisel carefully off the stone. Wipe off the oil, and check that you have smoothed out the bevel edge. If you have had reason to regrind your chisel, this bevel should be at 30 degrees to the flat face of the chisel [**1.1**].

Now look at the chisel again. You will see that right at the end there is another small bevel, probably about 2 mm wide. This will give you the sharp edge. It should be at 45 degrees to the face of the chisel.

To hone this edge, put the chisel back on the stone, and feel again for the bevel you have just made. When you can feel it flat on the stone, raise your right hand by one inch. This will lift the chisel on to the smaller bevel edge. Now swing your elbows again. This time it is more

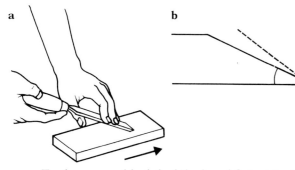

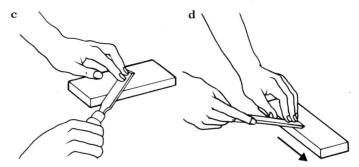

1.1a To sharpen a chisel, feel the bevel flat against the oiled stone, then move it steadily backwards and forwards.
b. The chisel should be ground and honed to give two angles, at 30 degrees and 45 degrees to the face.

c. Turn the chisel over, lower the face on to the stone, and rub it lightly to remove the burr.
d. Inexperienced workers might find it easier to sharpen the chisel with side-to-side movements along the stone.

difficult. The bevel is not long enough to feel, and you will have to keep it flat simply by coordinating your body movements to keep the chisel moving in the same attitude. Work at it until you can eradicate any tendency to roll the chisel on its edge, or to roll the chisel from side-to-side. Either will destroy the edge altogether.

Do this firmly and methodically for a dozen strokes, then take the chisel carefully from the stone, and wipe off the oil. You should have two smooth and shining bevels.

Now feel the edge with your thumb, both sides. The side that was uppermost as you worked will have a distinctly rough feel to it. This is the burr, caused by the edge being turned over in your sharpening action. To remove it, go back to the oilstone. Rest the flat face of the blade on one edge of the stone, then gently raise the handle, and lower the blade, until the flat face comes into full contact with the face of the stone. Now draw the chisel towards you. Repeat this. Do not jab the chisel into the stone, or you will wreck your new edge. Just lay it down gently, and draw it back. This will be enough to take off the burr, or at least loosen it, and you can carefully wipe away the fragments of metal on your palm. Some workers 'strop' the honed edge on the heel of their hand, to remove the remnants of the burr. It is

not a practice to be recommended to the inexperienced.

Now if you feel the edge you should be quite impressed. It will feel smooth and sharp, and you will be confident that you could work the toughest woods with it without the slightest strain.

But there is one more job to do. Take out your fine stone, squirt oil on to it, and go over the whole process again. Then you will have a really hard, compacted, firm sharp edge on the chisel.

Look after that edge. Do not leave the chisel lying on the bench. Not only is it capable of cutting you, but if you catch it with another metal tool you will knock teeth out of it and will have to get the chisel re-ground.

If you can perfect that simple skill, you will add a new dimension to your pleasure in furniture restoring, and you will produce work of a consistently higher standard than you can ever achieve with badly cared-for tools.

The most difficult part of sharpening is keeping the chisel at the same angle throughout. Keep trying, because it is the correct way to do it, but if you cannot achieve that, try turning the chisel through 90 degrees. You may find it easier to keep the angle consistent if you push it sideways and back, rather than back and forth along its length.

When the edge on the blade of your plane becomes

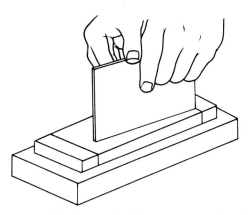

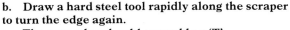

1.2a After 'stropping' the previous edge down, square off the cabinet scraper edge on a coarse stone, with forward and back movements.

b. Draw a hard steel tool rapidly along the scraper to turn the edge again.

c. The new edge should resemble a 'T'.

dull, sharpen it in the same way. You will have to use a perfectly flat oilstone for this. So always, when sharpening a chisel, vary the area on which you work. Otherwise you will cut a pronounced valley down the middle of the stone, and it will be useless for honing the wide blade of a plane.

If you are buying a new plane, consider one with disposable blades. Purists and traditionalists often frown on such developments, but many woodworkers who have tried them are won over. The supply of blades is not expensive, unless you are doing vast amounts of planing, and you will start each blade with a perfectly formed and perfectly sharpened edge. Their main appeal lies with the mobile carpenter, who does not have to worry about a blade going dull during a day's work and can save himself having to carry the weight of a spare plane or stone. But amateurs, even when working in the same workshop all the time, may still consider disposable blades a welcome time-saver.

There is one more tool that will need your attention. The cabinet-maker's scraper is a small rectangle of silver steel used for taking off unwanted old finishes, or very thin shavings from surface wood. Its use is explained in Chapter 3.

Working with it dulls the edge, and you will have to put the edge back on to restore it to effective working.

The process is almost opposite to honing a chisel. The edge on a scraper is bent over to form a kind of T-shape [**1.2c**], which you use as a hook. If you have bought a scraper new, used it, and found that it no longer works quite as well as it did, then clearly the hook has become worn down. Re-sharpening it is a three-stage process.

First lay the scraper on the bench with its edge near to, but not over, the edge of the bench. Press down on it with the knuckles of your left hand (if you are right handed) to hold the scraper firmly in place. You will now need some convenient round steel tool. The handle of a pair of pincers might do. A strong screwdriver blade is better. With this strong steel shaft, 'strop' the edge of the scraper back and forth a few times. You will completely flatten out the hook of the 'T'. Turn the scraper over and strop the other side, then turn the scraper round and strop both opposite edges, to give you four scraping surfaces altogether.

Now take the scraper to the oilstone, hold it firmly upright, and work it backwards and forwards a few times [**1.2a**]. This will flatten out any irregularities, and will also remove the flimsy part of the stropped-over edges, giving good firm corners to the hooks you are about to form.

Clamp the scraper in your vice, and stand at one end of it. Take up the hardened steel edge you used for stropping, and hold it at the far corner of the scraper, precisely horizontally and at right angles to the scraper. Hold it firmly against the scraper's edge, and draw it briskly towards you. It will set the scraper vibrating and ringing. Repeat three or four times. Then turn the scraper over and do the same to the other edge. [**1.2b**].

Now feel the scraper with your thumb and forefinger. On both sides of its two long edges you should be able to feel a distinct hook, strong enough to catch your skin slightly as you pull your fingers across it. It will be perfect for working on the surface of a piece of furniture without removing the quantities of wood that a plane removes, and without leaving the scratch marks that some glasspaper leaves.

2. STRUCTURAL REPAIRS

CHAIR REPAIRS

All householders know that the most vulnerable points in a chair are the joints where the side rails meet the back post. Every time a person leans back in the chair these two joints come under stress. Inconsiderate people often find it relaxing to lean back so far that they lift the front legs off the floor. The chair, and their own body, then balance on the back legs alone, and the load on these joints can amount to hundreds of pounds. Before long the glue breaks down and the joint starts to work loose. The chair is especially vulnerable if there are no bottom stretchers to help hold the frame square. Repairing these joints in an ordinary kitchen or dining chair is an excellent place to start furniture renovation.

Go round and examine all your chairs closely. Wobble the legs and back of each one. Unless you are extremely lucky, you will soon find one that is loose. If it creaks noisily, or if you can feel or see any 'play' in the joint, it needs repairing.

By the time you have completed this simple repair, you will know a great deal about several aspects of furniture restoration.

In some chairs it may be possible to pull the joint slightly apart, work glue into the gaps you have opened, then cramp up the chair until the glue sets. But that is an unrewarding short cut. It is better to do the job properly, and that means dismantling the chair, at least partially, cleaning away the old glue and re-gluing the chair correctly.

DISMANTLING A CHAIR

How far you need to dismantle any piece of furniture is a matter of judgement. With chairs, it is generally advisable to dismantle completely and put the chair in good order throughout, rather than make a partial repair and find you have to return to the piece because you overlooked a fault that had already begun to develop.

The first step is to mark the parts clearly so that you can reassemble the chair without difficulty.

Chair parts are rarely uniform. Even corresponding rails on opposite sides of the chair can be cut to slightly different sizes, and trying to reassemble the chair from a pile of unmarked parts can be very frustrating.

Mark each piece clearly but inconspicuously. You may later have to wash, sand down, or even plane away some wood, so pencil marks alone are not reliable. Cabinet-makers would be horrified to see a ball-point pen used on furniture, but it makes a clear and almost indelible mark. Best of all is to make a firm scratch in the wood with a sharp pointed tool, or even cut a groove with a chisel, then fill in the mark with a pencil. Mark the underside of each member, so that your marks will be out of sight on the reassembled piece. Mark all corner blocks, side rails, front rails – everything that would lead to confusion if you could not identify it.

You can work out your own marking system. Some workers use notches – one notch on all the pieces that fit together at one corner, two notches at another corner, and so on. Others inscribe letters on the wood, *rhf* for right-hand-front, for example. You will soon be able to see how far you need to take your identification, but in the early stages, be generous with marks.

At the same time, you will find a notebook useful. You can record in it all kinds of information: when you carried out the repair; how long it took; the cost; what work you did. Some people dislike such paperwork, but a notebook containing at least a sketch of the piece and a note of how you marked it can prove invaluable when you come to reassembly.

When you have marked the chair remove all the corner blocks. They may come free as you take out the screws. If so, clean them up by washing off the old glue with hot water. Put the blocks aside to dry naturally. If they remain glued in place, wait until you are ready to free the joint itself, then loosen the blocks at the same time by one of the methods described below.

Broadly, two kinds of joints are used in chairs. Good quality chairs generally have mortice-and-tenon joints. Less well constructed chairs, and many machine-made

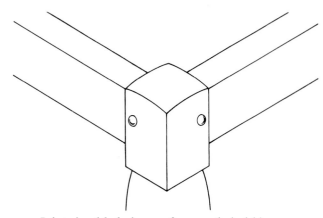

2.1 Joints in old chairs are frequently held by a peg through the mortice-and-tenon.

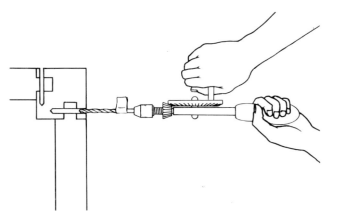

2.2 Tape the drill bit to clear the hole in the tenon, and drill out the centre of the peg.

modern chairs, have dowel joints, with either two or three dowels for each joint.

The mortice-and-tenon, especially in early chairs, may also be held by a peg let in through the tail of the tenon and glued in place [**2.1**].

REMOVING PEGS

If there are any pegs remove them from all loose joints and any other joints you plan to dismantle. If there is any suspicion that the joint is being held firm by the peg itself, rather than by the structural strength of the joint, remove it.

First take a sharp chisel and pare off the head flush with the surrounding wood. Now, with a small bit, say 1/8inch or 3 mm, drill a pilot-hole down into the peg. Next take a larger bit, smaller in diameter than the peg itself, but large enough to remove most of the peg without damaging the surrounding wood, and drill down into the peg.

If you are unsure of how far down to drill, hold the drill bit against the outside of the joint, with the end level with the far side of the member bearing the tenon. Wrap a short length of sticky tape (masking tape is best) round

the bit, at the surface of the mortice-bearing member. Drill down into the peg until the tape touches the wood. You can then be certain that you have cleared the tenon [**2.2**].

Next you will need a sharp narrow-ended tool. You may have to make it yourself – all craftsmen gradually develop a range of tools which they have designed and made themselves for specific unusual jobs. This one can be simply a small screwdriver, or a bradawl, with the end ground down to form a sharp chisel. Carefully cut away the sleeve of wood which remains on the inside of the hole after drilling. This process will clear the remnants of the old peg out of the hole, leaving the surrounding wood intact.

FREEING THE JOINT

It should now be possible to draw the tenon cleanly out of the mortice. But joints are rarely entirely clean, and swelling and shrinkage, combined with fragments of old dried glue, help to jam them.

To free a jammed joint, hold a block of softwood against the mortice-bearing part as close to the joint as possible, and tap it sharply with a hammer [**2.3**]. Do not

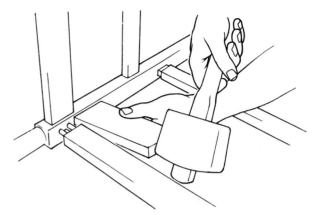

2.3 Hold a softwood block against the furniture and tap it gently with a mallet to aid dismantling.

be tempted to insert a chisel or screwdriver into the gap between the shoulder of the tenon and the other part. You will only damage the wood. Also avoid putting any 'bending' stress on the tenon. Work on both sides of the joint, tapping at each side alternately. And if you are dismantling the chair, work on the right and left sides alternately, so that the rails come out in parallel.

If sharp tapping still does not free the joints, it probably means that fragments of dried glue have wedged it firmly in place. If the original cabinet maker, and any previous restorers, have been kind to you, the furniture will be glued with scotch glue. You can free this easily by applying moist heat. It may be possible to soak a front corner joint for a few minutes in a bowl of hot water. To loosen joints in the chair back, and other inaccessible places, hold the joint in the steam from the spout of a kettle. Alternatively wrap a hot damp pad round the joint for a few minutes.

With any of these methods, providing old-fashioned woodworking glue was used, the glue should quickly soften and the joint come free. If it was assembled with pvc or other water-resistant glue, freeing it will be far more difficult. Persevere. Eventually you will soften the glue, even if you have to soak the joint in hot water for several days.

With the chair in pieces, clean all the joints ready for reassembly. First remove every spot of old glue. Chip off any remaining large pieces with a chisel, then immerse the joint in a bowl of hot water, or hold it under a running hot tap, until the glue softens enough for you to wipe it away with a rag.

Washing the parts should also clean off all the dust that has crept into the mortice, and any grime that has accumulated in the corners. If washing does not clean the wood completely, set to work with a stiff brush. If dirt still remains, scrape it away with a sharp knife or chisel.

Treat both the mortice and tenon, and the male and female parts of a dowel joint, to the same scrupulous cleaning process, then let all the wood dry out naturally.

Now there are several alternative courses to follow.

If you are lucky, and have chosen to work on a chair where the only problem was loose joints, you can begin reassembly at once. But it is more likely that the dismantling operation will have shown up several other faults which you will have to correct before you can reassemble the chair. Legs may have split under the pressure of dowels. Part of the tenon may have split away so that you cannot achieve a firm joint without inserting new wood. The back rail, or the back upright, may be split, in which case you will have to carry out serious structural repairs before you can contemplate putting the chair together again. Finding faults like this is an almost invariable consequence of the dismantling operation, but you will soon learn to contain your frustration, live with the chair in pieces for longer than you expected, and accept the challenge of a series of operations when you thought you would only have to carry out one.

Then there is the question of when to clean the wood, or strip off the chair for re-finishing – before or after you reassemble it. The order in which you tackle these jobs is not critical, but you may find it more convenient to strip the old finish off each member on its own, rather than work on the reassembled chair when some parts will be difficult to get at.

But let us assume that you have been lucky in your choice of chair and that you do not need to carry out any structural improvements or strip it while it is in pieces. You can go ahead with the reassembly immediately and enjoy the satisfaction of a completed job.

GLUE

Two main types of glue are available to the furniture restorer – scotch glue, the traditional woodworking adhesive, and white resin pva glue (Evostick Resin W is probably the most widely available).

Scotch glue is becoming increasingly difficult to find. Old-established ironmongers generally keep a stock, and it is worth locating a supplier. Buy half a kilogram, and it should last you for years of furniture restoration.

Pva glue comes in plastic bottles, and is available through all d-i-y shops. Buy the small bottle. It has a convenient pouring spout, and you will waste less through drying out.

Each type of glue has its advantages and disadvantages.

Some conscientious restorers – the purists – would never dream of using anything but scotch glue. Their main concern is future restorers, who will have a far easier time dismantling the work if scotch glue has been used. This can also be a great advantage to the beginner. If the assembly turns out to be wrong – and some of your efforts almost certainly will – you can dismantle the chair and start again.

The problem with scotch glue is that it sets by cooling. It is applied hot, and you must have the joint assembled quickly – within seconds rather than minutes – so that the joint is held firm and in the right place as the glue begins to cool. By the time the glue has cooled to room temperature, it has set, and in a few days it will be rock-hard. Working in a warm workshop, and closing all doors and windows to eliminate draughts, will help to slow down the setting rate.

Pva glue sets far more slowly. It needs no preparation, and you apply it straight from the container. It begins to bite within a couple of hours, and sets hard within about twelve. This gives you time to go about your assembly with greater care and far less risk of going wrong through hurrying. On the other hand, since the glue is water-resistant, you will face a long and tedious process of applying damp heat to soften it once it has set hard.

Have both sorts of glue available. Pva resin glue has its place, where you are letting in new wood and no future restorer is ever likely to want to take it out again, for example. Scotch glue, on the other hand, although it needs careful preparation, is more interesting to use. If you can learn to work quickly enough to get the assembly right, it is more rewarding, and certainly safer, for the amateur.

PREPARING SCOTCH GLUE

To prepare scotch glue, you will need a double heating system. Purpose-made glue-pots are available. They consist of an outer container in which you boil water, and an inner container in which the glue heats and softens. While professionals always use them, they get messy, and cleaning them can be unpleasant.

A perfectly adequate alternative for amateurs is a small saucepan in which to boil water, with a jam-jar or tin-can inside to hold the glue. Put a half-inch layer of glue pearls in the bottom of the jar, and add water to cover the pearls by another half-inch. Put plenty of water in the outer container or saucepan, and heat it slowly. Never put the cold jam jar into hot water, or add cold water round the hot jam jar, or it will crack.

Have ready what the modern marketing men call an 'applicator': a stubby brush is best. Your ironmonger may stock a special glue-brush, or you can cut down an old half-inch paint brush providing you clean it well.

The glue is ready for use when it runs easily off the brush. If it is too thick, slowly add boiling water. If it is too thin, add more glue. When your glue-pot becomes messy, throw away the jam-jar and start again. Glue sets increasingly quickly as it is repeatedly re-heated, so it is wise to work with small quantities and discard it from time to time.

When the glue is hot and runny, bring the workpiece and glue-pot close together. A gas ring in your workshop is ideal, so that you can keep the glue hot on the ring as you work. Otherwise, take the entire glue-pot, double boiler or saucepan, to the work. The hot water will help to keep the glue warm.

Wherever possible, take up the work and hold it over the glue-pot for gluing, so that excess glue runs back into the pot, not over the workshop floor or the work itself. If you are gluing a length of wood, run the wood along the top of the pot, holding the glue-brush steady. If you are gluing a joint, just brush a thin layer over it. Do not worry about gluing inside mortices. The glue will find its way under pressure to all the parts that need it, and the excess glue will ooze out of the joint.

CRAMPS

All major woodworking operations involve cramping up the work at some stage, and if you are going to take furniture restoration seriously, a good set of cramps is essential.

To cramp up a chair you will need two sash-cramps. They are available in various lengths; one pair of 36 inch cramps is enough for most jobs.

It is possible to save money by buying only the sash-cramp heads. You can then cut a piece of wood for each pair, the right width and thickness to fit through the heads. The head with the tightening handle fits on one end, and you can drill holes at 2-inch intervals along the length of the wood to accommodate the peg on the moveable head.

If you subsequently encounter a job for which your cramps are too short, you can cut more wood to make new cramps to the right length.

You will also need several softwood pads, to protect the workpiece from the metal faces of the cramps. Never cramp up the work without this protection: the metal will press ugly marks into the hardest of woods.

Since it is difficult to handle two cramps, the workpiece and four loose pads at the same time, wise craftsmen fit pads permanently on to the faces of their metal cramps. Soft pads cut from cork tiles, and glued to the faces of the wooden pads, help to put the kindest possible surface in contact with the workpiece.

Eventually you will also need at least one pair of G-cramps. Four-inch cramps are adequate for most tasks. But it is one of the clichés of cabinet making and related trades that you can never have enough cramps. If you are planning to restore several pieces, then buy cramps as the need arises. You will never find that you own too many. Remember to use softwood or cork pads with G-cramps.

If you really cannot afford sash-cramps, or if you intend doing only the occasional job, you can make up a tourniquet, or spanish windlass. This consists of a loop of rope, and a stick to twist through the loop to draw it tight [2.4]. Use softwood pads, since rope can mark wood as badly as metal. You may find that a length of

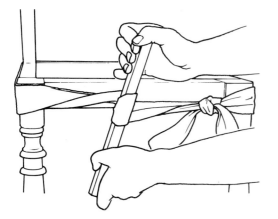

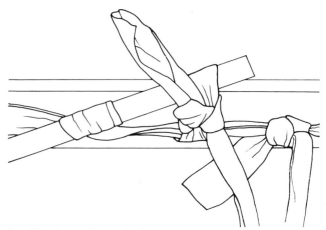

2.4a A tourniquet or Spanish windlass makes a reasonable substitute for orthodox cramps.

upholsterer's webbing, which gives even pressure over a wider area, is more successful than rope.

Tightening the tourniquet can produce an adequate cramping operation. But it is at best a makeshift device. Sash-cramps give controlled pressure at each of the joints. The difference is remarkable, so if you are at all serious, buy some.

REASSEMBLING THE CHAIR

First try a 'dry run' to ensure that all the joints go together. They should be a tight glove fit. If they are too tight, rub down the tenons or the dowels with glasspaper.

Set up the cramps, with the pads, to fit the workpiece. You will not have time to adjust the cramp heads once the glue is on the wood. Lay the cramps handily to the sides of the work. If you can, warm the joints slightly by putting the wood in an oven. It will slow down the cooling of the glue and give you more time to work.

With everything ready – and if possible a mate handy to hold the parts in place while you work – start glueing up the joints. Brush on the glue, and slot the joints home in turn [**2.5**]. Put on the cramps, and tighten them up:

b. Tie down the end of the rod to prevent the twist unwinding.

not too tight; the cramps are designed to hold the joints steady while the glue dries, not to compress them into a good fit. If excessive pressure is needed to cramp up the piece, the joints will come under a reverse pressure once you have removed the cramps and will soon work loose.

Once you have the cramps on, check them carefully. They should be in identical positions on each side of the workpiece. Check the levels. If they are pulling in non-parallel directions, the chair will tend to twist, and will set out of true. Make sure that the pressure from the cramps is directly against the joint itself, or again the work will be pulled out of true [**2.6**].

When all the cramps are in place and look right and 'comfortable', wipe away the excess glue with a cloth soaked in hot water and wrung out. You should leave the job untouched for twenty-four hours, then you can take off the cramps. The chair should have a satisfying sturdy feel about it.

All that remains is to replace the corner blocks and the pegs.

The blocks are rarely the exact fit that you would expect, and menacing gaps often appear between the blocks and chair rails. This is not vitally important. The joints themselves should be accurate enough to maintain

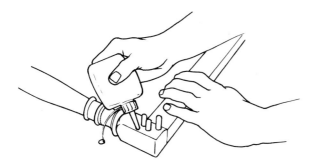

2.5 Brush or spread glue on the joint.

2.6 Cramp up the joints to a snug but not over-tight fit.

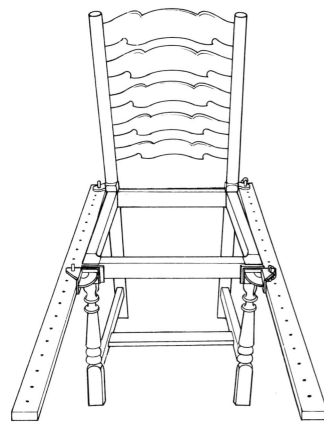

the 'set' of the chair, and the blocks are there merely to help to brace the joints. Fit the blocks dry first, then remove them, glue them where they make contact, and screw them home, just enough to hold and not enough to put the joints under stress.

To fit the pegs, buy a length of dowel corresponding to the diameter of the holes. Measure the depth of each hole with a convenient probe, and cut the dowel at least half-an-inch over length. Trim the end with a chisel so that the peg will slot home without chipping, and either trim a tiny sliver of wood off one side, or cut a shallow groove, to allow the excess glue to escape. Either dip the end of the peg in the heated scotch glue, or squeeze out a ring of pva round the end. Push the peg into the hole, and tap it home with a mallet. Leave it to dry before you trim it.

Some pegs are trimmed flush with the surface of the surrounding wood, especially in modern furniture where they are intended to strengthen joints. Other pegs, especially in old oak furniture, are designed to stand slightly proud and form a small wooden knob or dome. Your notebook sketches should tell you how your chair was originally made. If the pegs are to be left proud, trim them carefully with a sharp chisel.

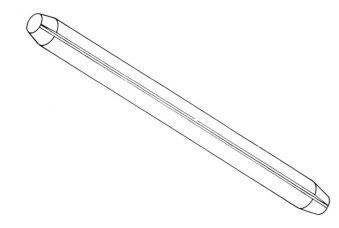

2.7 Trim the end of the peg or dowel and cut a shallow channel for the glue to escape.

Modern dowelling material is generally made from ramin, a wood that is strong and works easily. If you are restoring a high quality antique, however, you should use the same wood that the maker used. It will probably be the same as that of the chair itself – for example oak in an oak chair. This means that you will have to cut your own pegs, just as the original maker did.

If you have access to a lathe on which you can turn pegs, excellent. Most people will have to use simpler methods. Plane down a piece of wood to the same thickness as the diameter of the hole. Then saw and plane a length from it to form a square peg. Plane off the corners to give an eight-sided section, then run it through your hand while you hold a piece of medium grade glasspaper in your palm. You should produce a length of dowel, round in section and accurate enough to form a good strong peg. Cut it to length, cut a groove for the glue to escape, and fit and trim the peg as before [**2.7**].

A more accurate way of producing a peg involves a little elementary metalwork. You will need a piece of mild steel about 6 mm thick. A piece from an old bedstead is about right, or you may be able to buy a length at a local steelyard. About 200 mm is long enough to hold

in a vice. Drill a hole through it, using a high-speed metal bit of exactly the same gauge as the hole in the mortice. You can drill other holes for other sizes of pegs or dowels you want to make.

Now chisel out a rough peg from hardwood, a fraction larger than the size you finally want. Using a mallet, knock the peg through the drilled hole. The metal will neatly strip off the outside wood, leaving you with a peg of exactly the required size. In fact it will be slightly over-size, as the steel will have compressed it slightly as you forced it through the hole. It will then give a good tight fit when it is compressed once more on being slotted into the joint.

If you do not have a vice and sturdy bench to hold the steel while you manufacture your pegs, support the steel on a pair of slightly separated blocks or bricks on a solid floor.

There is one further complication. Many pegs are either purely decorative, or are designed merely to prevent a joint working loose. Some, however, especially in early hand-made chairs, are an integral part of the joint. The joint is drilled so that the holes in the tenon and surrounding wood do not exactly correspond, but are offset by about 2 mm of an inch. As the peg is hammered home it draws the holes into line, forming a joint as tight as a cramped one. During the dry run for reassembling the chair, look into the peg holes, and see if the hole in the tenon is offset. If it is, you will have to follow a slightly different sequence. Measure and cut your pegs during the dry run. During reassembly, as soon as you have the joints glued and pushed home, apply glue to the pegs and tap them in. If the chair is accurately made, it should not be necessary to use cramps at all, though they will help to hold the chair steady while the glue dries.

If you have carried out the steps so far described you will have learned a great deal about furniture restoration – dismantling, cleaning up, glueing, and cramping. However complicated these processes become on more difficult pieces, the techniques remain the same.

Your choice now is either to repeat the operation and

put right your other rickety dining chairs, developing your skills as you go, or to move on to more complicated or more dilapidated furniture, requiring a new range of skills.

LETTING IN NEW WOOD

To repair many of the more serious faults in badly dilapidated furniture you will have to replace parts of the old wood with new.

By this method, what looked like a terminal case can be brought back to perfectly sound condition. The procedure is far easier than it looks before you start, and if the job is done well only close examination will reveal that drastic grafting has taken place.

New wood is needed to correct a variety of faults. It may be a serious attack of woodworm, or simply rot, or a fracture in which dirt, splintered fragments, or missing wood make straightforward re-gluing impossible.

Each such problem makes its own demands. However, the principles behind letting in new wood are the same for all cases, and it is possible to demonstrate them in a few typical examples. You will find as you work through one operation that the steps apply to a wide range of jobs.

The most difficult decision is what wood to use, for you will have to identify the wood from which the furniture is constructed – not always easy under a covering of stain, polish, and layers of dirt.

There are no short cuts. You will simply have to learn your woods. Descriptions in a book are of limited use, and this book includes them in case no better information is available. A more reliable way is to buy a few samples from a hardwood dealer, and handle them until you can recognise the species wherever you find it. One book which sets out to deal with the problem is *What Wood Is That?* by Herbert L. Edlin (Stobart). It gives a comprehensive package of information, together with an excellent set of 40 wood samples. The problem is that these are small thin sheets of wood, and can obviously

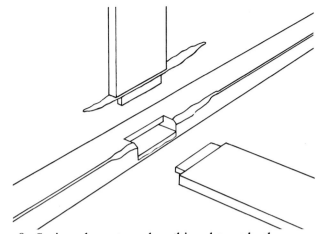

2.8 **Serious damage such as this, where a back upright has split, will require extensive renovation.**

only show the grain from one direction. If you can obtain small off-cuts of your own, you will see the grain on different surfaces. And if you start with reliable information on what they are, and keep them accurately labelled, you will soon learn to recognise the main types.

Use paint stripper to remove the polish from the damaged part of the surface, to reveal the grain without doing any harm. You can then find a sample of the wood with the nearest possible grain pattern. Make sure, of course, that the grain runs the same way. The new piece must be bigger in length, width, and thickness than the affected part that you intend to remove.

A serious problem which occurs on badly dilapidated chairs provides a typical example of the need to let in new wood. The fault occurs where the stresses have not only loosened the joint in the way already dealt with, but have broken wood away from the back, around the mortice [**2.8**].

Where two tenons enter the upright from the two sides, only a narrow strut of wood is left at the inner corner. So long as the joint is securely glued, the arrangement is perfectly sound, since each part of the joint derives strength from its adhesion to the other parts. But

2.9a Letting in new wood, a similar process for many types of repair, involves first cutting away old wood, using a mortice chisel and working to a straight line. Cramp a steel ruler to the workpiece, and tidy up the recess with a paring chisel.

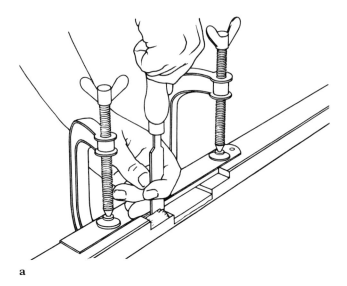

a

once the joint begins to work loose, individual parts have to take stress on their own. The narrow section between the two mortices is vulnerable, and rapidly deteriorates. The only solution is to take out all the damaged and weakened wood, and let in a new piece.

The first task is to determine how much of the old wood you should cut away. Do not be afraid to take out plenty of wood. The greater the surface area connecting the new wood to the old, the stronger the joint will be. On the other hand there is no point in making a new piece too big: the repair may become so obvious that you would be better advised to make an entirely new member. Also you must consider the value of the piece as an antique. The less furniture has been repaired, the more valuable it will be. Getting the right compromise between these conflicting interests is a skill which you can only develop with practice.

CUTTING OLD WOOD CLEAR AND PREPARING NEW WOOD

To clear away the damaged wood, first scribe lines along the chair's rear post using a straight edge. These form base lines, one for each new mortice to be cut. The best place to scribe the base line is exactly at the side of the original mortice, away from the damaged wood. The old joint provides the best guide and the new will be in precisely the same place.

Now chisel out the wood. The correct tool to use is a mortice chisel (also known as a sash-mortice chisel). This has a strong blade of constant width, and is designed to cut across the grain. Sharpen it well (see Chapter 1), then hold it exactly against the side of the guide line, and hit it sharply with a mallet. It will cut a wedge into the wood. Move it along, in the direction of its face, still using the scribed line as a guide. Make another cut, then a third, and so on. Each cut should break away a narrow wedge of wood. If the wood does not drop out, simply slide the chisel along under the chippings to slice them free.

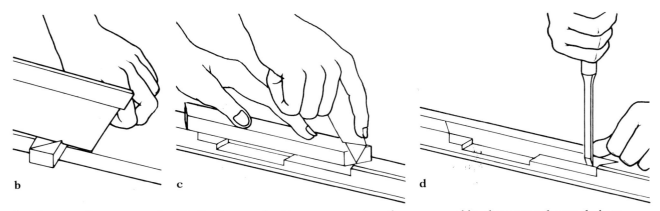

b.   **Prepare the new wood, with the face and edge planed perfectly flat, and cut it slightly over length, with the ends angled to form 'dovetails'.**

c.   **Lay the new wood in place over the workpiece, and mark the cutting angle at the ends.**

d.   **Cut out the angled recess.**

Go along to both ends of the damaged area, working from both sides if they are accessible. Work down to the depth required as accurately as you can.

Inevitably, working with the mortice chisel will not produce perfectly flat sides to the recess. So cramp a straight edge on to the workpiece, exactly on the position of the scribed line; a steel rule is ideal, and will bend to fit a curved surface. Then use an ordinary paring chisel to clean away the wood up to the line. The main problem is to ensure that the chisel is exactly upright; for this you will have to rely on your eye [**2.9a**].

At the ends of the joint, it is advisable to let in a 'dovetail'. The idea is to cut the ends of the joint at an angle, so that the load it will carry in use falls against the wood itself, and does not rely on the strength of the glue alone. Examine the workpiece, and see which way the load falls. In the case of a chair it will be in the front-to-back direction, so you should form the 'dovetail' on the side. First, however, prepare the new wood.

Plane an accurate face side and face edge on to your selected piece. It should be long enough to fill the new recess and thick enough to leave plenty over. Next, saw

the piece to length, cutting the ends to form the dovetail. The angle is arbitrary, but about 60° will give a sturdy joint. Mark one end, and saw it through. Hold the wood over the recess to give a cut slightly longer than the recess itself and mark and saw the other end. Clean off the 'feathers' – the tiny splinters left by the saw.

Now return to the chair back. Hold the new piece as accurately as possible in place, and mark the angles [**2.9c**]. Chisel out the waste [**2.9d**]. It may be tricky down in the corners, but care and perseverance will produce a clean cut. Now try the new piece in place. It should fit precisely, but still remain proud by a generous amount. This is to be removed later.

If it does not fall into place comfortably, pare away the excess. If there are small gaps, do not worry about them: you can fill them in later with wax or some form of 'stopping'. And your next attempt will be more accurate. If there are large gaps, contain your frustration, reject the piece, and make a new one. Do not try to make the new piece fit the existing recess. Cut it slightly longer, then re-work the angled ends of the recess to match the new piece.

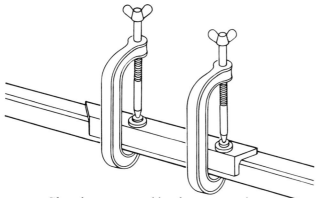

2.10a Glue the new wood in place, cramping it up firmly with protective pads.

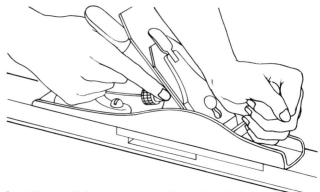

b. Plane off the excess wood level with the workpiece surface, on both the face and the edge.

FINISHING THE REPAIR

When you are satisfied with the fit of the new wood, glue it in place. Permanent pva glue is acceptable as this is not a part of the piece of furniture that will ever need to be dismantled and reassembled. If the repair ever proves faulty, a future restorer would cut away wood by the same process.

Apply the glue sparingly to the recess and slot home the new wood. Protecting the piece with offcuts of soft wood, cramp it in place from two directions with even pressure. Leave time for the glue to harden thoroughly, at least overnight.

When the glue has set, secure the workpiece in a vice, and plane off the excess wood. If other parts of the chair prevent you reaching the new wood with a plane, pare it down with a chisel. Theoretically you should stop when you have planed the new piece flush with the existing wood, but in practice it is worth taking a thin shaving off the old wood to ensure a perfectly uniform surface [**2.10**].

In many repairs involving letting in new wood you can now go on to re-finishing the piece.

If you are stripping off the old finish, spread stripper liberally over the existing wood and the new wood together. The stripper and any old polish and dirt will help merge the two surfaces. Wash the area down with methylated spirits. (See Chapter 3 for details of stripping procedures.)

If you are repairing broken chair joints, you need to re-cut the mortices, using a mortice chisel the same width as the tenon [**2.11**]. If you originally used the edge of the old mortice as your base line, then the edge of the new wood will provide the perfect line from which to work. Alternatively, providing the piece has a flat face and edge, you can use a mortice gauge. Set the points the same width apart as the thickness of the tenon, and slide the moving block along to the appropriate measurement from the face and edge of the wood, then turn the screw firmly to hold the measurement.

Naturally, if you are working on a curved piece of wood you cannot use its face as a guide. The simplest method then is to hold the tenon in place, slide a steel rule up against it, remove the tenon, and scribe a line against the steel rule.

Sharpen the mortice chisel, cut the new mortice in the new wood, using the wedge-chipping technique already described, and clean up the edges. Try the rail in place. The tenon should be a tight glove-fit in the mortice.

Turn the chair post over and cut the second mortice. But take care: completing the second mortice leaves an

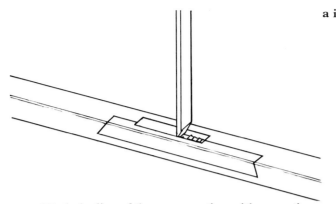

2.11 Mark the line of the new mortice with a mortice gauge, and cut the new joint with a mortice chisel.

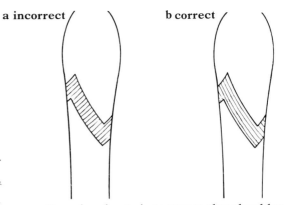

a incorrect   b correct

2.12 Examine the grain to ensure that shoulder of a splice does not include a 'short' grain.

extremely thin section of wood between the two joints. The best way to avoid breaking this is to keep your chisel razor sharp, and finish the cutting process by hand alone, without a mallet.

With any necessary re-cutting of the mortices complete, the chair should be ready for reassembly by the procedure already described in Chapter 2.

OTHER CHAIR REPAIRS

BROKEN LEGS

Broken chair legs often appear to be so drastic that the owner may be tempted to discard the chair altogether. In fact the repair is relatively simple. If the chair leg has suffered a clean fracture, it may be possible to glue and cramp it together leaving hardly any sign of a break.

More often you will have to cut away the splinters and let in a splice of new wood. The repair will involve dismantling the chair to use one leg as a pattern for the length and shape of the other. The splice should be cut on the slant, and the ends must incorporate a shoulder, or the faces of the joint would tend to slide across each other as weight was applied to the chair.

These shoulders can themselves be vulnerable if the

new wood is cut with the grain in the wrong direction. A weak shoulder, with a short grain, is shown in figure [**2.12a**]. A properly cut splice is illustrated in figure [**2.12b**]. Plane the wood for the splice first. It must be large enough to incorporate the shoulder, to cover the damaged wood, and to leave some spare for removing later. Scribe the two faces to be glued, and with a try-square, mark in the shoulders.

Secure the wood in a vice and saw along the two faces as far as the shoulders. Then turn the piece and saw through to make the shoulders.

With a marking knife, transfer the outline of the splice to the broken chair leg. If the leg is in two parts, tape the broken pieces to the good leg to secure them in their correct respective positions. Pack slivers of wood between the legs to accommodate any tapering. Saw along the lines, to remove the damaged wood, cutting in the shoulders exactly as on the splice itself.

The three parts should now fit together as in [**2.12a**]. Without doubt, this kind of freehand cutting will lead to fitting problems. Pare down all the high spots until the fit is perfect, taking care not to slice the shoulders off with over-enthusiastic use of the chisel.

Gluing the pieces together will test your ingenuity with cramps; in theory pressure from the ends should be enough to hold the joints closed while your glue dries, but in practice you will need to rig up a system that also holds the surfaces together. On a simple chair leg, you should be able to do this with a sash-cramp along the length, and two G-cramps at the joint. Check the set of the leg from every angle, to make sure that you are not building a twist into it.

When the glue is thoroughly dried, remove the excess wood with a plane on the flat surfaces, and a spokeshave on the curves. Stain and polish the finished leg, then reassemble the chair.

An alternative which some restorers prefer is to let metal into the leg to hold the joints together. Lengths of 6 mm round steel section, with the ends filed to remove any burr, are ideal. Cut them long enough to pass through the splice and about 40 mm into each part of the leg. With this method there is no need to cut shoulders, and sawing the mating faces also becomes easier. You cannot, of course, use steel where you will need to cut joints across the mating faces.

When you cut the splice, mark and saw its faces so that they are not precisely parallel, but form a slight wedge shape.

Now tape the broken leg on to the good leg to maintain its position, and scribe lines on to it to match the splice.

Saw the leg cleanly to make way for the splice. With the parts of the leg held firmly in position, put a spot of glue on one face, and slide the splice between the two parts until the wedge makes a firm contact on both faces.

The glue is designed to make just a temporary fix between the splice and one part of the leg. When it is dry take away the unglued part, and drill holes through the splice and the part to which it is glued. Make these deep enough to take the reinforcing rods but do not insert the rods yet.

First glue the other part of the leg to the splice, permanently. Continue to use the sound matching leg as your guide to length. Cramp the parts together.

When the splice and one part of the leg are firmly glued, hold the assembly in a vice, and break away the part that was temporarily joined. A tap with a mallet and softwood pad should do it. The holes through the splice will now be revealed, and you can drill through them into the permanently fixed part of the leg. Measure the depth of hole with a probe to make sure that they will take the rods. Finally, insert the rods, and glue the other part permanently, cramping the length and width. Plane, shave, and sand off the excess wood, and stain and polish the repair.

An adaptation of this method where no new splice is

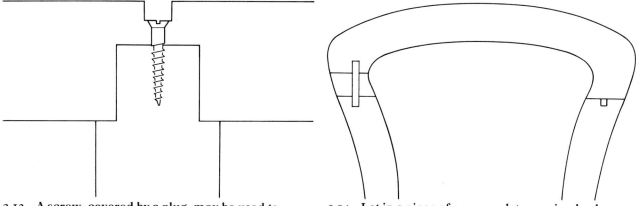

2.13 A screw, covered by a plug, may be used to draw a joint together and help ensure a firm hold.

2.14 Let in a piece of new wood, to repair a back which has broken in the region of the short grain.

needed is to reinforce a cracked or broken chair member with a bracing screw. If the crack is old, you may have to break it completely to clear out the accumulated dust and grime. If it is new, you may be able to prise it open to work glue into it. It may be possible to cramp up the joint without glue, drill pilot holes and a recess to take a plug, then use the screw alone to draw the joint tight after inserting glue. Otherwise, glue and cramp it, and, when the glue has dried, drill the pilot hole to take the bracing screw.

A pilot hole should be the depth of the screw, and wide enough to allow the thread to bite without splitting the wood. Before inserting the screw, drill out a small recess to take a plug, slightly wider than the screw head.

Carve a small plug to fit the recess, with the grain matching as far as possible the character of the surrounding wood. Do not cut the plug with the end grain showing.

As you glue and cramp the joint, screw home your bracing screw, glue in the plug, and when the glue has set plane it down to match the surface. Stain and polish it, and the repair will be barely visible. This type of repair is shown in figure [**2.13**].

If you have access to a woodworking lathe, you can turn your own pegs or dowels from hardwood, and use these in place of steel rods. This is a more elegant solution and you will add some strength to the joint by using material which, unlike steel, bonds with the glue. Do not use ready-made dowel; it is cut from softwood, or ramin, which is not strong enough to take stresses across its grain, and is likely to snap. Turn the pegs fractionally oversize, and cut a glue-escape channel in them.

Pegs can be used to mend breakages at almost any point in the chair.

Victorian chairs, for example [**2.14**] often break near the point where a curved top rail joins a curved back upright. Since the top rail is cut from a single piece of wood, the grain lies along the length on the main part, but runs across the wood where it curves at the corners. This vulnerable 'short grain' at the joints is under great stress and often breaks.

The answer is to peg in new wood. Try to match the new wood to the old. If only one side of the chair is broken, you will have to release the opposite joint to complete the dismantling. If this is well fixed, you may have to saw through it, losing a fraction of the wood, rather than wrench the joint and risk bruising the wood.

In the area of the damage, cut away the useless wood to make room for the splicing piece. Lay the chair out to form a pattern, and cut the new piece to fit between the end of the rail and the upright post. Then proceed as on the spliced leg. Glue the splice to the rail with temporary dabs of glue and drill it to take a hardwood or steel peg. Release it, and glue the splice to the top of the upright. Let pegs into these two parts together. Before you finally glue the joint, attend to the other end of the rail. If you have had to cut any pegs in dismantling, scrape out the remaining wood to leave the original holes clear and clean. Re-making the joint will then be easy. If damaged wood makes it impossible to use the original holes, drill new ones. To start them in the same place on corresponding faces, first make a small indentation at a suitable point on the face with a hammer and punch. Rest a small ball bearing in the indentation, fit the other piece as closely as possible, and tap it lightly with a mallet and softwood pad. The ball-bearing leaves a matching indentation. The real difficulty lies in drilling holes in the right direction – a test of skill and eye. If the faces are square enough you can put the pieces in a vice, and drill into them exactly perpendicularly.

When you are perfectly happy with a 'dry' assembly, glue the joints home.

SADDLES

Because chairs are not made up of rectangular members, cramping them can be extremely difficult, and if not done properly can lead to the finished job being warped.

Cramps must not be put on at the best available angle, and tightened up regardless. Instead, the curved lines of the chair should be converted into straight lines, to accommodate the stresses of the cramping operation, by making up 'saddles'. These are pieces of softwood cut to fit the curves of a chair, or any other piece of furniture. The outer side to which the cramps are applied remains straight and square, and the tightening action of the cramp is distributed evenly and in the right direction over the curved area.

Cutting saddles might seem a tedious business, as a

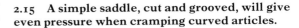

2.15 A simple saddle, cut and grooved, will give even pressure when cramping curved articles.

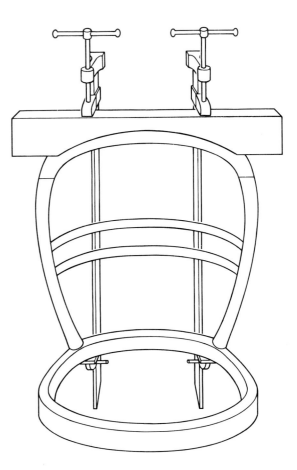

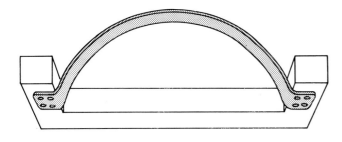

2.16 Alternatively a wood-and-leather apparatus can be rigged up to accommodate complex curves.

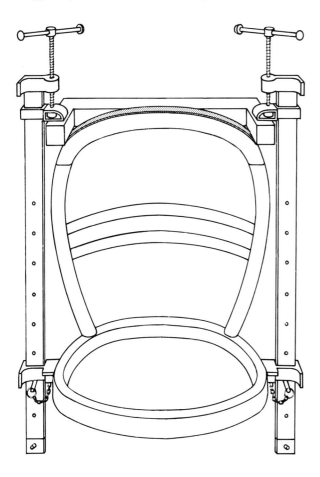

new one must be made for each operation. Fortunately, since the introduction of the power jig-saw, it has become a simpler job. Trace the outline of the chair-back on to a piece of cardboard, transfer the outline by means of pin holes on to the wood, and cut round the curve with a power saw. A few strokes with a spokeshave will remove any high spots, and give the saddle a perfect fit.

If you have wood-carving tools, you can cut a groove in the saddle to match precisely the curved section of the chair back.

The use of a simple saddle of this kind is illustrated in figure [**2.15**].

An alternative type consists of a piece of wood, recessed to accommodate the chair piece, and a length of leather nailed into position to fit to the curved shape of the back [**2.16**].

BROKEN JOINTS

If a chair has been subjected to excessive stress, the housing of the joints may stay firm, but the inner part crack and break off [**2.17**]. It is possible to repair this by letting new wood into the rail, effectively converting the joint into a double-mortice. First saw and chisel away the broken part of the tenon. Measure the original mortice, and mark it on the surface from which the tenon was

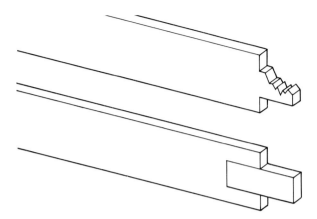

cut away. Chisel out this member to a suitable depth, and prepare a new piece of wood to fit the recess. Glued in place, the new wood should look exactly as the original tenon. Beech, which is not difficult to work, but has the strength and tightness of grain to carry the load of such a joint, is an ideal wood to use.

TABLE REPAIRS

Many of the problems which crop up in tables are similar to those in chairs, and can be dealt with by similar methods.

The operations follow the same sequence. First assess the job. Dismantle the furniture if necessary. Let in new wood to replace the damaged part, or make a new member entirely if the damage is extensive. If the surface is damaged, it will be a matter of regluing veneer, cutting in new veneer, or simply cleaning and re-polishing. All these steps are dealt with in other chapters.

However, there are other difficulties, many of them the result of shrinkage, which are peculiar to tables. A table is basically a frame, with a flat board fitted to the top. Most antique tables were perfectly satisfactory in the places for which they were designed – that is, rooms without central heating. Even if the rooms were well heated by fires, the draught of the fire brought plenty of moist air in from outside. Low humidity – the real cause of shrinkage – was not a significant problem, for when the coal fires died out at night, the wood was able to take up moisture from the cooler night air.

The introduction of central heating changed the balance drastically. Now, throughout the winter months, a table may stand in an atmosphere which is much drier than the outdoor air. Convector panels (radiators) do not need draughts to feed them, as an open fire does, and there may be negligible change of air. At night the heating might go off, but the air in the room remains virtually static, unlike the situation in rooms with open hearths and chimneys. Double glazing, while adding to comfort and reducing heating bills, can add to the problem by further eliminating draughts. In a double-glazed centrally heated house there is no nightly refreshing of the atmosphere.

The result is that the wood steadily dries out and over a long period, shrinks. Uniform shrinkage would not be a serious problem: the real trouble arises because wood only shrinks in one direction, across the grain. In other words, a plank becomes narrower, but not appreciably shorter. The construction of furniture, in an age when shrinkage was unlikely to be a problem, took no account of this, and cabinet makers happily joined together parts with the grain running in opposing directions. When bonded pieces of wood shrink at different rates, the stresses are more than any glue can stand, and it gives

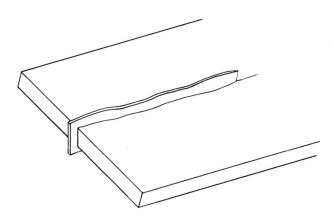

way. Veneers lift from their ground, parts separate from each other, or, where parts are well screwed in place, the wood itself splits.

REPAIRING SPLITS

There are two main methods of repairing splits; closing them up, or letting in new wood. The method you intend to adopt may help you decide whether to dismantle a table or deal with the repair in situ. It is possible to let in new wood with the table top in place, but if you intend to close the split up, you will have to separate the top from the frame. Generally, whatever the operation, working on fully dismantled furniture gives better results.

Often, when the table top is a single piece, it splits only part of the way across the surface: once as the stress is released, there is no need for it to split further. In closing up such a gap you will only revive the original stresses. In such cases the kind of repair illustrated in [2.18] is advisable.

First saw down the length of the crack. It would be impossible to make a piece of wood to fit accurately the narrow triangular shape this kind of split makes. The thickness of a saw cut is often enough to make the sides of the fault parallel. When the cut is made insert a small fillet of wood. Your success with this kind of repair depends on how closely you can match the thickness of

the inserted wood to the thickness of the saw blade. A better repair is made by using a narrow-backed saw such as a coping saw, or better still a fret-saw. Make the saw cut follow the curve in the split, which will itself follow the grain, and thus remove the minimum amount of wood. Now cut a slice of wood, such as a thick veneer, slightly oversize. Glue the mating faces, insert it in the saw cut, and cramp up the table top from both sides. When the glue has set, plane down the insert, and finally scrape it dead level, before polishing it.

If the crack is too wide to clean out with a single saw cut, first make a saw cut at the narrow end, where the saw does contact both faces. Insert the fillet glued on one side only. When the glue has set, make a second saw cut, working your saw carefully along the side of the first fillet. Slide a second fillet, glued on both sides, down beside the first.

Cracks are liable to develop on a table like the figured walnut library table illustrated in [2.19a]. The top is in two parts. The halves are joined together; the screws fixing it to the oval frame are concealed under round-headed knobs. Many of these elegant tables were designed to tilt vertically, to form a decorative screen. Central heating will shrink the two parts of the top, and leave a crack of two millimetres or more between the two halves.

To repair it, carefully ease out the plugs, and remove

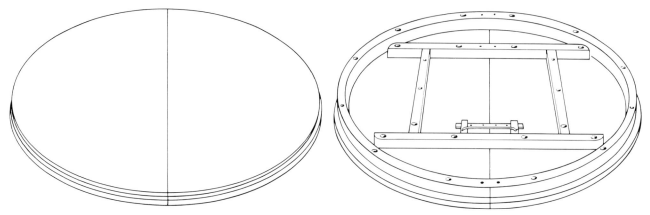

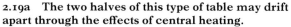

2.19a The two halves of this type of table may drift apart through the effects of central heating.

the screws holding the top to the frame. Then screw them home again with the gap closed up. If the boards are to be glued together, a problem will arise if the table is too wide to accommodate your cramps. You may have to cut new bars for your sash cramps especially for this operation. Alternatively lay the two parts of the table top on an absolutely flat surface, pass a rope, or better still a length of leather, round them, and cramp up the end. If the rope or leather is nailed to two blocks, as in the arrangement illustrated in [**2.19c**], you can draw the blocks together with G-cramps.

Alternatively the wedging system illustrated in [**2.19d**] may work. Again you need a firm base, such as a long plank of wood, or two laid parallel. Screw a block of wood at one end to form a fixed post against which the compression can act. Screw down a second block at the other end, about 150 mm further away than the width of the piece being glued. Cut a third block in half diagonally to form two triangular pieces. They will serve as wedges. Set them up so that the inclined faces work against each other, and tap them from opposite ends with a mallet. The 'rectangle' you have formed will gradually increase in width, forcing the two parts of the workpiece together.

When the crack is not serious, has not resulted in

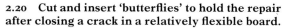

b. The top boards will have to be removed from the frame and re-fixed, with the two parts closed up.

warping, and can be pulled together without too much pressure, it may well be possible to repair the damage by simply holding the gap closed. Glue alone will not withstand the pressure, but the system illustrated in [**2.20**] usually works. The 'butterflies', forming a kind of double-dovetail, fit on the underside of the work. Cut them with the grain running from end to end. Use well-seasoned hardwood, so later shrinking across the grain will not loosen them.

Cut the butterflies first. Their size depends on the size and weight of the table-top being repaired; 50 mm–75 mm is generally appropriate, 20 mm–25 mm at the

2.20 Cut and insert 'butterflies' to hold the repair after closing a crack in a relatively flexible board.

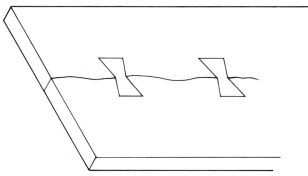

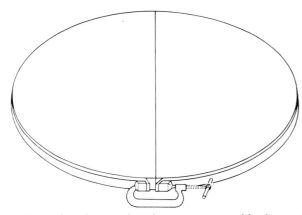

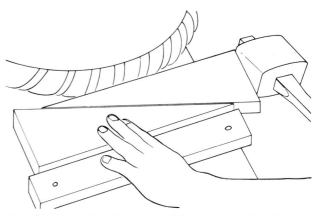

c. Cramping the repair using a strap, two blocks, and a G-Cramp.

d. Alternatively, rig up a wedging system. Tapping the wedges together will close the gap in the table top.

waist is about the right width. On most table-tops, they should be about 6 mm thick when in place. Cut them over-thick. Only the bottom face needs to be planed flat. The other face will be planed off when the butterfly is in place.

Cramp the table-top to close the split, and position the butterflies. Mark each one so that you know where it goes, and in what direction it lies. Then scribe round them. Release the cramps, and you can now cut the recesses to take the butterflies. The right tool to use is the mortice chisel, which will cut down into the wood of the table-top across the grain. When you have made the downward cuts, you can clean out the bottom of the recess with a paring chisel.

Cramp up the piece again, and check that the butterflies are a close fit. Release the cramps so that you can brush glue into the split itself, and on to the bed of the recess which takes the butterflies. Cramp it up again, put the butterflies in place, and weight them, protected with wax paper to prevent the weights sticking to the work. When the glue has dried, plane down the butterflies flush with the surface, and give them a coat of polish for protection.

When you have repaired a table-top by closing the split, you will find that the screw holes in the frame no longer line up exactly with the positions of the screws in the top, but are too close to the original holes for you to drill firm new ones. The solution is to turn the table-top right round. The old holes are unlikely to line up again and you can drill new ones.

HINGES

Drop-leaf tables, such as gate-leg tables, often suffer from the consequences of shrinkage and warping. In some examples there is no serious damage from the shrinkage itself, but the narrowing of the centre board of the table means that the outer leaves do not drop clear of the frame, and the hinge takes a considerable strain, finally breaking away. In other cases the centre leaf of the table is in two pieces, and they pull apart. Still other problems start when the gate leg is not opened fully, and weight on the outer section of the drop leaf leads to splitting.

First decide which of these faults is giving the trouble. Probably the table simply needs dismantling and re-assembling in a way that eliminates the cause of the trouble.

If the centre-part has split, you may be able to cramp it up and glue it, preferably with butterflies. This sol-

2.21 It may be necessary to let in new wood to repair the running part of a drawer which has become worn down.

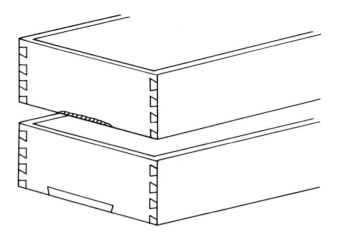

ution may also work when the boards of a drop leaf have come apart. However, if you deal with the centre section in this way, you will have to make sure that there is still room for the drop leaves to fall clear of the frame. If not, your solution may be to let in a separate piece down the centre gap.

If the hinges have pulled loose, you will have to re-fit them. It will almost certainly be impossible to fix the screws near their former holes, and you will have to move the hinge to a new position. Before you do so, clean out the old hinge recesses and let in a small fillet of new wood of the same type and character as the table.

CARCASS REPAIRS

A carcass is the trade name for a type of furniture which is basically a box. Most furniture is either a frame, such as a chair, or a box, or a combination of both. Boxes suffer especially when they shrink, because the large boards from which they are formed are interlinked, and the stresses are transmitted throughout the structure. By the time an amateur restorer has covered the run of repairs likely to be encountered on chairs and tables, he will have no difficulty in working on carcasses, even though they are generally bigger and less accessible.

DRAWERS

Most carcasses incorporate drawers. Over years of use the wooden runners on which they slide are worn down, sometimes to the point where they do not support the drawer at all.

Sometimes the drawer has simply warped, probably as the result of drying out due to central heating, and no longer runs freely. The answer is to plane wood off the part of the drawer which is sticking. Take care not to remove any unnecessary wood, and rub a block of bees-wax on the bare wood to help it run smoothly.

A more likely problem is wear. Generally drawers are of two main types. Either they run in and out resting on rails, or they have grooves cut in their sides, and the rails are set within the grooves.

Take out the drawer and examine its construction. If it has the grooves in the drawer sides, you will see whether the upper edge has worn, and whether the corresponding upper edge of the runner, fixed to the inside of the carcass, is also worn. To cure the trouble, recut the groove in the side of the drawer. You will find it easiest with a small circular saw, on which you can set the depth, with a batten cramped firmly to the piece at the right distance to hold the saw blade on the correct

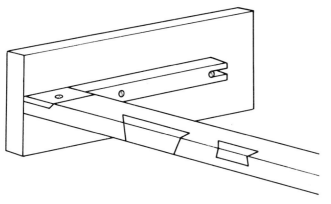

2.22   If the runner itself is worn, it will need to be replaced. Slot-screw it at the rear, to accommodate later shrinkage. If the wear extends to the front rail, cut away the worn part and let in new wood.

line. Then chisel out the surplus wood to give a smooth running surface. You will then have to remake the runner on the inside of the carcass. The best plan is to prise out the original, and either replace it entirely with a wider one, or set it higher in the drawer side, and turn it upside down to bring a fresh edge to the top. If you can, follow the original method of fixing. Rub both parts with beeswax to ensure free running and to cut down wear from friction in the future.

In furniture from later periods, the drawers sit on runners. Often there is a rail across the front of the carcass, and perhaps also a dustboard to separate the drawer compartments. If the side of the drawer shows wear on its lower edge, as in [2.21], repair it by cutting away the wood to square it up, and gluing another piece in its place. It will probably be necessary to cut and plane it to the exact size before fitting it, as the lip of the drawer will prevent you working with a plane when the new wood is in place. On the runner you will probably find a deep indentation along its entire length. It will have to be replaced. Ideally, the new runner should be glued in position at the front, and slot-screwed at the back to allow for expansion and contraction in the side-boards [2.22].

If the indentation extends as far forwards as the rail across the front, you will have to dismantle the carcass, cut away the worn wood to give you a square bed, and let in a new piece [2.22].

On most types of drawer, the rail and the bottom board should carry a couple of slivers of wood which form stops. If they are missing, serious problems can follow. The drawer itself may run right back and slam against the back of the cabinet. Or, especially on furniture of the early 18th century, the lip that was used to conceal the drawer opening will have taken the full force of the drawer closing, and will have broken off. The lip was commonly glued into a rebate round the front of the drawer, with a decorative veneered facing to the join. Curing the fault may involve drastic, but fortunately not complicated, treatment. It is not difficult to remove the veneer. Craftsmen used to lay the veneered surface face down for a few days in damp grass, but that technique can cause as many problems as it solves. A more controlled treatment is to cover the veneer facing in damp sawdust, so that the moisture seeps through to soften the glue. If the hurry to do the job is great, a damp cloth and an iron will soften the glue, and you can lift the veneer before the glue resets. After that, remove the lip and re-glue or repair it and glue the veneer back into position. Finally polish it.

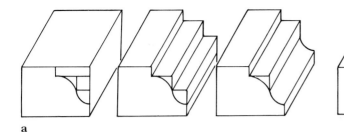

a

2.23a **The profile of a moulding, showing the cuts necessary to produce the shape on which the final moulding can be chiselled.**

MOULDINGS

Do not be dismayed at finding moulding broken and parts of it missing. It is a common fault. You can re-make mouldings using a power saw with a disc-type blade, either hand-held or inverted for use as a bench saw.

If you are making a complete length, fit the wood first, by measuring and cutting the mitre at the corners. You can then draw the outline of the moulding on the new wood, and proceed with the cuts.

If you are making several short pieces, draw the sectional outline of the moulding on to a piece of card, to use as a pattern. Draw over it a rectangle representing the width and thickness of the replacement wood. From this, at as many points as convenient, you can mark the distance from the face and edge, and the depth, of all the cuts. This will give you the approximate outline of the moulding. [**2.23a**] shows a typical example. The simplest way to complete the cutting is to work along the wood with a hand-held chisel with a rounded blade. The right kind of chisel is widely available, sold as a wood-carving tool.

More complicated and larger-section mouldings can be made by building up two or more pieces of wood together. [**2.23b**] shows two pieces glued to produce a large but simple profile. [**2.23c**] is a more complicated profile assembled from several separate pieces.

Other likely repairs include replacing parts of a cross-banding border, re-gluing and replacing cracked veneer,

smoothing out the 'ground' to take a re-glued piece. All these operations are described in other chapters.

REPAIRS TO SURFACES

Often, a well-made article of furniture will remain structurally sound, but will need repairs to its surface which go beyond stripping and repolishing.

LEATHER SURFACES

The leather surface of a desk or table top is less robust than the wood which surrounds it, and a new leather or 'skiver' will be needed periodically.

Making up the new skiver, with its border of decorative tooling in gilt, is a job for the professional. Locate a skiver-maker in your area, and give him the dimensions of the recess in your desk top. If it is not a simple rectangle, make a template of the recess. He should be able to match the existing skiver faithfully enough, or if you prefer a change, he will produce one to the right size in your specified colour.

Remove the old skiver with as little damage as possible to the surrounding woodwork. Start by tearing off the old and damaged skiver. Clean away the remnants of dried glue with hot water, used sparingly, followed by a scraper. Make sure the corners and edges of the recess are absolutely clear.

You will have to repair any defects in the wood, to provide a firm base for the new skiver. Fill any splits

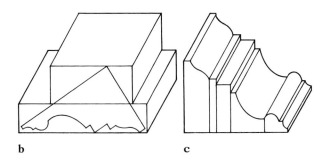

b

c

b. Large mouldings can be made more cheaply from two pieces of wood.
c. Complicated mouldings are simply assembled from several pieces.

with fillets of wood, and fill small holes with a mixture of glue and fine sawdust. Sand down the renewed surface carefully. It is worth giving the exposed area a dose of woodworm treatment as a precaution.

The standard technique for applying a new skiver is to glue it in place first, then cut it to fit. First try the skiver in place 'dry', to give you some idea of how the tooled border fits, and how much overlap there will be all round before cutting. Prepare four or five battens – lengths of thin wood – to lie across the width of the desk. They will help the inexperienced worker complete the job without spreading excess adhesive everywhere. It is also useful to have help during this operation.

Working fairly quickly, spread the adhesive sparingly over the recess, and work it well into the edges and corners. Lay the wooden battens across the desk, and the new skiver across them. Lower it at one end, leaving the overlap you established when fitting it 'dry'. Ask your helper to remove the lengths of wood from under the skiver as you progress along its length, easing it gently down on to the adhesive with as little movement as possible.

With all the battens removed, the skiver should lie in approximately the correct position. You can still make adjustments, sliding it on the adhesive, to move it to exactly the right position. Look for the imprint of the sharp edge of the surrounding wood showing through the skiver to guide your positioning. If the outline of the recess does not show, press all round with the back of a spoon, but not hard enough to leave a permanent creasemark.

When you have the skiver correctly positioned, smooth it out from the centre, but do not press fiercely or you will stretch and buckle the thin wet leather. You can then cut off the excess all round the edge. Start near a corner, and with a scalpel make a one-inch cut in the skiver, along the line of the surrounding wood. You will have to use extremely fine judgement to avoid cutting the wood, while at the same time cutting so close that the skiver falls precisely into the angle when you press it down. After the first short cut, protect the wood and cut away towards the edge of the skiver. Then you can carry on cutting, all round the edge of the recess, peeling away the strip of excess material as you go.

Press the skiver down into the edges and corners, and clean off any stray adhesive as soon as possible.

Some craftsmen prefer to cut their leather tops and skivers before fitting. This can make it easier to work with, but will not give the accuracy of fit you can achieve by cutting in place.

An alternative fitting method is to roll the skiver round a wooden rod, then, preferably with a helper, work it slowly along by unrolling it on to the pasted area, smoothing it from the centre to the sides as you go.

REPAIRING VENEER

Broken, chipped, cracked, or lifting veneer is one of the most widely encountered problems in furniture restoration.

It is worth looking for early signs of faults in a

veneered surface so that you can put them right before the damage becomes too drastic. The trouble invariably arises from the veneer becoming detached from the surface to which it is glued – the ground. Often it starts to lift at an edge, as the result of wear. Sometimes the lifting starts in the centre of the surface, where it can be caused by the ground and veneer shrinking at different rates through drying out, especially in centrally heated rooms.

Trace a fault by feeling for it. First go round the edge to detect any gaps. Then go over the surface, feeling for any bumps, tapping them with a fingernail to see if they are hollow underneath. Sometimes you can pass your hand across a surface and hear a slight hiss as you press air out of the gap.

Mark with chalk the areas to be treated.

Repairs of this kind, where you still have the original veneer, simply involve inserting glue between the surfaces, and pressing down the veneer until the glue sets.

However, both these processes can be slightly complicated. First you must wash out the debris of any old glue, which will probably be mixed with dirt. At the edge of the surface, lift the veneer cleanly and carefully and hold it away from the ground with a matchstick or similar small wooden strut. Use a soft brush and hot water to wash out all dirt.

In the centre of a surface, you will have to slice the veneer cleanly with a scalpel, to allow you to lift and work water under each side in turn. The veneer may be so badly buckled that you have to cut it anyway to make it lie down. A cut of this kind will not be seriously noticeable after the repair.

But if you want to avoid having to make a cut at all, for example on a highly valuable article, you may be able to drill two small holes from the under-side of the ground, up into the pocket behind the lifted veneer. Gauge the depth of the drill holes with extreme care, to ensure that you do not drill through the veneer and ruin the whole exercise. Use a syringe of some kind, first to run hot water through the pocket, to soften and wash out old glue, then to squirt glue into it. As you insert the glue through one hole, it should press air out of the other hole, until the whole pocket is filled with glue. Rub the area from the veneer side to ensure that the glue is well spread to the extreme edges of the pocket, and apply a 'caul' until the glue sets.

A caul is a device for exerting even pressure on a veneered surface, either during its manufacture or during a repair.

Devising a cramping system for holding the caul in place presents interesting problems. At the edge of the work, a simple G-cramp with softwood pads will do the job. For repairs away from the edge, a softwood pad held down by a wooden beam, with the pressure exerted by cramps at both ends, will generally work. Shape the caul at the back so that the beam does not exert excess

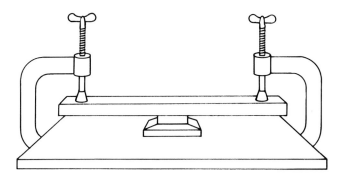

2.24 Use a shaped caul, bar, and G-cramps to exert pressure on a centrally placed veneer repair.

pressure at one edge. A typical arrangement is shown in [**2.24**].

However, near the centre of large surfaces, this kind of pressure can bend the ground, and when the cauls are taken away the surface returns to its original shape, putting the repair under strain right from the start. To avoid this problem, arrange a system of double cauls, so that your cramps exert equalising pressure at the back of the repair.

If the repair to the veneer does not 'take' well, you can complete the job with an ordinary household iron. This is a useful alternative method of repairing any fault where you can be sure there is no dirt behind the veneer. Use a wet cloth and iron firmly through it. The steam will heat and damp the wood, and soften the glue, and the pressure from the iron will force the surfaces together. If you switch off the heat from the iron just before you start work, the iron will soften the glue, then allow the glue to cool. All you need to do is keep the pressure on for a few minutes until the glue begins to bite.

Applying veneer to curved surfaces presents the additional problem of applying uniform pressure. There are three standard solutions, but no reason why you should not invent another of your own.

The first is to bend a sheet of hardboard to fit the curved surface, and keep it in place with several cramps, to exert even pressure over the whole surface.

The second is to fill a bag with sand, lay the workpiece on it 'cold', and mould the sandbag into the inverse shape of the workpiece. Apply the glue and veneer, and put the article upside down on the sandbag. Lay heavy weights on the work to press it well on to the face of the sandbag until the glue sets. Obviously, the bigger the workpiece, the less convenient this method will be.

The third method is to shape a separate piece of softwood into a curved caul to match exactly the curve of the veneered surface. This may appear to be a rather elaborate answer involving a great deal of work, but on a valuable article it may be worthwhile, and again the power jig-saw cuts down the work. First cut a cardboard template to match the curve exactly. Transfer the curve to the wood and cut it with the jig-saw, or with a coping-saw. Make any minor adjustments with a spokeshave, and finally ensure a perfect fit by rubbing the caul and veneered surface together with a sheet of sandpaper between them. Cramping this kind of curved caul on to the work is straightforward.

REPLACING MISSING VENEER

As veneer lifts, especially at the edges of surfaces, it tends to crack, and small pieces may fall off and be lost. You have to cut new veneer to replace it. Obviously, you should buy new veneer that matches the existing surface as accurately as possible.

2.25 Trim round the area of an edge veneer in the shape of 'donkey's ears' to provide a clean edge for the new veneer.

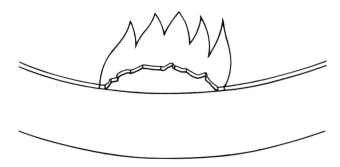

2.26a A simple type of banding. Square off the end of the centre type of wood, and saw sections. Glue the veneer for the outer type of wood to each side, to form a sandwich. Slice the sandwich with a knife or saw, to the thickness required for the banding. Glue the banding in place, building up the length required from the cuttings. Sand or scrape it down to produce a smooth finish.

b. To produce a chequered banding, glue two types of wood together, and cut segments from the end. Reverse alternate segments, and reglue them, with veneer to form the outer wood. Slice the banding as before.

Prepare the existing surface to take the new wood. First trim the area of the repair. Using a scalpel, cut into the area a set of 'donkey's ears', roughly in the direction of the grain [**2.25**]. Hold the scalpel with the blade precisely vertical. Ease up the wood you have cut away, and clear all dirt and old glue off the ground.

Tape down a piece of tracing paper large enough to cover the repair, using masking tape. With a soft pencil, crayon, or even a ball of cobbler's heel, rub in the outline of the repair, as if you were taking a brass-rubbing. Take away the paper, and tape it to the new veneer, again checking that the ears run in the direction of the grain. Now cut carefully round the outline with a scalpel. This time, lean the scalpel slightly away from the outline, to make the veneer fractionally oversize, and with a slight undercut. When you glue the new veneer in place, the angled edge will press firmly against the surround and produce a perfect fit. Establish the right stain and polish by trial on a waste piece of the new veneer, then stain and polish the new surface. The result should be a repair which, if not invisible, will be at least unnoticeable.

INLAID BANDING AND STRINGING

Articles of high quality furniture often include either banding or stringing. Banding is a patterned border of different woods in various colours and grains. Typically it is about 6 mm–10 mm wide.

Stringing is a single line of wood let into the surface usually a lighter colour than the background.

Both forms of decoration are vulnerable, as the glue tends to weaken with age. Then the decorative wood begins to pull out, gets snagged, and breaks off.

If it is lost, it will have to be replaced. Clean the recess of old glue and debris, and glue in new stringing or matching banding.

You may be able to buy banding to match exactly the portion that has survived. If not, you can choose between lifting out all the old banding and replacing it entirely, or making up small pieces of your own banding to an exact match. On valuable antique furniture, the less you replace the better. On less valuable pieces, a complete replacement is often simpler. How far you can go in making your own matching banding depends largely on the variety and suitability of small offcuts of wood you have available. The choice of approach depends mainly on how much needs replacing.

If you can buy banding to match, trim the broken end with a sharp chisel, and cut the replacement to length with a scalpel.

a

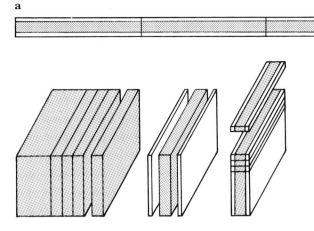

b

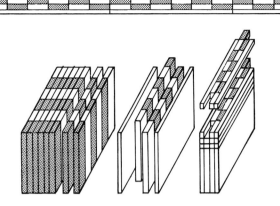

Glue it in place. Use an offcut to experiment with stains and polishes to produce a finish that matches the old wood. Normal everyday wear, and periodic household polishing of the whole area, will help the woods to blend together.

If you are replacing the banding completely, lift out the old banding with a chisel. Wipe out the recess with a hot damp cloth to remove traces of glue. Mitre the corners when gluing in the new banding, by overlapping one piece with the other and cutting carefully through both with a scalpel, protecting the surrounding wood with waste veneer.

To match unusually patterned bandings you may have to make up your own. First determine what kinds of wood you have to match.

Woods typically used in banding include satinwood, boxwood for thin pale yellow lines, and ebony for black-and-pale chequered effects.

Take as an example a simple three-strand banding. The main central strand is generally cut across the grain, making the grain visible and giving the surface plenty of character. Start by squaring the end of a piece of wood for the centre strand, as in [**2.26a**]. Cut a slice off the end to the width of the centre part of the banding. To each side, glue a veneer of the species of wood for the narrow

outer strands of the banding. From this 'sandwich', with a fine saw or knife, slice thin sections. Lay them end to end to build up the length of banding required. Any irregularities or excess depth can be sanded away when the banding is in place.

A more complicated but widely used banding consists of a chequered pattern. Start by gluing blocks of two types of wood together. Slice them into segments as thick as half the width of the centre banding. Arrange them in pairs to give a chequered effect [**2.26b**] and glue them together, with the veneers on the outer side as in the first example. When they are firmly glued, slice off the sections of banding as before.

Stringing is far simpler. A sharp spike is essential to clear out the recess of the old stringing. Work a hot damp rag into it to mop up any old glue. Brush new glue into the recess, and press the stringing into place, working from one end and forcing it well down into the recess inch by inch. When the glue has completely set, smooth the stringing flush with the surrounding surface, using either a cabinet maker's scraper or glasspaper.

It is hardly worth trying to make your own stringing, but in case you cannot find a suitable replacement, here is a simple technique. First plane a piece of the required wood square on all sides. Boxwood is used more often

2.27 Cut marquetry pictures with a fine fret-saw, from a sandwich formed from the picture segments, fine veneer, and a plywood base.

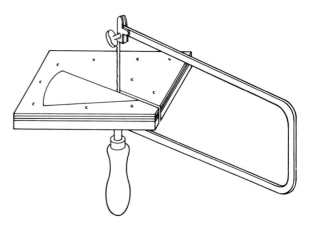

than any other wood for this purpose. Clamp a steel rule to one side, the same distance from the edge as the thickness of stringing that you require. If you cannot gauge that accurately, cut it slightly over-size. You can reduce it later with glasspaper to give a tight fit when dry.

Clamp the wood in a vice, and slice along it against the straight edge with a craft knife or scalpel, keeping both hands well behind the blade for safety. Turn the work on to its side, and clamp the ruler on again. Then make a second cut to meet the first. The stringing should come away cleanly.

Cut one length of stringing off each of the four corners of the wood. You may be able to cut off a second and third length all round. If not, plane the wood square again to give you four fresh corners to work on. But there are other methods of producing stringing, and you may well devise one that suits you better.

MARQUETRY

A restoration problem that is in many ways similar to banding occurs in much fine antique furniture. It arises when marquetry pictures become damaged. You may have to replace one part of a picture, or all of it. Bear in mind the general rule of restoration – that the more original an article the more valuable it is. But remember also that any furniture in a good state of repair is more attractive to look at than one which shows uncorrected damage.

Marquetry is similar to inlay. Both consist of veneer, but in marquetry the pattern is made up of several pieces of veneer, assembled into a picture or design then glued into place. Inlay consists of small pieces of veneer let into the recesses in the ground.

If you need to restore a complete picture in marquetry, first draw a reproduction of the original as accurately as possible. You may be able to take it from the remains of the damaged marquetry. If that is unrecognisable, draw up a new picture by referring to a photograph of a similar piece of furniture. Draw the design in a clear thin line, and take photocopies of it, one for each of the different woods in the marquetry. Give a numeral to each of the different woods, and mark the number for one of the woods on each photocopy. Then, referring to the original drawing, mark the number of the wood on each drawing on the separate sections of the picture. From each sheet, cut out the numbered sections roughly with scissors, slightly over-size all round. Paste these parts of the picture on a piece of waste veneer, with

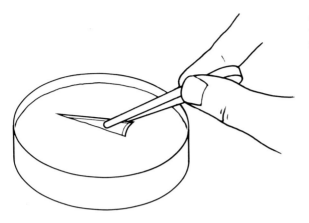

2.28 You can shade pieces of the veneer by dipping the parts into a bed of heated sand, to darken it slightly.

the pattern elements for each wood close together. Cut the waste veneer into separate parts – one for each wood – so that you have the pattern elements for each wood on its own piece.

Now make up several 'sandwiches' – again one for each wood. Put the waste veneer with the paper shapes pasted on to it on top. Underneath, lay the fine veneer from which you are going to cut those parts of the pattern. Underneath that you need a sheet of plywood, which will support the fine veneer while you cut it. The three parts of the sandwich must be held tightly together, so obtain some veneer pins, nail them right through the sandwich between the paper shapes, and bend over the ends. At this stage some skilful fine cutting is called for. Serious woodworking enthusiasts may have a band-saw or power jig-saw to work with. A hand fret-saw is just as good and gives plenty of control. Hold it upright, and cut round the outline of the shapes in each drawing [**2.27**]. The pieces of veneer will fall out, cut to exactly the size and shape required for the pattern.

Professional marquetry producers work this way, but put several pieces of fine veneer into each sandwich. Several thicknesses of the same veneer will reproduce the same picture several times. Different types of veneer

in each sandwich will produce different versions of the picture.

When you have cut all the pieces, assemble them on a copy of the original drawing. They should fit into place exactly, but any necessary adjustments are easy to make with a scalpel or glasspaper. When you are satisfied with the fit, paste them on to a reverse image of the drawing. You can easily make one of these with carbon paper. And now you can turn the marquetry picture over, and glue it on to the 'ground'. When it is dry simply wipe off the paper with a damp cloth. Finally sand down and polish the picture.

An interesting variation, which can produce remarkably beautiful marquetry work, involves shading the individual pieces.

Fill an old tobacco tin with fine dry sand. Heat the sandbox over a low flame. Holding the veneer with a pair of tweezers, push it slowly into the sand, about halfway [**2.28**]. When you remove it, you will see that the hot sand has darkened it permanently. If you experiment with offcuts, you can vary the rate at which you push the veneer into the sand, and the time needed to produce perfectly graded shading. Assemble the picture as before, and you may be surprised at the quality of the finished piece.

When only individual parts are missing from a marquetry picture or design, replacing them is similar to repairing veneer. With a soft pencil, make a 'rubbing' of the area to be replaced. Clean out the recess. Make up a 'sandwich' as in marquetry to cut the new piece, and glue it in place.

Making up your own inlay, banding, and stringing, and your own marquetry patterns may be 'fiddly' work, and may be more interesting to the woodworking enthusiast than to the ordinary householder who simply wants to keep his furniture in good repair. But if the time is available and you have the patience to take the job at the unhurried pace that is essential in so much craft work, then the improvement that you can bring to otherwise dilapidated furniture is dramatic. And it is just this kind of intricate and time-consuming repair work that is so prohibitively expensive, if you try to have it done professionally.

DISTRESSING

At some stage towards the end of the restoration, you will have to consider the problem of how to conceal and disguise your new wood or restored surface, before you come to stain and polish it.

If you have let in a substantial piece, or even replaced a complete member, you will have a fine new part looking startlingly out of character with the old. Its faces will be smooth, its edges sharp and true. In the reproduction industry, the process of making a newly manufactured article of furniture look as if it has been in use for a couple of hundred years is called 'distressing'. Some craftsmen regard it as an essential step in building furniture in any early style; others find the business of inflicting intentional damage on any newly made article a source of distress in itself.

On balance, it is perhaps advisable to opt for a complete concealment in restoration, and simulate the kind of damage the rest of the piece has suffered. The first thing to do is sand down the sharp edges, to reproduce the wear that any furniture will have suffered in years of use.

Around handles and door edges, the hundreds of tiny indentations that fingernails make can be simulated by tapping the surface for a few minutes with a wire egg whisk. Go over the surface lightly and fast as if beating a drum roll.

A device frequently used in the trade to reproduce bumps and bruises on old furniture is chain. A short length of fairly heavy chain, with about one-inch links, will make the right kind of shallow marks in a random pattern. Some distressers make up a kind of 'cat o'nine tails' with three lengths of chain attached to a handle. You can probably achieve equally realistic damage by dropping the chain a couple of feet on to your new wood.

An alternative is to tap the wood with a rough selection of tools – hammers, screwdrivers, chisels – in random fashion. You will soon have the new wood looking as worn as the original.

METAL REPAIRS

Faults to the metal parts of furniture may form only a small part of the amateur restorer's work, and many people who are enthusiasts for wood and its working take less pleasure in dealing with metal. Nevertheless it can be extremely difficult and expensive to find professional craftsmen prepared to do the work, and there is no reason to avoid this aspect of restoration. The tools are similar, and the operations run on the same basic lines – dismantling, removing damaged or worn material and replacing it with new, reassembly, and polishing.

HANDLES

The problem most frequently encountered is that of replacing missing handles on drawers and doors. If it is not possible to find a matching example in an antique shop, the nearest possible reproduction may be the only answer. You may be able to buy a similar item slightly over-size, and alter it to produce an exact match. You can file brass plate quite easily, and saw it with a hacksaw. If a swan-neck handle is oversize, you can easily reduce it, and this kind of exercise serves as a good starting experience for working in metal. The technique is similar to woodwork, but first you must anneal the brass. Heat it in a gas flame, then plunge it into cold water. It will lose any brittleness and you will be able to work it.

Cut out the excess, and file down the mating parts to the same diameter. If the faces meet well, you can solder them together without difficulty. Anybody who has done any household plumbing will have no trouble with this type of work. On a repair of this size, the best heat source is a modern butane-gas blowlamp. The old-fashioned pressure type, though attractive to look at, gives far too big a flame. You can buy nozzles in various grades for the bottled-gas blowlamp, and one which produces a fine flame will suit this kind of work.

First file the faces smooth and coat them with soldering flux. Fix the parts in a vice, with the faces in contact, and play the blowlamp flame over the joint until the area heats up. Now take a length of solder (it comes either on a spool or on a card) remove the heat source, and touch the solder to the join while the brass is still hot. The solder will melt and run into the joint by capillary attraction, and will seal itself to the two brass faces wherever you applied the flux. File away any odd spots of solder, and polish the brass.

This is not the strongest of joints. Other ways of working metal such as brazing and welding give a far stronger bond, but are beyond the scope of the average household furniture restorer. Even so, the solder should be strong enough to hold the handle together, and if you have worked with precision, nobody should see the join when the renewed handle is on the furniture.

INLAID BRASS

Inlaid brass occasionally causes problems, as the glue weakens and the corners lift, often helped by shrinkage in the wood, or even by an over-enthusiastic duster.

Take care not to damage the brass in repairing it. It is thin material, and liable to crease permanently if it is folded.

Do not try to pull it back to lift it. Instead slide a thin wooden wedge under it and prise it away from its bed. If the wooden base has shrunk it may be necessary to cut a small piece out of the brass, so that it drops back into place. When you have cleaned all the old glue out of the recess, you can glue the inlay down. Woodworking glue is not made to stick metal to wood. Use instead one of the modern adhesives which bond equally well with wood or metal. Make up some form of caul to press the inlay home firmly until the glue has set.

Some restorers help keep the brass in place with pins. The thinnest brass-wire tapered pins should be used. As you glue in the inlay, hammer the pins gently through the brass until they bind with the wood beneath, and hold the inlay down. When the bond has set firm, nip off the protruding ends of the pins with pincers, and sandpaper the whole area down flush and smooth. When you polish the finished work the pins will not show. If the trouble is simply a raised corner, ease some adhesive under it, and hold it down until it has set.

LOCKS

The most complicated metal item likely to give trouble is the lock. Often, the problem is simply that the key is missing. The restorer with average skill will find it easy to cut one to fit. If the cabinet was locked when the key disappeared it may be possible to take out other drawers to gain access to the screws that hold the lock, or to prise apart a weak cabinet to gain access. At worst, a complete dismantling operation might be necessary.

Locks made before 1778 were relatively simple, and

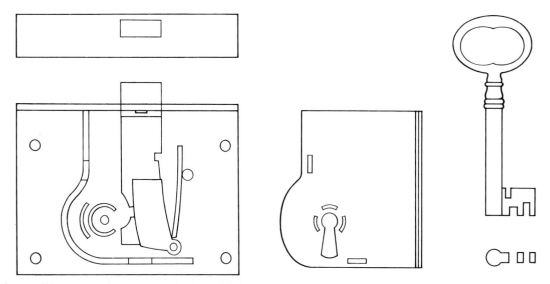

2.29 It is possible to cut a key to pass the 'wards' that protect early locks.

you may be able to make a key that will open one. Once you have got the lock open, you should dismantle it, and cut a new more accurate key with a saw and file.

Whether or not a key will turn in this type of lock depends on it matching a set of obstacles called 'wards'. If the slots in the key let it pass the wards, it will operate the bolt. The wards were simply fixed to the sides of the lock casing.

First obtain a blank that will fit the lock. A few minutes careful measuring, probing, and estimating will give you the length and depth of the key flange, and the diameter of the pin over which the stem of the key fits. Then hunt out a good locksmith or ironmonger who stocks blanks of the right size. Buy at least two – one (or more) for experimenting, and one for a finished job.

Mix up a paste from petroleum jelly and a suitable dark colouring pigment, such as powder paint. Spread a thin layer on the key flange, and start to turn it in the lock. The obstacles it encounters should show up as clear indentations in the layer of jelly. Mark them with a file and with the key blank held firmly in a vice, cut them out with a hacksaw and file.

A series of inventions after 1778 introduced a variety of locking systems, with tumblers, levers, and cylinders – each more complicated, more ingenious, and more secure than the last. Most of them are too tricky to pick or unlock from the outside, and you will have to remove the lock and dismantle it [**2.29**]. Once the lock is open and you can see the inner mechanical parts, it is possible to reproduce the key that will open it, and to replace worn parts to bring the lock back to working order. But this is advanced-level metalwork, comparable in difficulty to car mechanics. If you can work at this level, all you will need is a book on locks, and infinite patience.

3. CLEANING, STRIPPING AND REFINISHING

Some of the furniture in your home will have nothing seriously wrong with it, and there will be no reason to carry out any structural repairs or restoration. But many pieces in otherwise sound condition would benefit from careful cleaning. All but the best kept furniture responds to a little attention; as you see the results of simple cleaning you will find that you quickly learn to distinguish between maturity in a piece of furniture, and dirt. They are often confused.

The finishing processes described in this chapter are designed so that you can work out as you go just how radical a treatment your furniture needs. They start with a simple cleaning process, and move on by stages to the most drastic, a complete strip down and re-finishing.

This sequence also serves a second purpose. If you follow it, you will gain practical experience of refinishing, without damaging the furniture you are working on. If there is a finish worth preserving under several layers of grime and sooty deposit, you will be able to recover it in a few hours if you work carefully through this sequence. If you move too quickly, you will find that you have taken the piece back to bare wood, when all that was required was a simple clean up. Not only will you have made unnecessary work for yourself; you will also have destroyed the efforts of previous owners, perhaps even those of the craftsman who originally created the piece.

Working by stages in this way is a great advantage to the beginner in restoration. By the time you have completed a few pieces of your own, you will have less need to go through the processes one by one, and you will be able to judge accurately exactly what is needed from the look and feel of the piece.

One of the difficulties a beginner faces is deciding what finish is already on the furniture. Broadly speaking, finishes fall into two categories. Hard finishes coat the wood in a fine protective shell. They include french polish, or shellac, various kinds of varnishes, and various kinds of lacquers. So long as they remain unscratched they should protect the wood from dirt, and remain impervious to dirt themselves. Other finishes might be called 'soft'. The main one is wax polish, prepared according to a variety of recipes. Wax is a fine finish and hard enough to ward off ordinary dirt. Eventually, however, it loses its freshness, and gathers an accumulation of grime and old polish that turns it black and dull.

Until recently, rooms were warmed mainly by coal fires which, however efficiently they burned, wafted particles of dust and smoke into the atmosphere. These settled on all the furniture, and as the housewife carefully dusted and polished it, she rubbed a little more dirt each time into the layers of polish. Over the course of decades, wooden furniture can get so badly blackened that the grain and character of the wood are invisible. Then it is impossible to see the beauty of the furniture, and you can have no idea what kind of wood it is.

The best place to start cleaning, then, is on the blackest and dullest piece of furniture you can find. If the finish is wax, you will soon reveal the wood beneath. If it is black for some other reason – a sprayed-on black lacquer for example – your cleaning will have no effect and you can go on to the next step.

REVIVERS

The term used in the trade for a solution used to smarten up a wax finish on wood is a 'reviver'. It is possible to buy revivers, but it is perfectly simple, much cheaper, and far more rewarding to make up your own. Recipes for revivers were once closely guarded trade secrets. Now they are freely available, and like many aspects of this craft, there is always a choice from a wide range.

The simplest are generally effective, but it is worth experimenting with the more complicated recipes if you can obtain the ingredients. The simplest recipe of all is a mixture of vinegar and water, but water can have a slightly unhappy effect on wood through 'lifting' the grain. Vinegar by itself – or at least the acetic acid in it – can be moderately effective by cutting through grease. But more effective on most surfaces is a concoction known by many restorers as 'half-and-half'. It consists mainly of equal quantities of raw linseed oil and turps substitute (white spirit). Then a third ingredient is added – a dash of vinegar.

An eggcupful of each of the two main ingredients produces enough reviver to clean the average piece of furniture. Mix them up in a bottle, and shake it well before and during use, because the vinegar will separate out and float on top as the bottle stands. Label it clearly, and make a note of the recipe you are using, for future reference.

To use it on dirty furniture, work it round and round with a soft cloth, preferably muslin. Wipe the surface with a clean cloth, and repeat as often as you continue to get results. Use an old toothbrush to reach inaccessible parts of corners, mouldings and carvings. Often treatment with a reviver is all a piece needs to bring it back to life. The grain shows again, and you can keep the furniture in good condition for another couple of decades by simple polishing.

How the reviver works depends on the nature of the dirt you are trying to dislodge. But basically the acetic acid cuts through the grease, the white spirit dissolves at least the top layer of polish, and the linseed oil, as well as lubricating the whole process, seeps down through the polish and feeds the wood. Then it dries to help give a hard shine. But one word of caution: when linseed oil sinks into wood it darkens it considerably. If your furniture is dark enough already, you may want to avoid this. More important, your layers of polish may not be even. If it is cracked or patchy, the oil will affect some parts more than others, leaving a permanent 'skewbald' effect. If you are working on a cracked french polish surface, the oil will seep into the cracks and can leave a permanent and indelible stain recording exactly where the cracks were. Some restorers will not allow linseed oil near furniture, unless they are using it all over. It just shows how widely expert views vary in this trade. Go carefully on your own furniture.

Individual polishers also vary the ingredients they use in revivers. Some use methylated spirits instead of turps substitute. One recipe recommends equal parts of raw linseed oil, methylated spirits, and vinegar. Another gives only two parts methylated spirits, to 48 parts vinegar and 50 parts raw linseed oil. Clearly you can vary the exact measures to suit yourself. They seem to make little difference to the way the basic mix works.

Several other well established recipes use more obscure ingredients. If you can buy them, either from your local chemist or from a polish shop, you may like to experiment with them. Here are two:

1. 1 cupful vinegar
    1 cupful methylated spirits
    1 oz camphor
    1 oz raw linseed oil
    $\frac{1}{2}$ oz butter of antimony

2. 4 parts raw linseed oil
    12 parts vinegar
    1 part terebine

WIRE WOOL

Applied with a cloth, the reviver may not produce the finish you are looking for, for a variety of reasons. It may be that the wax has flaked off in parts and has become patchy, in which case you will have to remove it all. Alternatively the dirt may be particularly stubborn, in which case neither muslin nor any other cloth will be strong enough to dislodge it with any of the revivers.

If so, you will have to go on to the next stage in the cleaning process, and use one of the furniture restorer's most useful tools, wire wool. This is available in five grades in Britain: 5 is the most coarse; the finest is 000. Most hardware stores stock only the medium grades, but you will need the finest for several operations in furniture finishing, so it is worthwhile asking your local shop to order you a supply. Specialist polish suppliers stock it in all grades. Buy at least a large pack at a time;

you will be using and discarding it in fairly large amounts.

Try rubbing in a reviver with wire wool. Work with a feather-light touch at first, and the wire wool may take off just enough of the dirty and greasy surface to leave a finish of serviceable old polish. If results are slow in coming increase the pressure, but not enough to scratch the wood. Work round and round until the dirt begins to loosen, then finish with long smooth strokes along the length of the grain to clean out any dirt trapped there.

When the wire wool gets clogged, turn it to produce a clean surface, and when it is full of debris discard it altogether and make a new pad.

A slightly more drastic alternative is to use wire wool with methylated spirits alone as a solvent. When you finally wipe off the debris from the surface you may find you have achieved an adequately restored finish without expending too much time or effort.

If none of these methods succeeds, it may mean that the finish you are working on is some form of cellulose. Try using cellulose thinner with wire wool. Make sure you open the windows because thinner gives off potentially dangerous vapours. Wear rubber gloves, and give the surface to be stripped down a wash with the thinner, or a mixture of thinner and methylated spirits. You will have to experiment to find the most effective proportions for the surface concerned, and work quickly, because thinner soon evaporates. Keep rubbing and applying the solvent until you have reduced the surface layers to a sticky paste. Wipe this away, and give the surface a final wash down with a rag soaked in methylated spirits.

If the surface is too tough to respond to any of these treatments, or if you are confident you can do better by starting all over again, go ahead and strip it back to bare wood.

STRIPPING

In recent years the widespread practice has developed of stripping furniture by immersing it in a bath of caustic soda. This process rapidly removes all finishes, including paint.

The method is adequate for old doors, and perhaps to take the colour off painted pine kitchen furniture. But the treatment is too brutal for good furniture. It leaves a grey tinted surface, obscures the grain, and gives wood a dull lifeless look.

The owner who cares for his furniture, and has the time and patience to work on it, must use more discriminating techniques.

The aim is to take off the top layers of dirt and polish, leaving the lower layers intact, and not affecting the wood itself. You will also leave intact the basic work of the craftsman who originally polished the piece, and will save yourself several stages of work in re-polishing.

USING A SCRAPER

First take off as much of the unwanted finish as possible by purely mechanical means. The best tool for this is a cabinetmaker's scraper (see page 19).

Hold the scraper in two hands with the sharp hook away from you, the fingers wrapped round behind it, and the thumbs near to you. Now push it away from your body, in the direction of the grain [3.1]. A few strokes with the scraper will remove all the unwanted material. Do not allow the scraper to lean over at the edge of a surface. This puts a bevel on the corners and can cut right through a thin veneer.

You may find that scraping off layers of the old polish leaves the surface smooth enough for refinishing. But the scraper only works on relatively flat surfaces. On turned work, or on concave parts of the furniture, you will have to apply a stripping solvent.

STRIPPERS

It is essential to use a stripper that is spirit-based. Water-based strippers remove the unwanted finish but

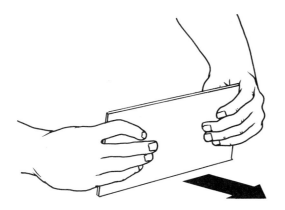

washing down the bare wood with water may 'raise the grain'. You can see this effect on a piece of untreated softwood after it has been soaked: it looks and feels slightly fluffy, and loses its hard smooth surface even when dry. If this happens with furniture you will have to smooth it down again with a scraper or glasspaper. You will also find you have dislodged any grain filler that the original craftsman used. In effect, you will have to start further back in the process than is necessary or advisable.

The containers used for commercial strippers rarely state whether the contents are water-based or spirit-based. The clue can be found in the directions for use. If they advise you to wash down with water, the stripper is water-based. If they advise washing down with methylated spirits or white spirits, they are spirit-based.

An example of a satisfactory stripper, made by Rustins, is Strypit. Wearing rubber gloves, apply the stripper with a brush. As soon as the top layer dissolves and bubbles up to form a loose dirty paste, clear it away. Use an ordinary paint scraper in the early stages on accessible surfaces. In the later stages and where you cannot manipulate the scraper, use wire wool.

After each application wipe over the surface with a rag or cotton wool pad well soaked in methylated spirits. Work quickly, to prevent the solvent working for too long and penetrating too deep. You can then control the depth your stripping goes to, and you may be able to stop stripping before the solvent attacks the lower layers of the polish, or the original bodying-in of the grain, or affects the colouring of the wood itself. All these will have remained unaffected by the dirt and grease of decades of use, and form an ideal ready-made base layer for your new finish.

On your first few pieces you may find it impossible to judge when to stop, and you will have to go right back to the initial stages. There is no harm in this, only a loss of time, and you will at least learn something of the full process of furniture finishing by starting from the beginning. Make sure you wash all surfaces well with liberal applications of methylated spirits to give yourself scrupulously clean and grease-free furniture to re-start polishing.

REMOVING INK STAINS

Ink stains on wood are almost inevitable on any antique desk or bureau.

They are easy to remove using oxalic acid which you should be able to obtain through your local chemist. Oxalic acid is highly poisonous, so lock it away when you are not using it. The chemist will sell it to you in the form of crystals. Dissolve a couple of tablespoonsful in half an inch of water in the bottom of a bottle.

Wear rubber gloves. Pour the acid generously over the stained area to form a small pool. Dab it in with a wad of cotton wool for a few minutes, then soak up the acid with a dry wad. Repeat the process, several times if necessary. It may take an hour or so of dabbing and washing, but eventually the old ink will be neutralised and the stain will disappear.

The treatment can change the colour of the wood slightly in the area where the acid has been applied. Pale mahogany, for example, turns from a yellow to a slightly pink shade, so once you have taken out the ink stain, wash the acid lightly over the whole surface. The colour may not be all the same, but the edges of the treated area will be less noticeable.

Some restorers recommend hydrogen peroxide, or ordinary household bleach, but these leave a far more drastic patch which you will have to re-stain to match the surrounding wood.

REFINISHING FURNITURE

Wherever you have let in new segments of wood, or replaced complete members, you will have to put a new finish on it.

Many craftsmen find refinishing the most satisfying part of all furniture restoration. You can begin to see your work come to fruition, as the furniture, once dilapidated and dull, starts to display a new beauty and vitality.

Unfortunately, the process can be bewildering as well as satisfying for the beginner. There exists a wide range of methods of finishing a piece of furniture. Some of them are simple; some appear complicated. And the problem of selecting from the varied advice available is likely to confuse rather than illuminate. Even when you have worked out which finish is ideal for your piece of furniture, according to the age of the piece, its value, and its future use, you will still find almost as many methods of applying each finish as there are polishers trained in the craft.

For the amateur and owner-restorer, the picture is further clouded by the commercial considerations. Some finishes which are ideal for the amateur have been neglected by the professional because they take too long. The professional restorer would either have to work on the piece over a long period of time, so that it remained in his workshop for several weeks before he could charge for the job, or the actual work would absorb too much of his time for him to be able to charge a reasonable fee and still make a profit.

The owner is mercifully free from these constraints. Presumably he is doing the work for pleasure, so it hardly matters how many hours the job takes and he can spend enjoyable hours on it. And it is not critical if the furniture has to be left untouched for a few days before moving on to the next stage. An owner-restorer should have enough time to devote to the work to produce the perfect finish. And the cost in materials in most finishing methods compared with the labour component in professional charges is almost negligible.

On the other hand, in strictly comparable operations the amateur can hardly expect to achieve quite the same results as the professional. It takes the polisher as much as seven years of apprenticeship to become a skilled craftsman. The amateur restorer, working in leisure hours only, and on just a small selection of his own furniture, is never going to attain the professional's range of skills, or his knowledge and experience of any single operation. The average owner's results will therefore be a compromise between the professional's skill, and the amateur's devotion.

To get the best results you should concentrate at first on a limited range of processes. That way you may get enough practice to achieve a finish virtually indistinguishable from that of a professional polisher. Once you have acquired a measure of skill, you can go on to experiment with some of the more unusual methods.

To aid the beginner, we have kept the list of finishing products short, and methods of applying them simple. Once you understand these, you can track down information on the more esoteric methods.

There are three basic steps in finishing. First colouring the wood: in the case of most restoration work you will be attempting the difficult task of matching new wood to old. Next filling in the grain ready to take the final polish. Lastly giving the final polish, both to enhance the appearance, and to protect the wood from damage in use.

STAINING

When you have let in new wood or made a new part for an item of furniture, you will have wood which is a different colour from the surrounding material. And when you have stripped or scraped an area, it will almost certainly need re-colouring back to its original shade.

You will have to colour the wood by staining it.

Old texts list the chemicals used on various species of wood to achieve all the colours and tones that the restorer might require. The problem that home craftsmen face today is that these materials are becoming increasingly difficult to obtain in their raw state. Specialist polish manufacturers can generally supply them, but they are designed mainly for the professional cabinet maker or polisher who will save money by being able to mix up the large quantities of any stain he may need from the basic raw materials. For the home restorer, who will have only small quantities of wood to colour on any piece of furniture, proprietory stains and wood dyes are perfectly adequate.

Manufacturers like Colron and Rustins produce a range of wood colouring liquids, at only a few pence for a small tin or bottle. You will rarely need more, as a thimbleful is generally enough to colour a chair leg, and an eggcupful will completely cover a new table top. So the cost of materials for this work is relatively low, and the convenience of being able to buy from the local d-i-y-store gives them the advantage over cheaper but more complicated chemicals bought on a special trip to Clerkenwell.

However there is one pitfall. For furniture restoration purposes, the names on the tins are virtually meaningless. Proprietory stains are made for the purpose of colouring pale softwoods such as pine and deal to make them look like the more interesting hardwoods. Although the grain is unlikely to be convincing, you can stain a pine table with a mahogany colour and to the uninitiated it will look more or less like a mahogany table.

If, on the other hand, you have let a piece of mahogany into the leg of a table to make a repair, staining it with a mahogany stain will have quite a different effect. It might even turn it bright red.

So, after buying the stains, ignore the names on the outside of the tins.

The technique, as always, is to carry out a trial run on an offcut of the wood you are using. And you should achieve the right colour by mixing two or more stains.

It is worth buying three tins or bottles of stain in the first instance. 'Medium oak' will give a standard brown colour, 'mahogany' will give a redder shade, and 'walnut' will give a slightly greyer, flatter tone. From these three you should be able to produce a blend that will give a good match to most woods commonly used in furniture.

To aid in estimating the effects of mixing any two or all three stains, it is useful to make a chart. Any piece of white-wood board will do, such as a floorboard offcut.

Mark nine small squares on it, and with a small pad made from a square of cloth wrapped round a wad of cotton wool, apply the stain neat to the first three squares. Label them clearly.

Next mix them in pairs in equal quantities. A few drops in a bottle-top will be plenty. Apply the mixes on the second row, and label them. On the bottom row make up a mixture of all three. That will leave two squares, on which you can experiment with different quantities, or with a diluted version of one that is near to your requirement. White spirits is generally a good dilutant, but check if any other is specified on the tin or bottle.

If you buy four cans of stain, you will need ten squares, and if you buy five, fifteen squares. You will probably find that some of the squares are not very different from others. And you must remember that you are experimenting on white wood, which will produce a different effect from the wood used in your work.

By the end of an experiment like this, you will know a lot about the effects of mixing stains, and you should be able to produce, quite quickly, the mix to give the right colour for your final wood. Test it first on the offcut.

Bear in mind also that when you are staining end grain, it absorbs more and shows up considerably darker than the sides and edges. So dilute it, or apply fewer coats.

FILLING

Before you apply the stain to your wood, you must consider whether you need to fill the grain or not. An open-grained wood like oak can be attractive with the grain left unfilled. Any stain you apply will tend to accumulate in the grain, leaving it slightly darker. Then the wax or polish that you apply will build up in the recess, and form an effective filler.

In french polishing the first application of polish fills most of the pores in the wood, and subsequent applications help to build up a hard surface, so that no filler is necessary. The problem is that this process, of applying the polish, waiting for it to dry, then cutting it back, takes time, and professionals like to use a filling material to shorten the early stages.

If you want to do the same, filling is a simple operation. The best and most convenient filler is plaster of Paris, but it is glaring white, so you will have to add a colour to prevent it showing through as white flecks.

The best material to colour plaster for most shades of wood is vandyke brown powder. Mix it into the plaster, using just enough to take away the glaring tone of the white for light woods, and more for dark woods.

To apply the filler, dab a damp cloth pad into the plaster so that it picks up a deposit, and rub it in circular movements over the workpiece. Before the plaster begins to set, lift off the residue from the surface of the work by wiping it across the grain with a clean cloth.

If there are larger holes to be filled, for example an old screw hole, or a bruise that refuses to come out with the damp heat treatment described on page 49, a more substantial form of stopping will be needed.

Several proprietary products are available, such as plastic wood, Brummer's stopping and Gedge's Durax woodfiller, all in a variety of shades to match surrounding wood. Work them into place with a spatula or putty knife, and sand them down to level when dry.

An alternative filler is stick stopping, which looks like sealing wax, and again is available in various shades from specialist polish manufacturers such as Gedge and Co.

Melt the wax with a hot iron (an old screwdriver heated in a gas flame will do the job) directly over the fault to be filled. The wax will drip into place. Level it with a scraper when it has set. To help fix the filler in place, prick the recessed area several times with a pin before melting in the wax. The wax will then penetrate the holes and form a set of 'roots'.

OIL FINISH

When skilled labour was cheap, oil was a popular finish. It has since fallen into neglect as it takes time, a lot of hard work, and demands long intervals between applications, but it is an excellent finish for much household furniture. It stands up well to ordinary household maltreatment. Hot plates and cups, spilled liquids, and scratches do little harm; and if it should need repair, it is perfectly simple to rub in a new coating.

Providing you can leave the piece out of commission for several weeks, and have the patience to wait for each application to dry, oil is the easiest finish to apply.

First colour the wood. Make sure that the stain is several shades lighter than the colour you finally want, as the oil will darken the wood.

Then rub in a light coating of linseed oil. Rub until the oil goes dry. Repeat after a few days. Eventually you will build up an attractive eggshell sheen.

Polishing experts disagree about which oil you should use – boiled linseed or raw linseed oil.

To produce boiled linseed oil, manufacturers boil raw oil for a certain period, and add other substances to reduce the drying time. Normally, boiled linseed oil will dry in about 24 hours, and you can then apply the next coat.

You can produce your own boiled oil. Simmer raw oil for fifteen minutes, and add one part turpentine to eight parts of the linseed oil, plus terebine to help the drying, in the proportion of one teaspoonful to a half-pint.

Raw linseed oil takes up to three days to dry (some experts recommend leaving it for a month), but once it is dry it produces a harder surface.

On balance it is best for the owner-restorer who can afford time for these long intervals between coats.

Apply the linseed oil with a cloth or pad of wadding. Be sparing. Give the surface just a thin coating. Rub it in well and hard. Some polishers use a brick or heavy wood block, covered in felt or velvet, to increase the pressure.

Leave the job until the oil dries. Repeat the process, every few days, for up to a month if you can, to build up a good hard coating. You could go on indefinitely; and applying the occasional coat of oil over the years gradually improves the piece, and keeps the wood in good order. It is comforting to know that you can do little damage to this kind of surface that is not quickly and easily put right.

An alternative technique is to apply a mixture of equal parts of linseed oil and turpentine for the initial coat. Brush it on thinly, rub it lightly, and leave it for a month. The coats that follow should contain a higher proportion of linseed oil, and each one should be left for several weeks to harden completely. This is a slow process, but if you can afford the time it gives a satisfying, deep polish.

WAX FINISH

Wax polishing is among the oldest treatments for furniture and was used long before the introduction of french polishing in the nineteenth century. Wax is therefore an appropriate finish for earlier furniture – oak chairs, oak gate-legged tables, old oak or walnut bureaux and chests. It gives a less shiny surface than french polish, without being dull, and many people prefer it. If applied correctly (which really means with enough hard work) it produces an attractive sheen which brings out the figuring of the wood.

First stain the wood to the colour required. It is not absolutely necessary to apply any filler. The wax itself will fill the cavities and crevices in the grain, but you might want to use a coloured filler on some open grained woods such as oak and mahogany, to produce an 'antique' effect.

Before waxing, brush on one, or preferably two, thin coats of white or clear french polish (see page 68 for an explanation of these terms). This simply seals the wood so that it does not absorb the wax. If it did, the dirt would eventually work its way through the wax and into the wood. Clear french polish will not have any appreciable effect on the colour of the wood itself. White polish may darken it slightly.

The work is now ready for waxing. You can either choose one of innumerable proprietary waxes, or mix your own. Mixing your own is easy, and some people find it satisfying to go right back to basics. You also know what ingredients you have put in and you can rely on it being pure.

Proprietary waxes are available coloured or clear. The coloured ones are designed as a short cut, to give an antique effect on unstained wood in a single process. You will have more control over your finish if you keep the staining and waxing stages separate.

To mix your own wax buy a quantity of pure beeswax (it comes in half ounce blocks and costs only a few pence; a couple of blocks should be enough to cover the average small piece of furniture) and a bottle of pure turpentine.

Place the wax in a container – an old shoe polish tin, well cleaned out, is ideal. Place this in a shallow dish of hot water and add enough turpentine to make an approximately half-and-half mixture. When the heat from the water has warmed the ingredients, mix them together. Then let the mixture cool and set. The exact proportions of wax to turpentine are not critical. The turps serves only as a vehicle and will eventually evaporate away. The mix should be the consistency of a thick paste or warm butter.

Professional polishers mix their wax in a double-boiler, the water simmering in the outer container rapidly melts the wax in the inner vessel. You may be able to devise a similar arrangement. Remember that turpentine is highly inflammable, and heating it over an open flame carries a serious fire risk.

Keep the tin of wax sealed when you are not using it or the turpentine will evaporate and the wax harden.

Make sure that the wood is dry, and if possible work in a warm room so that the wax will 'take' well. For the first application spread the wax sparingly on to the surface, with either a cloth or a scrubbing brush – a brush is essential for carvings and cavities, but wash all traces of dust out of it and dry it completely.

Polish the wax with a soft cloth and leave it to harden for a few days before applying the second coat.

The wax finish does not keep out dirt as well as french polish. But it is a simple matter, if dirt and dust are absorbed over the years, to clean the surface with an application of half-and-half reviver (see page 60), and apply a new coat of wax.

An alternative recipe, if you are able to obtain the ingredient, uses carnauba wax. This will harden the polish and improve its protective qualities. A well proven recipe consists of four parts beeswax, five parts turpentine and one part carnauba wax. Shred the carnauba wax with a knife before trying to mix it.

To keep the finish in good order, dust it off occasionally, and every couple of months apply a very fine coating of wax. Again, you can either use a proprietary brand, or you can make your own. One wipe of the cloth across the top of your tin of wax should be enough to polish a large piece of furniture, or two or three small ones.

FRENCH POLISHING

French polishing is without doubt the most challenging

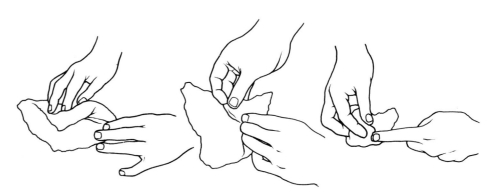

3.2 Fold a chunk of cotton wool into a pear-shaped pad with one flat face. Enclose it in a square of cotton and give the neck a twist. To charge the rubber, open up the neck and pour a generous dash of french polish into the cotton wool.

finish for both the professional and the amateur. The effect achieved can vary from an indifferent dull coating to a glossy, mirror-like finish which enhances the appearance of almost any wood and gives virtually permanent protection. It is not really suitable for furniture which will be in heavy use – dining chairs and tables suffer too much rough treatment to carry a finish which is vulnerable to heat and scratches – but for decorative furniture such as side tables, bureaux, hall chairs or library tables it is perfect.

French polish is a generic name for a range of finishing liquids made from shellac dissolved in a solvent, generally alcohol. You apply it in stages, and eventually build up a hard shell-like layer which gives the wood itself a deep burnished shine. Shellac itself is an encrustation surrounding an insect, *Lacciffer Lacca*, which lives as a parasite on trees in the Far East.

French polish comes in five basic versions. Theoretically they are quite distinct, though one polish from one manufacturer may be indistinguishable from a different polish from another manufacturer. You will have to experiment.

The standard type is known simply as *french polish*.

Garnet polish is a darker version made from garnet shellac instead of flake shellac. It gives a darker brown finish, and is suitable for oak and mahogany where deep warm brown tones are required.

Button polish is made from shellac in the form of 3-inch diameter buttons. It has nothing to do with polishing brass buttons. It gives a harder finish than standard french polish, but also produces a slightly orange effect. It is therefore useful for heightening the colour of golden-toned woods such as walnut. It is unsuitable for use over dark stains since it tends to obscure the grain.

White polish is made from bleached shellac. Because of its manufacturing process it does not dry as quickly as ordinary french polish. It has about the same darkening effect as water.

There is also a *clear* or *transparent polish* made from shellac which has been both bleached and de-waxed. It has the least darkening effect of all. It is useful for sealing very pale woods like pine before waxing.

It is possible to mix your own french polish using shellac and de-natured alcohol or turpentine. But like most materials used in furniture restoration, the polish is not expensive, and in the quantities likely to be used by the amateur restorer it is advisable to buy manufactured brands. If you can locate in your area a polish manufacturer who supplies trade polishers and shopfitters, you can buy the polish much cheaper than in small bottles through household do-it-yourself suppliers.

Specialist suppliers also make up various coloured french polishes, for example black polish and red polish. They are no longer common, and outside London and

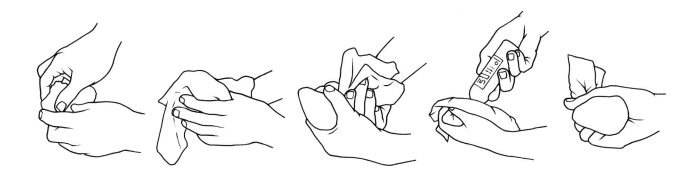

one or two other major cities, polishers will have to rely on d-i-y outlets and ironmongers stocking products from one or two main factories. They are unlikely to stock unusual polishes, and you will have to achieve the effect you want by staining the wood and applying the polish separately.

Whichever approach you adopt, follow the golden rule of testing your finish first on an offcut of similar wood, or failing that, on an unobtrusive part of the furniture.

Applying french polish is not difficult, but there are degrees of sophistication which you can achieve with practice. The more advanced are only necessary when working on valuable antique furniture. For non-valuable furniture – and the amateur should stay at the strictly household level until he has built up some experience – it is possible to reduce the process to three main steps. These will produce a perfectly acceptable finish which only an expert could distinguish from a professional craftsman's best work.

Once you have stained the wood satisfactorily and applied any grain filler you want to use, the basic steps are: fadding, bodying and finishing.

For successful french polishing, you will have to arrange certain workshop conditions. It is important to work at a reasonably warm temperature, and in fairly dry conditions. Central heating, with a temperature above 65 degrees fahrenheit and all the dampness taken out of the air, produces the ideal atmosphere. If you have to work in an unheated outdoor workshed, you will have to confine your french polishing to the period from late spring to early autumn in the British Isles, unless you can arrange an effective heating system. In hot climates summer conditions are often quite unsuitable for french polishing, because of the humid atmosphere.

Try to arrange your workbench so that it stands between you and the light. You will spend some time looking along the workpiece to pick up reflections, and this is impossible if the light is behind you.

First make a rubber. You will need a chunk of cotton wool big enough to fill the palm of your hand, and a piece of cotton or linen cloth about nine inches square. The type of cloth is important. It must be white, so that no dyes seep on to the work, and it must be plain, because any fancy textures can leave the imprint of their pattern on the work. Old cotton or linen white shirts are ideal, as are men's white handkerchiefs. The weave should not be too open, or it will allow too much polish to pass through. Lawn is an ideal material, if you have it.

Carefully fold the cotton wool [3.2] into a pad with a pointed end and a flat side. Try to arrive at a shape like a pumice stone. The inside of the pad should be fairly big when dry, because soaking it with polish will shrink it considerably in size.

Pummel it against your hand and on a table top to give

a roughly flat side, and feel it to make sure there are no excessive ridges or hard spots in it. When you have a consistent hardness and a roughly satisfactory shape, place it face down in the middle of the square of material, and gather up the corners to make a small bag. Work it carefully to preserve the pointed end. The point is important to get the polish into tight corners.

Now twist up the neck of bag and feel the rubber in your hand. With your forefinger on the pointed end, the body of the pad should fall comfortably between your thumb and second finger. It may take two or three attempts, but you will soon find a shape and size that suits your work.

Now carefully open out the pad on your palm, so as to expose the lump of cotton wool. Try not to disturb its shape or put creases on the face. Pour a good dash of french polish from your bottle into the middle of the cotton wool. Later you will need only the smallest quantity to charge the rubber, but for the first filling you can be fairly generous. Fold the rubber into shape again, and dab it on a hard flat surface such as a tile or a sheet of glass, or the back of a sheet of glasspaper on a table top.

Dab the pad until the polish feeds out through the front of the rubber on to the flat surface. If none at all appears, open the rubber and add more polish. During the polishing process, you will be using controlled pressure from your fingers to feed the polish at the required rate out of the cotton wool, through the weave of the cloth, and on to the workpiece itself.

Once polish appears through the face of the rubber as you dab it, you have enough polish in the cotton wool.

Expert french polishers have some variations on the basic process. For the initial application of polish – the first 'fad' – they do not use a rubber. Instead they fold a piece of wadding into a similar shape, soak it in polish, leave it to dry, soften it again with methylated spirits, and apply the polish using the wadding without a rag cover. They call this wadding pad a 'fad', to distinguish it from the 'rubber' which has the cloth cover. The problem is that wadding is not easily obtainable, and cotton wool used in this fashion would break away and stick to the work surface. The professional system is designed to save time, but for the home polisher the practice of using a rubber for the first application is perfectly satisfactory.

Put your rubber in a tin or jar with an airtight lid whenever you are not using it to stop it drying out. Making rubbers is not expensive, but it is time consuming and it can be inconvenient to have to find material and build a new rubber when you want to get on with the polishing itself. Also, you will waste polish if you leave a rubber lying about to go hard. Once a rubber hardens, throw it away; it will be of no further use. The small amount of polish you use on the furniture itself costs only a few pence, but the amount used to charge a new rubber is significant, and with an airtight jar and tidy habits you can achieve useful savings.

For the first fad, simply slide the rubber on to the work and begin to move it back and forth in long strokes following the grain. Squeeze it between your fingers so that polish exudes on to the face of the rubber. And use a fair amount of pressure at this stage to force polish down into the open pores of the grain, but leave only a thin layer of polish on the top of the work.

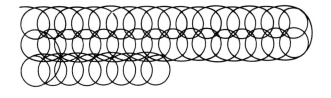

3·3

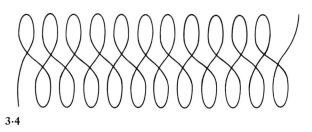

3·4

The details – and even the name – of the next step, are a source of disagreement among experts. Some regard the fadding as finished once a sealing layer of polish covers the wood. They then go on to the next process – bodying. Others apply several fads, working each one into the grain until the surface is flat. For them, bodying is then a process of building up a thickness of polish. Experts in the first school regard a thickness of polish as unsightly, and prefer to stop adding polish as soon as the unevenness and crevices of the grain have been made flat.

For the home polisher, however, there is no real difference between fadding and bodying. He goes on applying layers of polish with a rubber until the surface is flat.

Once you have applied the first coat using long strokes and fairly heavy pressure, and it has dried, you can apply succeeding coats with a variety of strokes. The basic french polishing action is a rhythmic movement in small circles, working along the surface and back, overlapping each line with the one before it [3·3]. Keep an even pressure on the rubber. If the movement away from your body is stronger than the inward movement, the circular lines will show, and any unevenness in the build-up of polish can be difficult and tedious to eliminate.

As a variation on the circular stroke, move the rubber in a small figure-of-eight motion. The different stroke will help to avoid the build up of polish in permanent circles [3·4].

You will find that your first fad is dry to the touch within about fifteen minutes of applying it, depending on the weather and the thickness of polish.

Before applying the second fad (or starting on the bodying process – whichever name you adopt) you must 'cut back' the polish.

Take a small sheet of extremely fine glasspaper (flour grade is ideal) and gently rub down the surface. The glasspaper will remove the 'pips' or 'nibs', which are small particles of dirt stuck in the polish. More importantly, it will also remove the high spots of the polish itself, leaving a good thickness in the crevices of the grain, and none over the peaks. If you take off the peaks between each application, the end result will be a completely flat layer of polish, with all the relief caused by the grain eliminated. That is the object of french polishing. As an alternative to fine grade glasspaper, ooo grade wire wool is perfectly satisfactory.

As you cut back the layer of polish, you will see pools of orange or light brown dust building up in the crevices. This dust is useful in showing how far you must go to achieve the flat surface you want. But remove the dust with a soft brush before applying the next layer of polish.

Once you are absolutely certain that you have applied a complete sealing layer over the wood, the process changes radically. From now on you will be using oil to aid the application of the polish. If there is the slightest crack in the early 'fad', the oil will seep down into the wood. This will not only produce dark stains, but will also prevent the polish adhering to the wood. Before long it will start to crack and peel off, and you will have to strip that area down and start again, and the oil will still affect the wood.

Assuming the wood is completely sealed, take a bottle

of oil. White oil is best. If you have difficulty in obtaining it, raw linseed oil will do.

The oil serves two purposes. Firstly it lubricates the already polished surface. Secondly it prevents the rubber lifting the polish already applied. You will learn by experience how much oil to use. Professionals seem to use a fair amount. Home polishers would be wise to use as little as possible. The oil does not form part of the finish, and must be removed at a later stage. Removing it is itself a skill, and if carelessly done can ruin the work. Professionals also sprinkle oil on to the work and are quite happy to see a heavy smear as they apply the rubber of polish. This can be disconcerting to the beginner, so again it is wise to use as little oil as possible. A simple and reliable method of applying oil is to place your finger over the end of the bottle, tip it up, and slide your finger across the rim. You will be left with a smear of oil on your finger. Dab it on to the front of the rubber, and it will lubricate the work just enough.

Now begin to work a new layer of polish on to the surface. Use the circular and figure-of-eight patterns described earlier, and let your wrist do the work. As you go through this stage, you will begin to grasp one of the essential elements in french polishing – pull. If you have too much oil on the surface your rubber will slide over it. You may find yourself applying a good new layer of polish, but it will only lie on the surface, and will build up eventually into a thick coating rather like sticky varnish.

With 'pull', on the other hand, you can feel the new polish making contact with the surface of the old layer. The object is to blend the two together to form a cohesive coat. As you work the new polish on with the correct pressure, the new polish acts as a solvent on the top surface of the old, and the two blend together. Too little pressure, and you will simply lay new layers of polish one on the other. Too much pressure, and the rubber will grab, so that you pull the old polish right off the surface, and especially out of the grain pores. Then you will have to go back to the beginning.

You can only find the right pressure by experience. As a rough guide, it feels rather like pulling your hand across a pane of glass. If your hand has the normal amount of sweat on it, it will set up an action with the surface of the glass. If you wash your hand, and dry it with powder, it will slide across the glass with no adhesion. If you let it get too sticky, you will set up a 'judder'. In french polishing, the ideal lies in the middle of this range, and the art of french polishing lies in the right combination of these variations. There are no hard rules, only a set of guidelines to work from. Using them, you will have to establish your own techniques and develop your own individual craft. You can vary the amount of polish in the rubber, and the pressure you apply to the work, and the amount of oil on the surface, and the amount of cutting back you do.

To summarize the work you have done so far: you will have applied the first fad, with a moderately wet rubber and some degree of pressure; you will have cut back the surface with glasspaper or wire wool, and brushed every trace of dust off the surface; you will have applied a second fad, and perhaps a third, to ensure that the wood is completely sealed with polish. You will then have gone on with the bodying stage, applying a coat of polish with a variety of strokes, lubricating the job with a smear of oil. You will have cut it back, applied another coat, cut it back again, and applied another coat, until you have a flat and reasonably shiny surface. You must leave at least twenty-four hours after applying each coat, before cutting it back and applying the next coat. You may find it still contains traces of the oil, in the form of dull smears. You now come to the last stage in the process, called, appropriately, 'finishing'.

There are at least three methods of finishing a coat of french polish. The easiest and most widely used is called 'spiriting off'.

Make up a new rubber, and charge it sparingly with methylated spirits. With the face of the rubber nearly dry, work it over the surface of the work with a light stroke, starting with small circles, and finishing with long straight strokes. The methylated spirits in the rubber lifts off any oil that remains on the surface. At the same time the rubbing action with the almost dry spirits re-works the fine top layer of the polish to burnish it into a bright fine finish.

The art of spiriting off is to judge how dry to make the rubber. Too wet, and the excess spirits will simply dissolve the polish, and you will have to go back to the bodying process to recover the flatness you need. Too dry, and it will be like a piece of rag rubbed over the work, leaving a dull surface, with nothing achieved.

As a variation, some polishers simply invert a bottle of methylated spirits in their hand to leave a smear in the palm, and dip the polishing rubber into it, to pick up a surface layer of spirit. Lightly running this from end to end over the work will pick up the oil, and leave the work burnished to a good shine. Other polishers achieve a gradual change from polish to spirits by charging the rubber with methylated spirits in the later stages of the job. The spirits follows the polish through to the face of the rubber, and works the final body into a flat shining surface.

You can try these various methods on practice pieces to see which suits you before you start work on your best furniture.

The second method, known as 'stiffing', does not use methylated spirits, and is really an extension of the bodying process, it is useful where there are no oil smears to remove. You can use your ordinary bodying rubber, or keep one specially for this operation. The key to success is to have the rubber almost dry. Charge it with polish very sparingly. Twist the neck firmly to force all excess polish out of the face, dab it away on to your tile or the reverse side of the glasspaper sheet. As you relax the twisting action you will see that the polish seeps back into the rubber leaving the surface almost dry.

Now, with a very light stroke, work the rubber in long straight lines from one end of the work to the other. This time the rubber itself will lift any smears of oil left in preceding stages and at the same time pull the polish into a good shine. As you work, you will find that with no oil, and the rubber almost dry, the 'pull' will become more and more stiff; hence the name.

Various other methods have evolved during the 170 years since french polishing was introduced, all aimed at removing the oil and producing a final hard shine. They are fairly complicated, and involve buying extra materials, many of which are no longer freely available.

The 'acid finish' uses a solution of one part of sulphuric acid to seven parts of distilled water. Mix it thoroughly. Make up a pounce bag filled with Vienna chalk (if you can get it). A pounce bag is like a rubber, but you can dispense with the pointed end, and tie the neck with string. Spread the diluted acid on to the surface of the work with a cloth, then dust the vienna chalk on to the work by dabbing it with the pounce bag. Rub the chalk over the work with a chamois cloth, and when it all dries out, dust the surface off with a clean soft cloth. The principle is that the acid absorbs the oil used in bodying, and the chalk then absorbs the acid. Just how old-fashioned the method is can be judged from the recommendation given in the handbooks for a final shine after the acid finish. It involves using a few drops of clarified ox-gall, obtained from a 'butcher's slaughterman'. The ox-gall must be put into a wide-mouthed bottle and filtered through crushed bone charcoal held in a core of white blotting paper, before use. It can be used until it goes bad.

An alternative finish is known as 'glazing'. It involves using gum benzoin diluted in methylated spirits, burnishing with burnishing agents, and converting the shiny surface to a dull sheen by using a variety of abrasives, including crocus powder.

Any enthusiast anxious to experiment with these obscure methods of polishing will enjoy researching the details in old craftsman's texts in a library.

4. UPHOLSTERY

A DROP-IN SEAT

The ideal place to start building up your skill as an upholsterer is with the same simple dining chair that gave you a start in the craft of restoration and repair. It should have a drop-in seat.

Push out the seat from underneath. On top it has a cover made of either fabric or hide. Turn it over. You will probably find a sheet of hessian or black lining tacked over it with upholsterer's large-headed tacks. Does it sag in the middle? A few years of sitting on it for two or three meals a day may well have taken the tension out of the support. Turn it back again. Does the top look as firm as it should? Or is there a pronounced dip that corresponds to the sagging on the underside? Is the fabric itself soiled from years of use and ready for re-placement? Or would you simply welcome a change?

If any or all of these problems arise, the seat is ripe for re-covering. Once you have finished a simple job like this, you will have learned much of the art of upholstery. A few bigger and better chairs, some with springs, one or two refinements in the form of sophisticated stitches, and you will be able to tackle the most formidable job and produce a highly satisfactory result.

RIPPING OFF

The first task, in almost every upholstery operation, is to strip the chair down to the bare frame. On some occasions you might want to carry out a minor repair which does not warrant a complete strip down, but that can be more tricky than starting from scratch. In any case, fully re-covering a chair is the best way to learn.

For this operation you will need a ripping chisel, and a mallet. A ripping chisel costs a couple of pounds. They come either straight or with a cranked blade. Which you buy is a matter of preference. Or you can follow many upholsterers and use an old screwdriver. If the screwdriver blade is badly worn, grind it down to give a well squared-off end. It should not be so sharp that it cuts through the tack and leaves a spike of metal in the wood.

Work on the underside first. Secure the seat either to your bench with a G-cramp, or in a vice. Start near one corner, push the end of the chisel against the head of a tack, or under it if you possibly can, and hit the chisel firmly with the mallet. At the same time, drop your hand a couple of inches. This will have a levering effect on the tack, and it should flip out neatly. It may take one or two blows, the first to bend up the head of the tack, the second to force the tack out of the wood. Take care to knock in the direction of the grain, that is along the length of the seat frame, not across it. If you try knocking the tack across the grain you will probably either split the wood or break the tack.

Work round the seat, removing the tacks that hold the hessian or black lining in place. Lift off this cover and lay it to one side.

Now you will probably see how the top covering folds over to the underside of the seat, and is tacked down. Notice how, at the corner, the cover is pulled over, trimmed, and nailed down with an overlap. If you are just beginning upholstery, you would do well to make a rough sketch of the way the corner is formed. This will help you (assuming it is done correctly) when you come to replace the covering. You will also be able to see how far the covering has faded by comparing it with areas that have been protected from daylight.

Work round the piece again, knocking out all the tacks that hold the covering in place.

Removing the covering will expose either a layer of wadding – a white fluffy material like loose sheep's wool (if so lay this aside) or a taut covering of white calico. If the latter, knock out any tacks holding it. You will then see the wadding underneath.

After the calico and wadding have been removed, you will come to the stuffing. With all upholstery operations, it is worth looking closely at the stuffing of a chair.

The type of stuffing you should look out for is horsehair. It has an indefinite life and in most craftsmen's opinion gives the best finish. Being also rare, it is extremely valuable. A professional upholsterer can get it

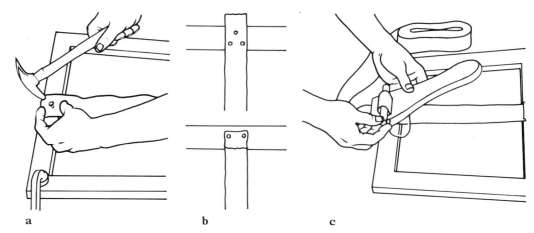

4.1a Tack home the free end of the webbing roll over the centre of one side of the frame.
b. Locate the tacks in a 'W' to ensure strength without splitting.
c. Loop the webbing through the stretcher, and insert the peg.

a   b   c

carded (combed out free of tangles) to use again and may pay you a small sum for yours. Or you might be able to get it carded yourself and re-use it. If you can't get horsehair you will turn to one of the three forms of stuffing most widely available today – sea grass, fibre, or hog's hair.

If foam rubber comes out of the chair, in any condition, reject it. No-one yet knows how long the life of foam rubber is in furniture. One upholsterer found yellow powder crumbling out of a chair in large quantities. Mystified, he asked the owner what it might be, and it emerged that only fifteen years previously the chair had been stuffed with foam rubber, which was now beginning to disintegrate. With one or two exceptions, the techniques described in this book call for the use of traditional materials.

Finally, in stripping down your chair, you will come to the upholstery support. This may be a set of springs, but in a seat of this size is more likely to be simply webbing. Go round the frame again, knocking out the tacks, until you have ripped off all the old webbing and you are left with the bare frame. If there are flat springs screwed securely to the frame, leave them in place.

If you happen to break the heads off any of the tacks, try to pull them out with pincers, or gouge them out. If you cannot do either, knock them well in with a fine

punch. You do not want any jagged ends to damage your new upholstery.

Before you start replacing the upholstery, you must make sure that the frame is sound. It is too late when you have fitted comfortable new stuffing and an attractive new cover, to find that the chair itself is loose and rapidly getting looser.

If the joints are loose – and you must test them by vigorous wobbling – take them apart, clean off the old glue, and glue and screw them together. While you must make the structure strong, you do not, of course, have to worry about appearance.

If parts of the frame of a drop-in seat or upholstered chair are rotten, replace the wood. The carpentry, which is not difficult, is described in chapter 1.

There will also be tack holes. These may look innocuous, and in any case will not be seen in the finished chair, but they can be a problem. If you should happen to hammer a line of new tacks in among an existing line of holes, you will produce a neat perforation that could cause a large piece of the frame to split away. Then you will face a major repair job before you can continue the upholstery. Mix up a thick paste from sawdust and glue. Either resin glue or heated scotch glue is acceptable. Using any suitable flexible blade, press the paste into the holes all over the chair. Use a damp cloth to wipe away

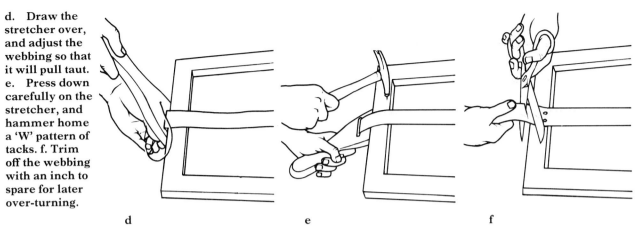

d. Draw the stretcher over, and adjust the webbing so that it will pull taut. **e.** Press down carefully on the stretcher, and hammer home a 'W' pattern of tacks. **f.** Trim off the webbing with an inch to spare for later over-turning.

d   e   f

the excess before it dries hard, and leave the chair for at least a day before you work on it again. You will find you have improved both the appearance and the structural soundness of the chair.

REPLACING THE WEBBING

Almost all upholstered chairs use webbing as a base, even if the seat also has springs. So fitting the webbing is the first task in re-upholstering them. It also teaches you how to handle some of the tools, and boosts a beginner's confidence: mistakes will not matter, as you can correct them without leaving any visible signs.

You will need the following tools and materials, none of which are expensive:

Upholsterer's hammer. This is a small hammer with a thin handle. Versions are available with a magnetic head, used for picking up tacks and holding them for hammering in. It works as an extra hand, and is recommended. There are two types. One has a claw opposite to the hammer head, for removing badly placed tacks. The other has a magnetic head for starting the tack, and a solid head for knocking it home. You will soon get used to flipping this type of hammer over in your hand.

Upholsterer's nails. These are blue metal tacks, available in various sizes. Upholsterers use 10 mm, 13 mm, or

15 mm according to the job they are doing. They also come in two versions; 'improved' tacks have large heads; 'fine' tacks have smaller heads. A box each of all six sizes will cover the full range of operations.

Webbing Stretcher. For a couple of pounds you can buy a tool made for the job, in one of two main designs. The correct tool is worth having for the control it gives. As an alternative you can use an offcut of wood, say a 100 mm or 150 mm length of 50 mm × 40 mm.

Webbing. Buy the strongest available. Most upholsterer's stockists sell rolls of English webbing, which is perfect for any job. Jute webbing from the Far East is also available, but can only be used when perfectly dry.

FIXING THE WEBBING

The illustrations [**4.1**] show just how simple it is to apply the webbing. Until you develop an eye for spacing, mark the positions on the seat frame. If you are having an odd number, start at the middle; otherwise start spacing them on each side of the centre. Work on the front-to-back webbing first. It is easier to get the first webbings properly spaced for equal balance on each side. Hold an end of the webbing over one of the frame members, leaving an inch of overhang. Put in the first

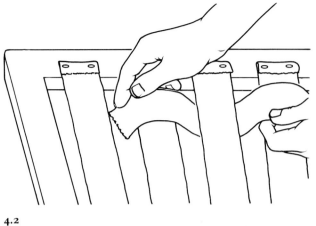

4.2

4.2   **Thread the free end of the webbing roll through the fixed strands of webbing.**
4.3a   **Tack down a square of hessian to cover the webbing, with a half inch over-turn.**
b.   **At the opposite side, tack down the webbing and hessian together.**
c.   **Trim the corners of the hessian to ensure that it lies flat.**

tack just outside the centre line of the wood. Put two more tacks just inside the centre line, to form the bottom points of a capital letter W. Now turn the overhang of webbing back over these tacks, and nail in two more on the line of the first one, to form the top outer points of the letter W. They should be close to the edges of the webbing. The pattern is shown in the illustration, although the first three tacks will not of course be visible.

The tacks are staggered, because five in line would tend to split the frame; they should lie comfortably over the centre line of the frame for strength.

Take care how you knock in the tacks. Each one should be level with the surface. If it bends over, even very slightly, pull it out and knock in another. The sharp rim of the head of a bent tack will cut into the webbing and in time weaken the seat.

Now thread the webbing through the webbing stretcher and tighten it in the way shown in the illustration [4.1].

Take up a tack on the end of your hammer, and gently lever down the end of the stretcher. It will draw the webbing tight across the frame. Do not over-stretch it, or you will pull the webbing out of shape and weaken it. Aim to keep it under uniform tension across its width. This will give a firm base for the stuffing.

If you have decided to economise and work with your home-made stretcher, wrap the webbing over the end of the block of wood. Grip the two tightly together, lever the block down against the side of the frame to pull the webbing taut, and hammer home the tacks.

Whichever system you use, hold the webbing in place with five tacks in the W pattern already shown. Some upholsterers knock in three tacks, and add the other two later with the hessian. But it is vital to get the webbing under tension right across its width, and this can only be done if the webbing stretcher is used for all five tacks. Knock in the outer two close to the edges, and cut off the webbing leaving 25 mm of overhang.

Nail on the other strips of webbing, leaving about a 13 mm gap between them. Smaller seats may take four strips, larger ones five. If the seat is wider at the front than at the back, fan the webbing out slightly to give even support.

Nail on the side-to-side webbing in exactly the same way, but thread the webbing through the first strips to give a woven effect before fixing it [4.2]. When finished, the webbing should be tight like a drum.

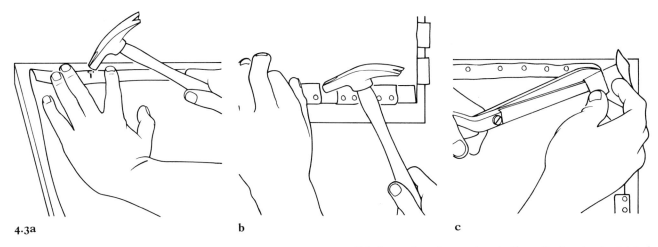

4.3a   b   c

THE HESSIAN COVER

Now take a piece of upholsterer's hessian. Lay the frame on it, and cut it tidily to fit round the outer edge with an overhang of about 13 mm.

With the upholsterer's hammer and some tacks tack it down one side – 10 mm improved are right for this job, as the hessian is not meant to take strain, only to stop the stuffing falling through the webbing.

You have two choices of tacking method. Either you can fold the hessian over first, and tack it down through the double layer, or you can tack down one layer, then fold it over, rather as you folded the webbing itself, and tack down the fold, with the second row of tacks alternating with the first row, and only the second row showing [**4.3a**].

Now pull the hessian taut across the frame. You will have to do this as best you can by hand, tensioning it at the point you are tacking, unless you have another simple tool, a hide stretcher. This a pair of pincers with long square jaws which grip about 75 mm of material so that you can pull it taut by a levering action. They make the job much easier. The reason for tacking half under and half over the fold should now be obvious. You can get much firmer tension on the hessian if you pull it from the edge and tack through the single thickness. On two of the sides, you will have an end of webbing hanging loose. Turn this over along with the fold of hessian, and tack the two down together [**4.3b**].

The tacks in the hessian should be at about 200 mm intervals, outside the rows of tacks holding the webbing. This gives a tidy finish, and avoids the risk of splitting the wood by having too many tacks in line.

A complication arises at the corners, where you will find yourself with a fold of excess hessian. It is possible to fold it square on each side as you go, but this produces a bulky wedge of four layers of material which looks inelegant and will make a lump at the corner. Together with similar lumps from covers still to be put on, this could stop the frame sitting comfortably on the corner blocks.

It is better to trim off the hessian at the corner. Either snip off the diagonal, then fold the two corners over to form a mitre, or cut out the corner square and turn one fold over the other [**4.3c**]. Either method will give a tidy finish.

BRIDLES

The next step is to put in some bridles – loops of twine

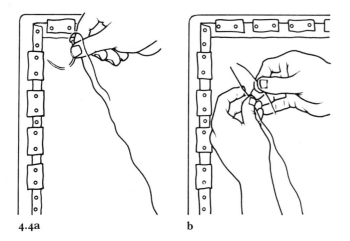
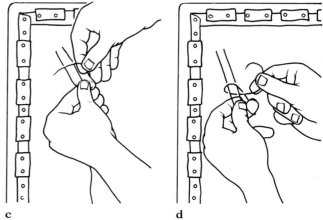

4.4a   b   c   d

that will hold the stuffing firmly in place. You will need a curved needle and some upholsterer's thread. If the thread is too thick for the eye of the needle, hammer the end flat, or use a larger needle.

First secure the end of the twine. Push the needle into the hessian about 60 mm diagonally in from one corner of the frame and back up through it, picking up about three strands of the hessian. Pull the thread through to within 100 mm of the end. Now tie an upholsterer's slip knot; [4.4] show the technique. Just turn the short end round to form a letter D, loop it over and up through the D, and over and up through the D again. Pull the long end of the thread, easing the knot snugly down to the hessian with your free hand.

Now start making bridles, along one side of the frame. Form a big looping stitch about 75 mm long, push the needle down through the hessian and back up a few strands away in the direction you came from. Pull the stitch just taut enough to allow you to get three fingers under the thread.

Continue the bridles (some upholsterers call them stuffing ties) along the side of the frame, turn, and go along the other sides. Then put some in the centre of this square. Either cross the diagonal, though this could cause an imbalance in the stuffing in time, or form a

second small square. An alternative is to stitch the bridles in parallel lines.

STUFFING

The stuffing for upholstery comes in plastic bags, and at first you will have to take your supplier's advice on how much you need, but will soon be able to judge fairly accurately how much chairs of various sizes take.

There are, as mentioned earlier, three main kinds of stuffing available: sea grass, coconut fibre, and hog's hair. Horse hair is unreasonably expensive. The best policy is to use the highest quality stuffing material you can afford, preferably hog's hair. Even this may seem expensive as the chair appears to take more and more. But you will be saving your labour costs, and the difference in cost between cheap and relatively expensive material, in the context of the whole operation, is not great. The satisfaction you obtain from doing a good job yourself with the best material is worth the investment.

Pull a handful of stuffing off your supply, tease it out neatly, and tuck it under the first bridle. Make it fairly firm, but not enough to pull the slack out of the other bridles. Go on tucking handfuls under all the bridles,

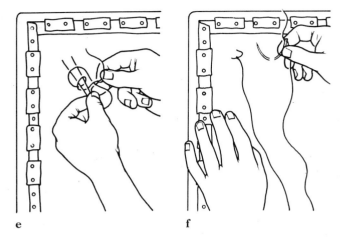
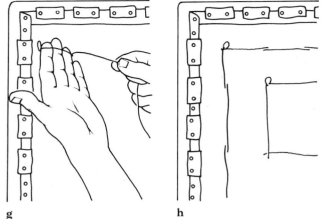

e   f   g   h

4.4a   With upholsterer's twine and a curved needle, start sewing a pattern of bridles.

b.   Secure the twine with a slip knot. First draw it through to within four inches of the end.

c.   Turn the short end over both parts of the twine to form a letter 'D'.

d.   Pass the end of the twine up through the open loop of the 'D'.

e.   Pass the short end over again and up through the 'D' for a second time. Draw the knot tight.

f.   Sew a stitch along, back, and up through the hessian to form the first bridle.

g.   Draw the bridle tight enough to accommodate three fingers flat against the hessian.

h.   A well balanced pattern of bridles will hold the stuffing in place all over the seat.

until you have a pattern of stuffing held firmly in place. The aim is to anchor this stuffing on to the hessian, so that the whole finished upholstery does not drift off to one side and throw the seat out of shape when it is in use.

Next, lay more stuffing in between the rows you have tied down, and then on top, until you have a good dome shape. It is impossible to specify exactly how much stuffing any seat needs. You will have to develop your judgement as your experience grows. In the first instance, it is advisable to err on the generous side, as the stuffing will be compressed down in use. A pile 125 mm–150 mm high is not too much to produce stuffing 50 mm thick when the seat is finished.

CALICO COVERING

Now you must hold the stuffing in place. Either tear off, or cut off, a square of calico, big enough to cover the stuffing and overlap the side of the frame by 50 mm. Lay it over the stuffing. Taking care not to pull the stuffing out of place, knock in a tack half way along one outer edge of the frame. Knock the tack only half way in. Turn round the frame, ease the calico taut, and knock in a tack half way along the opposite edge [**4.5a**]. Then put a tack in each of the other two edges. These four tacks will hold the calico nicely in place, and you can handle the seat without the stuffing falling out.

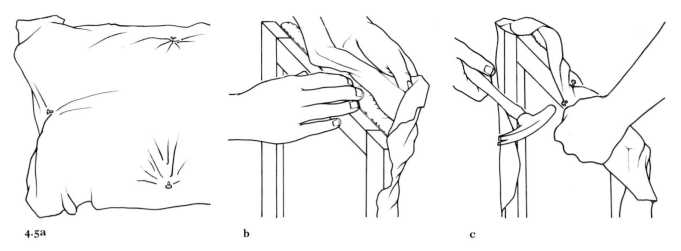

4.5a　　　　　　　　　　　**b**　　　　　　　　　　　　　　**c**

Lay out a few tacks and your hammer on the workbench. The right tacks for this job are called 'fine' tacks. Calico is a fine-weave material, so their small unobtrusive heads are adequate. A suitable length is 10 mm.

Turn the seat on to one of its edges, holding it in your left hand. Holding the calico in place, take out the tack on the top edge. Now take the end of the calico in your right hand, and start to ease it taut across the top of the stuffing with your left. Do not pull the calico; you will only stretch it out of shape. Instead, hold the calico steady with your right hand, and compress the stuffing, drawing your hand firmly across it, with your left. As you compress it the tension will ease, the calico will slacken, and you can simply take up the slack with your right hand. Do not pull too hard at this stage; there is still the opposite side to work on. Use your right hand to tuck the stuffing back into the seat as you go. Avoid leaving any hair hanging over the edge; it may leave ugly marks, and could make the chair frame too wide to fit back into the chair. When you are satisfied you have eased the calico to a fair tension, without over-strain, nail it down temporarily, with a tack knocked half way in, on the underside of the frame. Add another temporary tack 25 mm along towards one corner, and a third 25 mm along towards the other corner.

Turn the frame over, and do exactly the same job on the opposite side, finishing with three temporary tacks. These tacks should be in line about an inch in from the outer edge of the frame. Turn the frame round, and complete the other two sides [**4.5b,c**].

Now add the remaining tacks, 25 mm apart all round. Work from one set of three, towards the corner away from you, then towards the corner nearest to you. Compress the stuffing, ease your hand over it, tuck in the hair, take up the slack, and knock in a tack. Keep up this operation, coaxing the material into a smooth curve, until you get close to the corners. You will then be left with a fold of material at each corner [**4.5d**].

Dealing with these corners is one of the first real problems you will encounter. You will see that the calico must turn over and back under, on adjacent sides, round an angle which is rarely a true right-angle. It would be easy to deal with if you could cut away all the excess material, but this would leave raw edges against the edges of the frame, which could either fray or pull away, leaving the stuffing inadequately covered. The problem could also be solved by turning the material under itself, as if wrapping a parcel, but this would leave far too many layers and produce ugly bumpiness.

The answer lies in a compromise. First stretch the

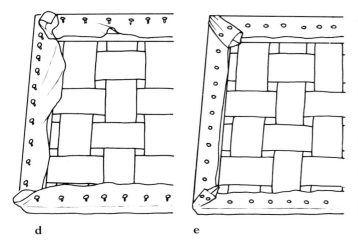

d   e

4.5a Cover the hair with wadding, then tear a square of calico, and secure it initially with a single temporary tack on each edge.

b. Stand the frame on an edge, and begin smoothing out the calico. Tuck in the wadding so that it does not overhang the frame.

c. Hammer in a temporary tack to secure the calico on the underside of the frame. A line of three, centrally placed, will secure one side while you work on the other three sides.

d. Work towards the corners, until you have the calico well smoothed out and secure.

e. Draw the calico up into a neat fold at the corners. Trim off any excess. Tack it down at each side of the fold for a firm, neat, flat finish.

calico over the corner, pulling it towards the centre of the seat frame, and tack it down. Now, to make the job easier, cut away all the excess, level with the inner edge of the frame. You will now have two small folds, one on either side of the first tack. Pull the first fold up, roll the material under itself towards the first tack, and lay the fold neatly down towards the outer edge of the frame. Tack it down. Do the same on the second fold. Trim off the excess material. This operation is among the most difficult to do well, as calico stretches easily. Fortunately the final result does not need to be too neat, as it will be invisible on the finished chair [**4.5e**].

Finally, knock home all the temporary tacks, and trim off the calico to a neat line all round the frame.

WADDING

The drawback to upholstery stuffing is that prickly ends of hair find their way through the weave of calico. Wadding, which forms a barrier which the hairs or fibres cannot penetrate, cures the problem. One layer of wadding should be enough; some upholsterers prefer two.

Some upholsterers also prefer to put the wadding next to the stuffing, under the calico. Both methods are perfectly acceptable.

Tear the wadding to fit exactly to the outer top edge of the frame, and lay it in place. A similar material, called linter's felt, is also used for this job.

THE COVERING

The final covering is fitted in much the same way as the calico. Make sure it goes on straight: if it is plain material get the weave dead square, or the seat will never look right; if there is a pattern, make sure it is both square and central. The great advantage of the first tack on each outer edge of the frame is that you can hammer it in while the frame is flat on the workbench, making sure that the material does not move out of true as you go.

With the material secured, turn the seat on to its edge, knock in the three temporary tacks, all round, then work to the corners. Check that the material is still square, since you may have eased it out of place as you took up the slack. If so, take out a few tacks and ease it back to the other side.

The corners are different from the calico corners. If you have a very stretchy material, you can take up any folds by pulling it over the corner and securing it with a central tack. This time, fold the excess under itself towards the outer edge of the frame, and turn the material

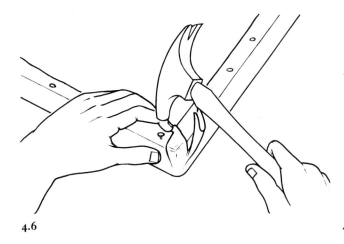

4.6

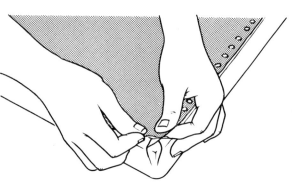

4.7

back down to form a mitre. Tack the first fold. Turn the second fold under, and tack it down. On the front corners of the seat these two folds tend to overlap because of the slightly acute angles. Try to pull them towards the centre of the frame to form a flat mitre. If you cannot, simply tack them down and go on to the next corner.

You may find that the material has ruckled slightly along the outer edges of the frame: this is almost inevitable with this technique and will not show once the seat is dropped into place in the chair.

If you have a material which does not lend itself to stretching, you can adopt a folding technique although this will not work well on some very thick coverings. First fold the material down the side edge of the frame. Then fold the front edge under itself at an angle of 45 degrees. The crease thus formed will lie neatly down the corner of the frame. On a drop-in seat, you can leave the crease open, but it looks much neater if you sew it down using the slip stitch. This will also be good practice for the time when you have to sew this type of pleat on bigger chairs, and any faults in your first efforts will hardly show.

Now turn the trailing edges under the seat frame. There will be at least four layers. As you have sewn the material, you can cut away the excess carefully up to the sewn edge, and fold down the spare as you did in the other method to form a neat mitre. Tack it in place [4.6].

Some upholsterers like to leave a drop-in seat finished in that condition, so that they can see any faults developing from the underside. A neater finish is achieved by adding a dust cover, for which a special black lining is available. Cut the black lining about 6 mm bigger than the frame all round. Turn it back under by about 13 mm, so that it lies 6 mm inside the frame. Tack it all round with 6 mm tacks, set 25 mm apart. The corners are easy. Simply fold the material square, and square again, and tack it down. This material lies quite flat, so there is no need to worry about forming mitres or trimming away bumpiness [4.7].

The job is finished.

STUFFED-OVER SEAT

The next type of seat represents a major step forward in upholstering technique, but still brings into play the experience gained in working on the drop-in seat. It is the simple upright chair, called a 'stuffed-over' seat, in which the upholstery not only covers the top of the seat, but also reaches down the sides. This type, which is quite common. It may be part of a dining suite, an

4.6 The top cover is fitted by the same method as the calico except at the corners. Draw the central part in, and tack it down. Draw the sides in to form a double pleat. Trim off the excess.

4.7 Add a dust cover of black lining, folded square at the corners.

occasional chair, or perhaps a desk chair. Make the frame structurally sound, fill in old tacking holes with glue and sawdust, and chisel a 6 mm bevel all round the outer edge of the frame.

Because there are no springs in this seat, the webbing must be fixed to the top edges of the frame. Follow the same procedure as on the drop-in seat. Judge for yourself how many strands of webbing the seat will need. Remember that an extra strand of webbing is not expensive, and it is not worth risking strain by laying too few too far apart.

Add the hessian, fitting it either with the same tacks as the webbing, or with an extra row of tacks outside the line of the end of the webbing. The hessian is there to prevent the stuffing falling through the gaps in the webbing, so you must take care to cut it snugly up to the corners. In the type of chair frame illustrated, you will see that the tops of the front legs stand higher than the edge of the frame. You need to fit the hessian neatly into that corner, either with a mitre, or with a square cut, folding in the excess neatly.

Now go round the seat exactly as you did before, applying the bridles. Start 75 mm in from a corner, and work along the edge. Follow each edge in turn and then fill in the centre. The pattern is not important. But take care to sew in the bridles symmetrically so that the finished seat will not, in time, become lopsided. Do not place bridles closer than 75 mm from the edges of the frame. Later, you will be 'regulating' the stuffing – moving it about inside the partly covered seat by poking it with a sharp tool through the cover – if the ties are too close to the frame this operation will be impossible.

FIRST STUFFING

In most chairs except the simple drop-in seat, the stuffing is installed in two stages. The first stuffing, held firmly in place under a covering of hessian, forms a solid base for the upholstery. The second stuffing gives the seat its final shape.

When you have a satisfactory arrangement of bridles, with just room to slip three fingers under each one, start fitting the first stuffing. Tease out the hair to a consistent thickness, and fit it neatly under the bridles.

At this stage, work just enough hair under the bridles to produce a layer of uniform thickness, with enough tension under the bridles to hold the stuffing in place. Then push more stuffing down between the lines. You should now have a roughly square area of stuffing covering the centre of the seat.

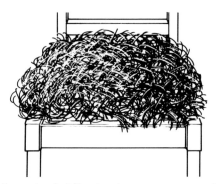

4.8 On a stuffed-over seat, apply webbing, hessian, bridles, and a layer of stuffing as before. Tuck hair

Next pack out the stuffing to the edges of the frame.

Start taking palm-sized chunks of stuffing, tease them out to an even consistency, and tuck them in under the bridles that run round the outer edge of your square. Work with lumps of stuffing about 100 mm long. Tuck them under the bridle so they reach towards the chair frame and overhang it slightly. Work round the seat keeping the stuffing well balanced. Push each additional lump under its predecessor, until the outer edge has built up to a fat springy lip round the frame [**4.8**].

Keep pressing it with your hand, firstly to ensure that it feels the same all round, secondly to estimate the thickness it will make when it is compacted later in the upholstering process.

Most chairs take more stuffing material than the in-experienced upholsterer would expect. The aim is to have two thirds of the hair in the first stuffing, and one third in the second stuffing.

When you have formed a substantial lip, and it holds well away from the frame when you compress it with a hand, cover it with scrim. This is the popular name for an open-weave hessian. The open weave allows flexibility; you can ease and pull the scrim to a variety of curves without it coming under strain. But this also makes it difficult to work with; it can take up shapes you did not intend.

First cut a piece of scrim big enough to cover the seat

under the outer bridles to give a generous roll all round the frame.

and hang down the sides to the bottom of the frame. Cut it square to the weave; the lines of thread are important guides in keeping the upholstery even.

To make a square cut in scrim, hessian, or calico, first 'draw' a thread. Nick the selvedge with scissors, and pull out one thread. It will leave a line for cutting which is square to the weave of the fabric.

Lay the scrim over the seat, ensure that the weave runs squarely front-to-back and side-to-side, and lies without any wavy lines. Tack it with three temporary tacks into the sides of the frame. This will hold the lip of stuffing in place for the time being [**4.9**].

The next job is to put in 'through-stuffing' ties of upholstery thread to anchor the central body of the stuffing, and the scrim over it, to the base of the seat. You will need a double ended needle, a long powerful instrument, sharp at both ends, with the eye at only one. It is designed to go through thick layers of stuffing, hessian, webbing and any covering material, and then back, without having to be pulled right through and turned. It is easy to forget that the end from which you are pushing is as sharp as the 'front' end so be careful how you use it.

Double-ended needles are available in a range of sizes. A medium size (about eight inches) will be suitable for this job. Thread it with about a metre-and-a-half of medium twine.

Take a piece of chalk and draw a line on the scrim, four

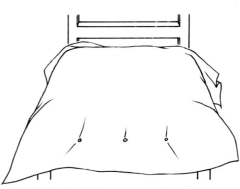

4.9   Cover the hair with a square of scrim, temporarily tacked down at the sides.

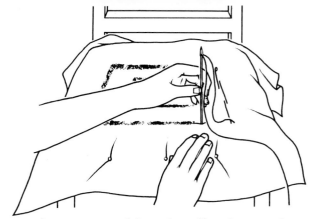

4.10   Sew a pattern of through-stuffing ties over the central part of the seat.

inches in from the frame all round. Beginners would do well to measure it carefully. Professional upholsterers generally work by eye, but complete symmetry is important in all upholstery operations, and it is worth taking care with marking the shape.

At one corner of your square, push the needle down through the scrim, hair, hessian and webbing. Pull the twine through to within six inches of the end. Now push the needle back up through the layers, about 8 mm away from the downward thread, and pull it out at the top of the seat. Tie an upholsterer's slip knot in the end (see page 82), and draw it up tight.

Now make the first stitch, along one side of the square. Follow the principle used in tying bridles. Divide the length of the line into a convenient number of stitches, say three or four on the average drawing room chair, and make each stitch to this length. Push the needle down through the stuffing, out at the bottom, and back up about 8 mm in the direction you came from. Then go on to the next stitch. The stitches will then loop over each other to give the strength and 'hold' you are looking for. Make a similar overlap at the corners, and continue round the 'square' [**4.10**].

How you deal with the centre of the square is a matter for discretion. It depends largely on the size of the seat centre. On a small seat you can simply turn towards the centre, add one stitch, and finish in the centre of the seat.

On a larger seat you can stitch in a separate little square of through-stuffing ties. However you do it, pull the ties tight as you go, then finally check them, pulling them tight again all round, and knot off the last stitch with several half-hitches.

You will now have a firm pad in the centre of the seat, forming a shallow depression as shown in [**4.10**].

Lay your double ended needle carefully back in your tool box, with a cork on each end to prevent accidents.

PREPARING TO SEW A HARD EDGE

For the next operation you will need your upholsterer's hammer, and a supply of the 10 mm improved tacks you used for tacking down the hessian.

Remove the temporary tacks from one side of the hessian. Draw it over the edge roll of hair, and check that you have the right amount of hair in place. As you work on your second and subsequent chairs, you will have a better idea how far a given quantity of stuffing will reduce under compression, but on your first chair you will have to try to visualise what the finished seat will look like when all the stuffing round the frame has been tightly compressed. You must have enough hair in there to still overhang the edge, and rise to a point just below the final height of the centre of the chair seat when the job is complete.

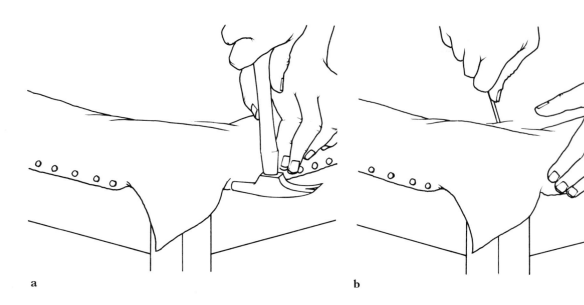

a

b

You must also work out the right tension for the hessian round the edge roll: unfortunately, this is almost impossible to judge until you have worked through the next stage of the operation, and stitched the hard edge itself. You will then know how tightly the stitching will draw the edge, this is another case where your later efforts should show marked improvement over your first. For your first job draw the hessian taut over the stuffing, then let it out by about 6 mm. The stitching in the hard edge will take up the slack.

When you have worked out the tension, try to visualise once more, whether you have enough stuffing under it. If it looks too mean add more now, before you have nailed down the scrim, this is the best time although you can do this later from the ends.

When you are satisfied, cut the scrim accurately about 25 mm below the top of the frame. You will recall that the stuffed-over seat has a bevelled edge on the outer top side of the frame. Fold the scrim under the stuffing, and knock in tacks through the double layer, into the bevelled edge. The tacks should be about 25 mm apart. At this stage knock them half way home. Temporary tacking

allows you to make alterations easily if you have to.

You will now see the value of keeping the scrim square. On the front and back of the chair, you can follow a line of the thread, to ensure absolute symmetry, and you will soon see whether your stuffing is packed into the chair evenly at each side, by the amount of slack the scrim shows. On the sides of the chair, if it has a non-square frame, you will not be able to follow a single line of thread. But you can judge, from the pattern of tacks crossing the weave, whether you are following a consistent line, or whether your stuffing is out of balance.

Go round all four sides, folding under and temporarily tacking down the scrim on to the bevelled edge. Leave the corners open for the time being. The result should look as in [**4.11a**].

The lip you have now formed should also be straight, viewed at eye level from the sides and front. Stand back and see if you can spot any waviness in the levels.

If the roll is not level, now is the time to correct it. The four sides are open at each end. If any part needs more stuffing, take handfuls, tease it out, push it in at the ends, and move it along.

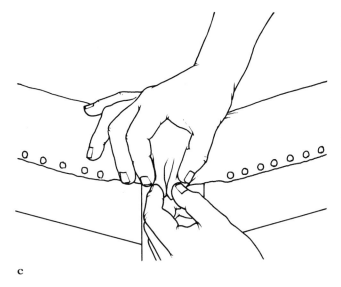

c

4.11a Fold the scrim under, and tack it to the bevelled edge of the frame to produce a bulbous roll all round.

b. Regulate the stuffing well forward, and well down on to the frame.

c. After inserting any extra stuffing from the corners, close the ends with a pleat, tacked down and sewn.

To do this you will need a regulator, a long strong spike with a sharp point at one end and the other end flattened to form a handle. Stab it through the scrim into the stuffing and lever the stuffing along with it. You will find that you can adjust the levels of stuffing quite considerably with this useful tool [**4.11b**].

When everything looks nicely even and well shaped, hammer home your tacks finally into the bevelled edge.

The four corners now remain to be finished. The rear corners, where the scrim meets the back uprights of the chair, are the easier. With scissors, carefully cut into the corner at a 45 degree angle. Stop just short of the chair back. Turn each side of the cut under, and fold it away beneath the scrim as you go. Trim off the excess, fold it under itself along the bevelled edge with the remainder of the scrim, and tack it down. Do this at both rear posts.

The method of dealing with the front corners will vary with the design of chair. The one illustrated has front legs which stand slightly above the chair frame. In this case simply cut and turn the scrim under to follow the outline of the legs, and nail in a tack half way along each to hold the scrim in place. You will be left with a large flap of excess material. Pull this flap taut and check that you have enough stuffing in the corners.

Stitching the hard edge will draw the front corners back towards the centre of the seat, so you must have plenty of stuffing there. The corner should overhang the frame, seen from both the front and the side. If there is not enough, push in some more under the corners, and work it into place with your regulator.

Now turn the flap inside out, and tuck in the excess material so that the fold is formed inside the chair. You will have two folded edges that come together [**4.11c**]. Thread a curved needle with fine upholstery twine, and sew these edges together. You may have practiced this piece of sewing on the calico of your drop-in seat. If not, it is a simple ladder or slip stitch, shown on page 137.

When you have sewn far enough down, fold the scrim under, and put a tack through the folds to hold it on the exact corner of the seat frame. Trim away any excess. Hammer home the temporary tacks all round.

You will now have a bulbous border, filled like a sausage, covered rather loosely with scrim and firmly tacked in place ready for the next stage.

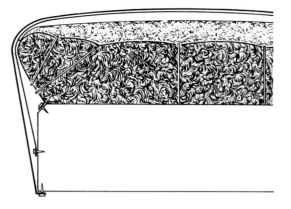

4.12a Section showing the composition of a hard edge on a stuffed over seat.

SEWING A HARD EDGE

A hard edge all round a seat is important. It gives comfort and support to the sitter, and keeps the upholstery firmly in place. The hard edge is in the form of a compact roll, made by moving the stuffing into position, then securing it by sewing lines of stitches through it with upholstery twine.

First regulate your stuffing into the correct position. It is not possible to produce a perfectly even filling during the stuffing process itself, nor to lay the scrim perfectly over the stuffing. You can only achieve a perfect roll after the scrim is in place. The regulator therefore serves not only to correct mistakes you might have made earlier, but to move the stuffing into exactly the place you want it. You will be surprised at how you can control the stuffing and make a well sculpted shape with the regulator.

Again, stab the regulator into the top of the thick 'sausage' of stuffing you have formed. With a circular action, lever the handle away from you so that the pointed end draws the stuffing forwards towards you. Be bold. Do not 'pick' at the stuffing with this tool, but make big movements of large wads of stuffing. Move the stuffing to one side or the other to equalise any unevenness. But most important, pull it forward to fill out the roll of scrim directly above the edges of the seat frame.

The outer curve of the stuffing should overhang the edge of the frame by about 6 mm to 13 mm. Then, when the calico and top cover are later applied, they will lie clear of the edge of the wood. [**4.12a**], showing a section through the frame, illustrates this point.

When you have drawn the stuffing well forward, push in the regulator from the front, and with the same circular motion, pull the stuffing down, to pack it on to the top of the frame edge. Fill this space with a compact layer of stuffing. Remember that this edge will take much of the weight of the person using the chair, and the front edge must hold steady, without any tendency to wander up and down. A firm full edge, right to the front and bottom of the roll, is what you are aiming for.

If you do not have enough stuffing in the roll, open up one end and add more, working the whole mass along from the ends with the regulator. Work all round the edge of the chair – front, sides, and back – to produce a straight line. You may have some difficulty using the regulator on the rear edge, because the chair back itself will present an obstruction. Fortunately, this matters less than at the sides and front, because the rear edge will not take any direct weight.

At first you can try to get all the edges level. But as you gain experience you will be able to slope the side down-

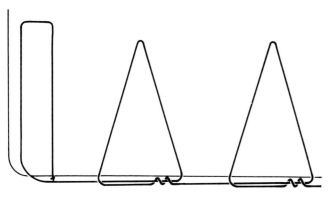

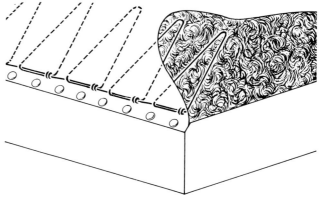

b.   Plan of the path of blind stitches through a hard edge.

c.   The stitches do not come through the scrim.

wards from front to back, to give a more elegant 'set' to the chair seat. The best way to achieve this is to regulate the front and back first, to give the right respective heights, then regulate the sides in turn between them.

When you are satisfied that you have a full roll all round with a straight top edge, well compacted on to the frame itself, and overhanging slightly all round, lay aside the regulator.

The next step is to stitch the stuffing into a firm roll all round, to produce the hard edge.

Two types of stitch are used: 'blind stitches', and 'top stitches'.

BLIND STITCHES

Take up your double pointed needle (the eight-inch model will do for this edge) and thread it with about a metre of upholsterer's medium twine. Turn the chair so that the back is facing you. If you work on the rear edge first, any defects in your first efforts will be less noticeable, and you can correct your mistakes before you come to the more visible sides and front.

First fix the twine with a single stitch. Almost all upholstery stitching is done from left to right, so start 13 mm in from the left-hand corner, and well down close to the wood of the frame. Push the needle in through the

stuffing, at an angle of about thirty degrees above the horizontal, so that the point emerges about 75 mm in from the edge of the frame. Pull it right through. Now go back towards your left, 13 mm, and push the needle back through the stuffing so that it emerges right down in the corner, 13 mm back from the point where you started. Pull the twine through, and tie it in an upholsterer's slip knot. This will give you a firm starting stitch [**4.12b**].

Now begin your first row of stitches. This row consists of 'blind' stitches, so called because the twine does not come right through the upholstery.

Estimate about 40 mm along from the knot you have just made. Measure the first stitch if you prefer. But you will soon be able to judge the correct distance and produce a row of equally spaced stitches. Push in the needle, again close to the wooden frame, and at the same 30 degree angle as the first stitch. But, instead of pushing it straight in at right angles to the chair frame, angle it backwards slightly to your left, so that the point emerges about 13 mm back along the line.

Pull the needle with one hand and push it with the other, but not right through. Ease it forward until the eye just begins to show through the scrim. Now re-angle the needle, turning the point towards the right so that the eye-end points towards the left. Push it back, the threaded end leading, through the stuffing. You will see

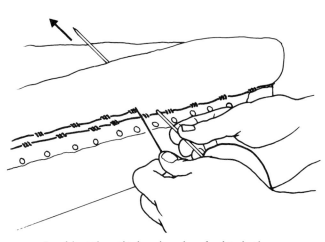

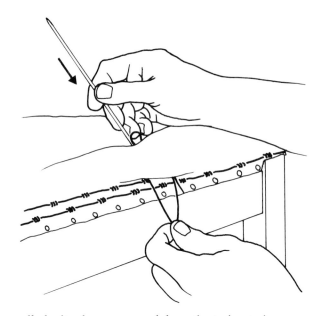

4.13 Locking the stitches in a hard edge is the same technique for blind and top stitches. Return the needle by its sharp rear end, loop the twine twice around it, then withdraw the needle and take it away

now why a double-pointed needle is essential. Keep it at a consistent angle so that it emerges just above the edge of the frame, and 25 mm along from the point where it went in. The twine will now have followed an angled path through the stuffing, without emerging from the scrim [**4.12c**]. When you pull that stitch tight, it will pick up a wedge of stuffing and draw it into a compact mass.

Now to form the stitch itself. Draw the needle out of the stuffing towards yourself for about 50 mm. Pause. Take up the twine in your left hand, about six inches from the eye of the needle. Make two turns in this twine round the protruding end of the needle in the anti-clockwise direction. Now pull the needle the remainder of the way through those loops, and out of the stuffing. You will find you have produced what looks like a tangle of twine, but the reason will soon become clear.

Pull the needle away to your right, and jab it firmly into the upholstery well out of the way on the right hand side of the chair. Now you can work without snagging your hands on those sharp points.

Now take hold of the twine, pull it through the stuffing to take up the slack, and finally tug it firmly to the right. Two things will happen. The twine passing through the roll will pull tight, starting to draw the stuffing into a firm and compact hard edge, and the tangle of twine will snap into a neat rolled stitch, resembling a piece of twirled candy. The twists you put in with that double looping motion will prevent the stitch working loose. Each stitch will then take the strain individually and even if one stitch should break in later years, the remainder will stay firm [**4.13**].

Now continue stitching, moving 40 mm along to the right for each stitch, inserting the needle at an angle back towards the left, pulling it through until the eye shows, pushing it back through at an angle to the left, so that it emerges 25 mm back from the point where it went in. Twist two loops round the needle, anti-clockwise. Pull the needle through, secure it safely out of the way, and pull the stitch tight. Repeat along the row.

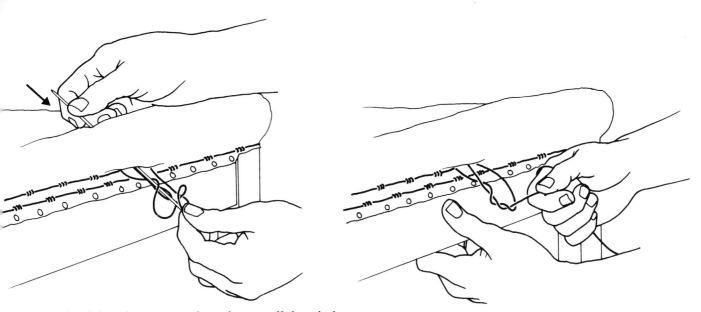

**to the right. Give a tug on the twine to pull the stitch
to a firm locked loop.**

By now you will know whether your hands are tough
enough to pull the twine into tight stitches, or whether
you need a pair of good strong leather gloves to stop the
twine cutting into your fingers.

As you move along the row of stitches, you will find
you are forming a compact roll. Try to keep it even. The
stitches should be at the same intervals and the roll itself
free of bulges. If uneven patches appear, use your
regulator to pull more stuffing into weak areas, or take
it away from over-stuffed parts.

When you come to the corners, follow them round as
accurately as possible. On the last stitch of an edge,
instead of working back to your left, turn the needle the
opposite way, and push it back to emerge right down in
the bottom left corner of the next edge.

At various points in the course of a row of stitching,
you will come to the end of your length of twine. Cut off
your next convenient length, and simply tie a reef knot
in it, as close to the scrim as possible. Then carry on
stitching. The knot should fall between two stitches,

with no superfluous loop.

Carry on stitching, turning the seat as you go, round
the four sides of the chair. When you get to the end of the
final edge, pull the last stitch tight and secure it with a
couple of knots stitched in with the needle.

In some seats, the hard edge will be so fat that a second
row of blind stitches is required, about 13 mm above the
first. This generally applies in thickly padded comfortable arm-chairs. In the case of a stuffed-over seat, unless you have been extremely generous with the stuffing,
one row of blind stitches will probably be enough, and
you can go on to top stitching.

TOP STITCHES

Top stitching is similar to blind stitching in many respects. Start the row similarly, at the left-hand end, with
a slip knot. This row of stitches should be approximately
6 mm above the row of blind stitches. This time, move
just 25 mm to the right to begin each stitch, and push the

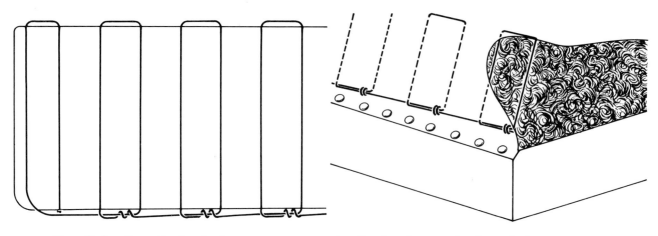

4.14a   Top stitches through a hard edge.

b.   Section shows path of top stitches.

needle directly through the stuffing. Do not angle it to the side. Make sure it follows the same angle to the horizontal as the blind stitches. The needle should emerge about 13 mm nearer to the frame. Pull it right through and out on the other side of the scrim. For this type of stitch, as you have pulled the needle through, you can obviously turn it round and use the non-threaded point. Move back 13 mm along the row, and return the needle back through the stuffing towards you, parallel with the ingoing twine. It will emerge 13 mm to the left. Loop the twine twice round the needle, exactly as before. Pull the needle through, stick it into the upholstery well to the right out of harm's way, and pull the stitches tight, with a good final tug to the right [**4.14**].

At this stage, examine carefully the roll you are making. This is the last stage at which you can determine the shape of the hard edge, and any unevenness that remains will disfigure the finished seat. As you draw the top stitching tight, the edge should be firm, well stuffed, well secured, and absolutely even all the way along. It should be dead straight along the front and back, perhaps sloping slightly down towards the back of the seat on the side edges.

Several faults may appear. The stuffing may still not be evenly distributed. You can correct that with the regulator. The roll may fall like a lip over the edge of the frame, when you press it with a hand. Correct this tendency by stitching the top row on a lower slant, so that the needle emerges closer to the centre of the chair seat, and pulls the roll back. The roll may sit on the top of the frame, without the necessary overhang. Correct this fault by inserting your needle nearer to the vertical. Pulling the stitches tight will then move the roll towards the edge of the frame. Finally, the roll itself may be weak and insufficiently padded. There is no way to insert more stuffing at this stage. The best plan is to go along the weak edges and insert another row of top stitching an equal distance above the first. The extra stitches will pull the roll right. Of course, having to do this means that you should have catered for the problem earlier with that extra row of blind stitches. But only experience will show you how to decide how many rows you need.

Work right round the seat as you did on the blind stitched row, and knot off the twine as before. You have now completed the hard edge.

The technique of sewing a hard edge is among the most widely employed skills in upholstery. You will find you have to put these stitches, either blind or top stitches, into dozens of seats, and in dozens of different locations. They appear in stuffed-over seats, along the front of large upholstered chairs, round the wings of wing-chairs, on the arms of chairs of almost all types, and round the padded backs of many chairs.

The size of the hard edge varies considerably from one chair to another, but the process remains the same. As you get practiced in using the regulator and the double ended needle and twine, you will learn to judge exactly how much stuffing you need to apply, and how to achieve exactly the effect you are looking for. Then you will be able to produce attractive and durable upholstery on any furniture. It is worth working until you get the technique of sewing a hard edge exactly right.

SECOND STUFFING

You will have reached the stage where the chair seat is in the form of a dish, with a firm edge slightly overhanging the frame all round.

Now add the second stuffing. Start by sewing in a few more bridles, using your curved needle to loop the twine through the scrim and back on itself, as you did on the hessian for the first stuffing. A run of bridles between the through-stuffing ties and the hard edge may be enough. But test the through-stuffing ties themselves. If you can lift them slightly, use them to secure the second stuffing.

If they are too tight, sew in another set of bridles among the through-stuffing ties.

Now add the final third of your stuffing. Tuck it under all the bridles, then fill in the gaps. Pay particular attention to the space between the outer bridles and the hard edge. Fill it well, especially just behind the front edge. There is a tendency for stuffing to drift back down this recess in use, and leave an uncomfortable gap which allows the hard edge to cut across the legs of the person sitting on the chair. Fill it firmly.

Now tear a layer of felt or wadding, big enough to cover the curved dome of stuffing, and reach well on to the hard edge. This is to prevent the hair coming through, so take care not to tear it off too short. Lay it in place.

Follow it with a calico covering. Cut the calico fairly generously, and begin fixing it with two or three temporary tacks on each side, about one third of the distance down the side of the frame. Try to recollect the procedure you followed on the drop-in seat. Of course, you cannot turn the complete chair in your hands conveniently. But you can still press down on the top of the seat to take up the slack. Work steadily round the frame, using temporary tacking at first. You may find the calico has a tendency to distort as you smooth out the slack and

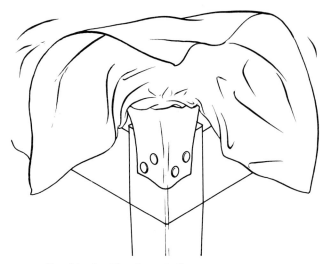

4.15 Card tacked in place to form a neat corner.

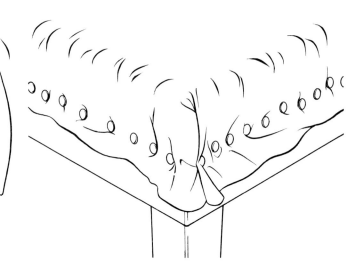

4.16 Calico tacked in place.

tack it down. At any point where this occurs, take out the tacks and keep working the material against the direction of distortion, to get it as straight as you possibly can. Tack from the centre of each side, to within about two inches of the corners. Use the weave of the calico as a guide to keep the covering square.

Now employ a neat little trick to produce tidy front corners. Take a sheet of light card, postcard thickness or slightly stronger, and cut a small square out of it. Fold it in half, and wrap it round the corner of the stuffing between the underlip of the hard edge and the top of the frame. [**4.15**] shows how. Tack it in place, tucking a small lump of wadding behind it. This will help give a firm appearance to the chair once it is covered.

Now you can complete the calico corners. First the back. Cut into the corner again, diagonally until you meet the inside back of the chair. Fold each side of the cut away under the calico, and again trim off the excess. You will find a new use for the regulator here. Turn it round, and use the flattened end to tuck the material neatly into the corner where it meets the chair leg. You can hold the material taut with one hand, and fold and

tuck the calico with the flat end of the regulator. You will achieve a far better finish this way than by using your hands and fingers alone. Finally tack it in place.

At the front, carefully draw the calico taut over the corner, and push the fold from the front round the side. Then pull the side calico down over that first fold. You will be left with a pocket, visible from the front, but not from the side. Tidy up the fold with the flat end of your regulator, remaking the fold as many times as necessary to get a neat pleat from the crown of the corner directly down the angle. Then tack the calico in place. Finally sew up the open end of the pocket, using an ordinary slip stitch [**4.16**].

Now the chair is ready for its final covering. Choose carefully; you have put a lot of work into the restoration and upholstery of the seat, and it would be a pity to spoil it with an unsuitable material. The chair illustrated is basically Georgian in design, so a good satin stripe, or a patterned brocade, would be suitable. If you are unsure, visit your local museum, or investigate in your library, to find what material originally went on the kind of chair you are working on. When you have chosen the material, you must work out how much of it you will need. If it has a pattern, you must have enough to fit the design symmetrically, either centrally if it is a large motif, or evenly balanced on both sides of the chair if it is a smaller one. Material generally comes in 125 cm or 140 cm widths, so consider whether you can buy material suitable for more than one chair. Measure the chair with a flexible linen tape measure in both directions, over the calico, down the faces of the frame, and underneath the edges of the frame, to see how much material you want.

Fitting the material is relatively easy. You have done the hard work in fitting the calico. For extra comfort, and to stop any stray hairs from the stuffing coming up through the cover, it is worth fitting a new layer of thin wadding on the chair. Lay it in place, running it down the sides of the frame, and under the edge, so that it will soften all the wooden corners. If it is not wide enough to cover the whole chair, lay it in parts, separating the layers where the edges of the wadding melt, and re-laying them interleaved, as though pushing together two halves of a pack of playing cards.

Now apply the top cover, making sure you lay it on straight, and that the pattern is well balanced. If there is a top and bottom to the pattern – a flower for example – the top is at the back of the chair and the bottom at the front. Fixing is almost the same as with the calico cover. Temporarily tack it on the centre of each side, on the underside of the frame, then cut diagonally into the back uprights. Tuck it away with the flat regulator end, and continue the tacking to the corners.

At the front, either follow the procedure just outlined for the calico, to leave a single exposed pleat. Some upholsterers leave this open. Generally speaking, it makes sense to sew it, as you did the calico cover, using a suitable matching coloured thread. Otherwise the pleat tends to gape and look unsightly when, after a few weeks of use, the material stretches.

Alternatively, you can finish the top cover with a double pleat. Draw the material down over the corner, leaving two folds of excess material, one at the front and one at the side. Tuck the excess neatly away, along the front and the side respectively, behind the facing part of the material, using the flat end of the regulator. Trim off the excess. You will now be left with two pleats, both of

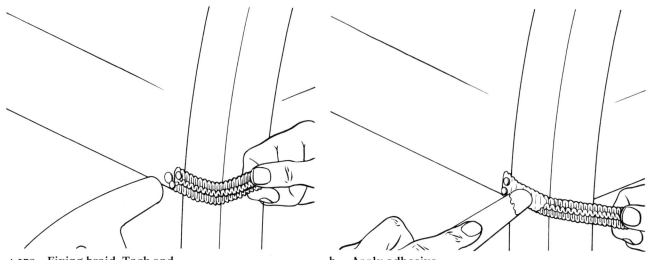

4.17a Fixing braid. Tack end.

b. Apply adhesive.

them shorter, because of the way the material falls, than the pleat on the single pleated treatment. Now tack the material securely in place on the underside of the frame.

Finally, buy a suitably coloured braid to trim the bottom of the face of the material all round.

To fix it in place, pin one end to the chair as shown in [**4.17**], with gimp pins. Hold the braid well away from the chair, and sparingly apply a cloth adhesive such as *Copydex*. Take care not to spoil your material by getting unwanted traces of this glue on it. Carefully press the braid into place, working round the chair. Cut the braid when the line meets wood, for example at the back uprights. Finally, using a curved needle and suitably coloured thread, sew the top and bottom edges of the braid to the material, using small, almost invisible stitches.

All that remains is the optional step of covering the underside of the chair with a square of black lining, tacked in place exactly as it was on the drop-in seat.

Your finished stuffed-over seat will have introduced you to many of the more difficult operations in upholstery.

A SPRUNG CHAIR

Now you are ready to learn to fit springs to a chair. Start simply and choose if you can a small chair with a plain back, and with springs in the seat only.

If you have no chair of this kind, but only a chair with a sprung back, the process is slightly more complicated and you should read this chapter through, fit the springs to the back as described on page 160, then return to the beginning of the chapter to follow the procedure for fitting the springs to the seat.

If you have to start work on an elaborate chair, such as a winged armchair, refer to page 142 to see how to upholster the wings, then return to this section to work on the rest of the chair.

The simple sprung chair described here has been chosen because much of the work on it is exactly the same as that already described in the last chapter. The only unusual feature is the sprung front edge, which is not used on many chairs. You can either install one, or build the hard edge directly on to the frame as in the stuffed-over seat.

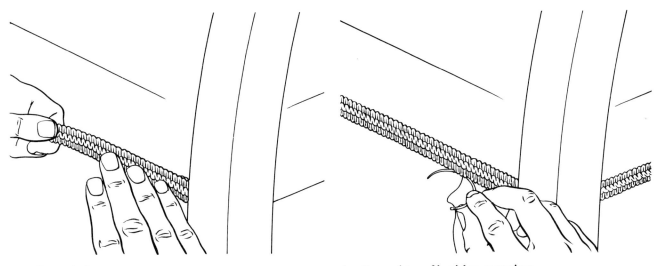

c. Smooth down.

d. Sew edges of braid to covering.

Bear in mind that even chairs of the same type vary vastly in the detail of their construction. At several points in the sequence of operations you will have to decide how to adapt the processes described here to fit your particular chair. There is no need to be nervous about the work. If you move carefully through the operations, taking one cautious step at a time, you will soon be able to tell when you have completed a stage correctly.

First strip down the old chair in the usual way. It will be helpful if you can make a sketch of the chair before you start to remove the old covering. The last person to upholster it was probably a professional, and your sketch will form a convenient reference for the way it should be restored. If you can take off the old coverings cleanly one at a time, you will also be able to sketch the constructional details of each stage. This will give you a full set of stage-by-stage reference drawings for the re-upholstery which you can use in conjunction with the drawings in this book.

But do not worry if, like most upholsterers, you find it impossible to take the coverings off in perfectly ordered layers. Even a general note of its final appearance should, in conjunction with the general descriptions of the chair given here, be enough.

When you have removed the old upholstery and springs, make good all the joints. Steam them apart if they are the slightest bit creaky, and re-glue and cramp them. Strip down all the old show wood, unless it is in perfect condition, which is highly unlikely, and re-polish it by one of the techniques described in Chapter 3. Most importantly, take care to fill in all the holes left by the tacks of previous upholsterers. And make sure all the edges are bevelled to take the tacks for hard edges all round.

Now you can start upholstering. Study the chair carefully. You will see that the kind of chair we are now dealing with has four basic parts – the back, the seat, and two arms.

Look at each of the parts in turn [4.18]. Start with the back. You will see that it consists of four members, the two uprights, the top rail, and a piece of wood across the bottom called the bottom tacking rail. The seat also has four members, the front and back rails, and two side

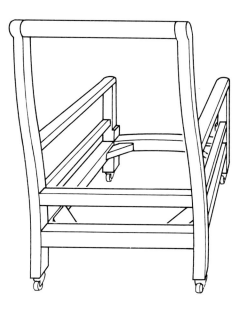

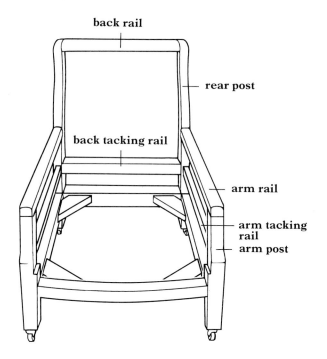

rails. Each of these sets of four parts forms a frame, not so different in many respects from the frame you have already learned to upholster on the drop-in seat and the stuffed-over seat. If you can picture these parts of the chair as separate entities, you will have gone a long way towards clearing up the confusion that faces many beginners and makes the prospect of re-upholstering a chair so daunting.

The arms are slightly more complicated. On most chairs they have only three wooden parts – the tacking rail at the bottom, the arm itself at the top, and the front face of the arm. The fourth part, which would form a rear tacking rail, is missing. All it needs is a simple substitute, described below.

As you look at the chair, visualising how the various parts separate out, you must settle the question of which part to begin work on. There is always a great temptation to finish the seat first. Avoid this. If you install the springs in the seat too early, you will find that working on the back and arms becomes almost impossible.

The best procedure is to work on the back and sides of the chair first, taking them to the point where you are ready to apply the first stuffing before you fix the seat springs in place.

First, as in the drop-in seat on which you began, you must fix the webbing in place.

On the back, the position of the webbing depends on two main factors – the shape of the back itself, and whether it is a sprung back. Whether you have springs or not depends largely on the preference of the owner and user. Back springs are soft and flexible, and give the seat a gentle, soft feeling. A back without springs, but properly stuffed, gives firmer support. Springs are almost always used on very big chairs, so the chair's size may determine your choice. Perhaps the best guide, until you have accumulated enough experience to judge for yourself, is to restore the chair the way you found it, with or without springs.

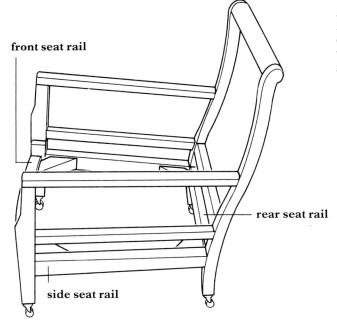

front seat rail

rear seat rail

side seat rail

4.18   Names of the component parts of a chair frame may vary considerably according to the detailed design of the frame, and among different upholsterers. However, the terms used here are generally accepted and widely understood.

If you are installing springs in the back of the chair, apply first webbing as in [**4.19a**]. The side-to-side webbing strands fit on the outside edge of the frame. Then the upright strands are fixed to the front of the frame. This draws the webbing slightly forward, so that the sprung back does not show as an unsightly bulge when the webbing ultimately begins to sag in use.

In the small chair illustrated the back is not being fitted with springs, so the webbing is tacked on to the front edge of the frame. In this chair, the back has a pronounced curve, so it is advisable to fix strands of webbing side-to-side only. Any webbing fixed top to bottom would tend to even out this attractive curve. And since the webbing will take only moderate pressure, and not have to carry any directly downward weight, the single strands will be strong enough to take the strain.

You can fix the webbing to the seat itself at this stage. It will not get in the way of any of the work you have to do on the sides and back. You will be using springs in the

seat, so the webbing is fixed to the under-side of the frame. Use strong 15 mm improved tacks, set in the usual staggered 'W' pattern, and pull the webbing taut with your webbing stretcher. The tacks should sit centrally over the frame member to give the greatest possible strength.

The general layout of the webbing will be similar to that used on the drop-in seat, but may vary slightly, according to the number of springs you use. The aim is to get the springs to sit squarely on the webbing.

It makes sense to apply plenty of webbing. It is not expensive material, and since you are doing the work yourself you can afford to spend a little more time on this part of the job. If you are using the springs in the 3–3–2 pattern shown in the illustrations, one strand will have to go down the middle of the seat frame.

A useful variation, uses doubled strands, the two lengths of webbing lying about 13 mm apart, one central pair and others at about mid-point between the centre

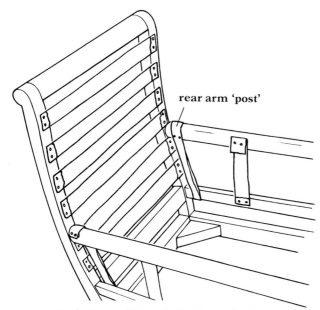

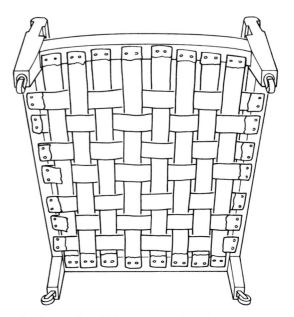

4.19a Apply the webbing, including a folded strand to form a rear arm 'post'.

b. Fit plenty of webbing to provide a firm base for the seat upholstery.

strands and the outer frame. Keep these strands of webbing parallel and ignore any widening effect towards the front of the seat. The two rear springs should then lie fixed between the centre and outer strands. The position of the springs must also relate exactly to the front edge springs. The main seat springs should lie in line with the gaps between the two front edge springs. Place the webbing as accurately as possible. Diagram [**4.20**] shows the springs arranged in a 3–3–2 pattern and twine fixing them to the webbing.

Apply the side-to-side strands next, weaving them between those already in place. Do not locate the two rear springs too close to the back of the chair. They will give little support there and their usefulness will be lost under the stuffing of the chair back.

You will probably find a rough sketch plan of the webbing and spring position, useful in these early efforts.

Finally turn to the arms. These do not have to carry any weight at all, so a couple of short lengths of webbing running vertically will be enough. However, there is a complication. Since the rear part of the arm does not have that fourth tacking rail, you will have to create a rail to fix the various layers of material on to. Take a length of webbing, long enough to run from the bottom tacking rail of the arm, to the arm itself. Fold it double along its length, and tack it to the arm, top and bottom, about two inches from the back upright and parallel to it. This will give sufficient support for the stuffing on the inner sides of the arms.

Now begin to apply the hessian to the arms and back. Fold over the edges of the hessian, and tack it down along the line formed by the ends of the webbing strands, using 13 mm improved tacks, at 25 mm intervals.

On the webbing post you have fixed to the arms, sew the hessian in place. Use upholsterer's twine and any convenient upholstery needle.

Next sew the familiar rows of bridles, or stuffing ties, into the hessian of the back and arms. Pull the twine tight enough to cover three fingers, as usual, starting the row with a slip knot and ending with several half hitches to stop the work ever coming undone. By now you should be able to judge the kind of pattern to use for your bridles. Since these bridles are designed to stop the stuffing sliding vertically down the inside of the chair, you can benefit from having more rather than fewer bridles.

Now start to fix the scrim in place on the chair arms. Normally you would fix the stuffing to the chair before the scrim, but you must change the order of operation now, to give yourself convenient access. If you have stuffing on the arms of the chair, you will not be able to fit the springs to the seat conveniently. And if you fit the springs first, you will have difficulty in wielding the hammer to fix the scrim to the bottom tacking rail of the arms. So tack the scrim to the bottom tacking rails, and a few inches up the upright of the arm at the front, and sew it to the rear webbing upright which you have made.

Take care over the dimensions of the scrim for the arms. The pieces must be cut generously, at least 150 mm of extra height and 75 mm of extra length, front to back, because the scrim will cover the inside of the arms, the stuffing on top, and the outside of the arms, before being tacked in place.

Cut the two arm pieces together, to help you to produce an even shape on the two arms when you come to the stuffing.

Also cut the scrim for the back, and tack it in place along the tacking rail and 100 mm or so up the back uprights.

Temporarily tack all three panels out of the way on top of the arms and back. Then you can begin fitting the springs to the seat.

FITTING THE SPRINGS

The chair illustrated, like many chairs of this size and type, has two sets of springs. A group of eight lies on the seat itself. And at the front, quite separate, is a line of four smaller springs, fixed to the front edge of the frame and linked together with a piece of malacca cane.

First determine whether any of the old springs can be re-used. To test a spring for wear, stand it upright on a firm level surface, and cover it with the palm of your hand. Now press directly and firmly downwards. If the spring tends to tilt over and collapse, or bows outwards at the centre, it is worn out and should be replaced. Some springs remain even, but are simply weak. There is no quick way of testing this: but try to imagine it, along with its fellows, taking the weight of your body. Do you think it would manage? If not, trust your judgment and replace it.

Do not replace one, two or three springs from the front edge. Because of the way they are lashed together, they will probably not show signs of individual wear, but will all have weakened at the same rate. Because of this you may find them stronger than some of the rear springs, and be able to save and re-use them. But if you decide to replace any of them, replace all four.

Fortunately, springs are still relatively inexpensive, and if you can afford it it is best to spend the couple of pounds that replacements for the whole chair will cost. They will give a far better finished article and prolong the life of the restored chair.

The length of the springs is important. When they are in position, all of them should lie with their tops at the same height. So the front edge springs, when compressed, must be shorter than the main springs, by the depth of the front member of the frame. Do the simple subtraction sum before you go to buy the springs, but remember that the front edge springs will carry less weight, and will be compressed less and can therefore be even shorter than the measurement you have just calculated.

Your best guide is an old spring. Take one of each – front and seat – for your supplier to match. He will produce the right length and the appropriate gauge. Failing that, you can use the table opposite as a rough guide.

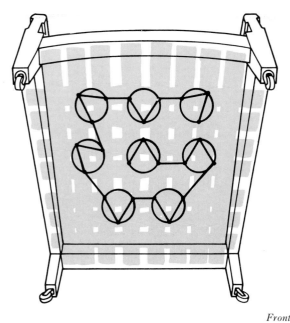

	Seat	Front edge
Sprung stuffed-over seat	150 mm	
Small arm chair	175 mm	125 mm
Wing chair	200 mm	150 mm
Deep arm chair or Chesterfield settee	250 mm	200 mm

Next, determine where the springs should be located.

Lay all twelve springs in place first. If you did not keep a note of where they were located follow this pattern: place the four lighter springs on the front edge, the outer ones 50 mm in from the armposts, the other two evenly spaced between them. The front of the springs and the front edge of the frame should coincide, so that the springs overhang the back of the frame.

The seat springs are located in a 3–3–2 pattern, going from front to back. The first two rows should lie in line with the three spaces between the springs in the front edge. The rear two springs will then lie in line with the spaces in the two front rows. The layout is shown in [**4.20**].

When you are satisfied that the seat springs will give all round support to the chair user, mark their positions with chalk on the hessian.

Now turn the chair over so that you have access to the underside, and sew the springs to the webbing. Start with the one at the centre, hold it in place, and with your curved needle and twine, sew a loop through the webbing and round the metal base of the spring. Tie it in place with a simple knot. Move obliquely across the base of the spring, sew another stitch and knot it. Then go across for a third stitch and knot, so that the spring is held in three places, and the twine forms an equilateral triangle underneath the webbing. Do not cut the twine, but move on to one of the outer springs. On each of these outer springs make sure that the metal join at the top (known as the 'knuckle') points towards the centre. This will help to preserve the balance. Sew the spring in place with three knots, and continue this process until you have gone all round. Knot off the twine firmly after the last stitch [**4.20**].

Lay a length of webbing down over the bottom coils of the four springs along the front edge and tack it firmly home with 13 mm improved tacks, two tacks on each side of the wire at each side of the spring. Remember to make the front of the spring and the front of the frame

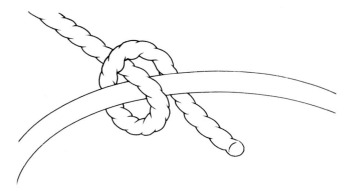

4.21a Locked loop.

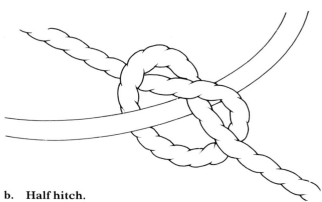

b. Half hitch.

coincide. And make sure that the knuckle at the base of each spring is towards the back of the chair.

Now all these springs must be lashed in place. When you first encounter a set of seat springs lashed down, the whole assembly looks impossibly complicated. But it is perfectly straightforward if you take it one step at a time, and if you have put the springs in their correct places in relation to each other.

The aim of lashing the springs down is to hold them in position, and to ensure that they all move in unison in response to the weight of the sitter. Otherwise one spring would depress where the pressure was greatest, leaving the others to form uncomfortable edges. Also it would cause serious problems if one spring, under pressure, should be forced out of position, and not be able to return to its correct place.

For this part of the operation you will need a ball of laid cord – a soft but strong cord designed specifically for this purpose. Do not use twine. It is too thin to stand up to the pressure of the metal springs.

You will also need a supply of 15 mm improved tacks, or, as an alternative, 15 mm wire staples.

As you will see from the illustrations, the springs are lashed together by knotting the laid cord on to them at the front and back of each, at various points up the coils of the springs.

To do this you will have to use knots which may be new to you.

Standard upholstery practice is to knot the first side of the spring with a locked loop, then the second side with a clove hitch. Some upholsterers use a half-hitch on the second side.

These knots are not difficult, and a few minutes practice should give you the dexterity needed to slip on the knots with barely a pause.

The locked loop is simple. Just take the leading end of the cord over the coil and back under, over the cord itself, under the coil, and away [**4.21a**].

The half hitch is also simple. Run the leading end of the cord over and back under the coil, then roll the end over and under the taut part of the cord. It is exactly the same as the first part of tying a shoelace [**4.21b**].

The clove hitch is slightly more complicated, but far more elegant. Take the leading end over and back under the coil, and bring it up on one side of the taut part of the cord (properly called the 'standing part'). Then take the leading end over and under the coil again, and back up on the other side of the standing part. Keep this second loop loose. Now pass the leading end through this loop you have formed, and away. Draw the knot tight. It sounds complicated but is perfectly simple in practice.

It is satisfying to abandon the locked loop and the half

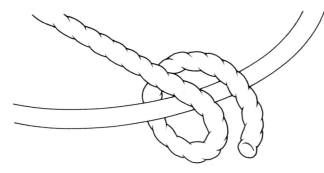

c. Clove hitch.

hitch, and tie the clove hitch to both parts of the spring. It takes no longer, and gives a far more secure feeling to the entire spring structure. The only disadvantage is that it is more difficult to loosen to adjust. So you will have to compress the springs to the right tension first time [**4.21c**].

Compressing the springs can seem extremely difficult at first, and you may feel you need a helper. But once you master the art, you can work perfectly well alone.

There are two ways of doing it. One is to tie on all the knots loose, then go back and compress each spring in turn, adjusting the knots and drawing the cord tight as you go. But this is rather fiddly.

A better way is as follows. Put your fingers and thumb on the spring at the two points where the knots will be. You will see where this should be shortly. Push down to compress the spring to the required depth. Steady your elbow on the frame to hold the spring in this position, and bring the laid cord to the position of the first knot, as taut as possible. Slide the cord under your finger or thumb, release the other side of the spring, and pinch the cord and spring together. Now, so long as you keep the cord and the spring pinched tight, you can let the spring come out of position, while you tie the knot. Slip on the two loops of the clove hitch, draw them tight, and relax. When you pull the cord taut again, the spring will come

back to the right position, determined entirely by the length of the cord from the anchor point where you started to the knot you have just tied.

Go across the spring and tie the next clove hitch on the other side. Now go to the next spring. The key to this method is that you need not compress this spring at all. It will lie the same distance from its neighbour at the top as at the bottom. All you have to do therefore is judge the length of the cord between them, lean the spring over, and tie the knot that distance away. In practice it will help if you check the right lengths for the lashing, by pressing the two springs down together, with the palm of your hand if your hand is big enough, or with a small piece of board.

Lashing the springs remains a fairly difficult job, so do not be afraid to work out some of your own variations on these basic techniques. Any method that you find comfortable is permissible, providing it achieves the right end result.

You may also find it difficult at first to judge how far to compress the springs. As in so many upholstery and restoration operations, there are no firm rules, and experience is the best guide.

Generally, however, if you have selected the right spring you can depress it about 40 mm and not go wrong. Remember that the seat will take about 50 mm of stuffing

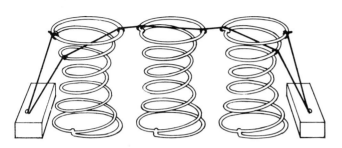

4.22   **Lashing the seat springs.**

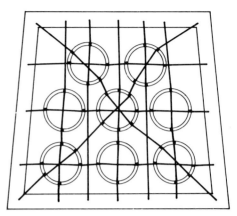

4.23   **Pattern of the seat-spring lashings.**

above the top of the springs, so if you can visualise how you want the finished seat to look, and subtract the thickness of the stuffing, you will know how high the top of the compressed spring should lie.

Start by lashing the two seat springs that lie on the central line of the chair from front to back. Cut off a length of laid cord, long enough to run over the top of the springs from the front to back rail, plus half a metre of spare.

Knock in a 15 mm tack on the front edge rail. It can be on top of the rail between the front edge springs, or down on the inner side of the rail, whichever is more convenient. Knot the laid cord round it 300 mm from the end. Now bring the other end up, compress the first spring, and knot the cord to the coil next to the top, with the clove hitch you have been practising. Now take the laid cord across to the opposite side of the spring and tie it to the top coil

Compress the next spring, and lash the cord to the near side, on the top coil. Go across that spring, to the coil next to the top, and lash on the cord with a clove hitch.

Take the laid cord down to the back rail, knock in a tack, and tie the cord to it. Lastly, take the two ends of the cord, bring them back up to the top coil of the nearest

spring and tie them on. The layout of the corded springs is in [4.22]. The path of the cord, running to a point part-way up a spring, across the tops, part way down, out to the tack, then back to the top, holds all the springs in their correct positions.

Securing laid cord to a tack can be difficult; it is thick and even the head of an improved tack may not be the most secure fixing for it. You can make a sturdier anchor point with a 15 mm wire staple (not the flimsy type that you fix with a staple gun). Knock the staple half way home, pass the cord through it. Draw the cord to the correct tautness, and then knock the staple in the whole way. Then tie a half hitch in the cord to hold it fast. Remember that staples are more difficult to remove than tacks, so get the tension right before you hammer them home.

Go on to the other springs, lashing down from front to back first. The single springs, at the rear of the seat, will have lines of cord of their own, running directly to the top rung of the spring at both front and back. Then lash the springs from side to side by exactly the same method. Finally, put in a couple of lashings diagonally. The whole seat should then look as in [4.23]. If any springs are seriously out of line, take off the cord and do them again. It is far better to spend an extra few minutes

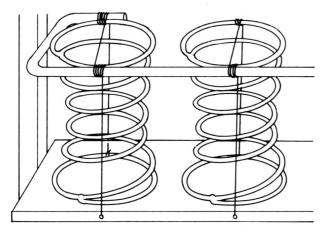

4.24 Front edge springs: lashed front to back independently, and to the cane.

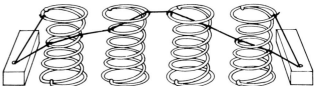

4.25 Side to side lashing for the front edge springs.

at this stage than to have a permanently uncomfortable seat.

For your first effort, you can aim to get the tops of the springs lying in a perfectly flat plane. The tops should be level with the tops of the front edge springs. When you achieve some measure of control, you will be able to improve the 'set' of the springs by adjusting them to form a slightly domed shape. Then they will take up the weight of the sitter without dipping quite so much, and add to the comfort of the finished seat.

Now lash the front edge springs, front to back first. Cut a length of cord about half a metre long. Tie one end to the bottom coil of the first spring, at the back where it overhangs the seat. Bring it up to the top of the spring. Compress the spring to level with the top of the seat springs, and at the same time draw it forwards about 25 mm so that it overhangs the frame itself, and knot the cord round the top coil. Bring the cord to the front of the spring and knot it again. Finally, bring the laid cord down the front of the spring, compress the spring by the right amount, and secure the cord about 25 mm down on the front of the frame, with a 15 mm tack or staple.

Compress and lash all four front edge springs by this method [**4.24**].

Now lash the four springs together with cord laid

from side to side. Cut a length of cord about one-and-a-half times as long as the width of the chair. Secure one end of it down in the corner where the front edge meets the arm post. Use either a staple or the tack-and-loop method. Take the cord to the bottom-but-one coil of the first spring, and lash it on. Now take it across the spring to the next coil up, and lash it on. Go on to the second spring. Lash the cord to the top but one coil, and go on to the top coil for the final knot. The cord should follow a steadily rising path through those two springs. Go across to the next spring, knot the cord and start going down, knotting the cord on as you go until you emerge at the corner opposite to where you started. Adjust all the knots if necessary to make sure all the springs are up-right, then secure the end of the cord by the tack or staple. The path of the side-to-side cord through a set of front edge springs is shown in [**4.25**].

There is an extra piece of support, to ensure that the front spring assembly continues to overhang the front edge of the seat. Cut short lengths of webbing, fold them double, and loop them over the second turn of the spring. Pull them taut, and tack them to the front edge of the frame.

Finally, lash all the four springs together to the malacca cane. If you have managed to rescue the old

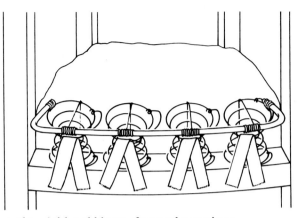

4.26a Add webbing to front edge springs.

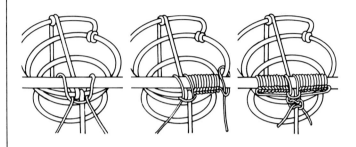

4.26b Detail of lashing of front edge spring to cane.

cane while stripping the seat, re-use it. If you can buy malacca cane, measure it carefully to determine where it should bend, and scorch it over a flame at the bending points. The heat will weaken the cane, and you can bend it into shape. If you have no cane, use $\frac{1}{4}$-inch section round-steel rod, and bend it to shape in a vice.

Now lash it down to the springs with twine. First make a loop over the back of the cane and spring together, and pass the free ends of the twine through the loop. Then start making hitches in each direction outwards from the centre towards each side. About 25 mm in each direction will be enough. Finally bring the two ends back to the centre, and tie them firmly together. Trim the ends. Do this on the front of all four of the springs, and at the sides of the two outer springs [**4.26**].

HESSIAN

With the springs all lashed securely in place, you can fit the hessian over them. (Use the same heavy hessian that fits directly over the webbing on other parts of the chair.) Calculate the length carefully. When fitted, the hessian will cover the springs, and also fit down in a well or gutter between the front edge springs and the seat springs [**4.27**] that allows the two sets of springs to

operate independently.

So lay a flexible tape measure over the springs from the rear seat rail, tuck it down into the gap behind the front edge springs, and take it on to the front rail. That determines the length of the hessian. To measure the width, run the tape measure over the springs between the two side tacking rails.

Tack the hessian, with 25 mm folded over all round, to the top of the tacking rails. Secure the rear first, then the two sides. Do not stretch it too tight over the springs. The springs must be held under tension by the laid cord lashings, and not by the hessian. You may find it difficult to hammer in the gap between the seat rail and the bottom tacking rails at the side and back. The solution is to hammer the tack in at a slight angle, and to tack near to the outer edge.

Cut the hessian tidily into the corners as you go.

THE WELL

When you come to the gap just behind the front edge springs, tuck the hessian down into it to form a valley. Let the front part fall over the front edge springs, but do not tack it down. Cut a length of laid cord 150 mm longer than the width of the chair: lay this over the hessian,

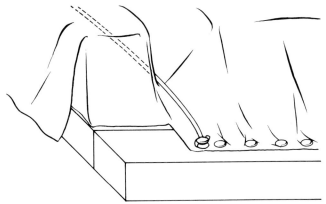

4.27 Cover the seat with hessian, with a strand of laid cord to form the well.

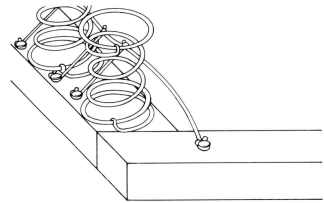

4.28 Fasten guy cord to the laid cord.

across the seat inside the well, tie a loop in one end, and tack it to one of the side tacking rails. Draw the cord to a snug fit, but not too taut, and tack it down at the other side of the chair. You may use 15 mm wire staples for extra security if you prefer.

Now fold the front portion of the hessian back over the well, so that it lies over the seat springs, and conceals the length of laid cord.

You will be able to feel, through the hessian, the laid cord you have just fixed in place, lying along the bottom of the gutter. Now you must secure that cord with a number of 'guy' cords. In this case there will be six, two in each gap between the front edge springs. Cut six lengths of laid cord about 250 mm long. Thread the first one through the weave in the hessian, round the well cord, and out again. You will not be able to thread a needle with the laid cord. The easiest way is to open up the weave of the hessian with the sharp end of your regulator, and push the laid cord through the holes by hand. If you cannot manage this, use the strongest grade of twine that you have and any convenient large needle.

Tie a slip knot in the guy cord, and draw it tight round the well-cord. Then tack or staple home the other end to the top of the front edge, between the front edge springs. The guy cords should look as in [**4.28**].

When all six guy cords are in place, bring the hessian forward over the front edge springs, and tack it in place on the face of the front edge of the frame, about 25 mm down from the top, and with 13 mm of overturn.

You will now be left with a generous fold of excess hessian at each side of the front edge springs. Do not cut it off. Instead push it carefully back between the outside spring and the arm on each side. Form it into a pleat at the top, and sew it neatly to the hessian where it lies along the side part of the malacca cane. At the bottom, draw the pleat through and tack it down to the top of the seat tacking rail, just behind the front arm post.

Finally secure the hessian to the seat springs and front edge springs all over. First sew it with twine to the malacca cane, along the front and round the sides. Either use a blanket stitch, working with a curved needle, or sew a series of separate half hitches.

Now sew the hessian to the seat springs. You will recall sewing the springs to the webbing on the underside of the chair, starting with the centre spring and sewing a triangle of twine with three knots in it, then going on to the others. Sew the hessian to the eight seat springs similarly with a single length of twine. Then sew it to the four front edge springs with another length of twine.

Now prepare the hessian to take its first stuffing. Sew bridles into all the areas where they are needed. You may be able to use the securing twine to hold the stuffing if it is not too taut. Alternatively sew some bridles between the springs. And you will need a few bridles on the slopes round the sides of the seat springs.

You should already have bridles in all parts of the arms, and in the back of the chair.

FIRST STUFFING

Now you come to the really creative part of upholstery – stuffing the chair. It has been relatively straightforward on the drop-in seat and stuffed-over seat; simply a question of giving the seat a gentle curve or crown.

On the more complicated sprung chair, you will have to build up a variety of curves, depending on the style of the chair, its size, and even the shape and taste of the person who is going to own and use it. Part of the value of doing your own upholstery is that you can tailor the seat, arms, and back to measure. For example, the width of the seat will be determined by the amount of stuffing you put into the two arms. Well stuffed arms will be suitable for a slim person. Whereas if the chair's owner is bulky, you can understuff the arms to give the user plenty of room.

With these considerations in mind, begin the stuffing. As always, the stuffing will be applied in two stages: first stuffing or understuffing; and second stuffing or over-stuffing.

The procedure is almost the same as on the stuffed-over seat. On each of the four parts of the chair, you must fix stuffing all over, and then cover it with scrim, and secure the scrim and stuffing in place with through-stuffing ties. On most parts of the chair, you will build up a hard edge with blind stitches and top stitches. Then you will add the second stuffing, into the various dished areas you have formed, and cover them with felt, calico, and finally the top cover.

The Arms. Start by stuffing the arms. You will recall that you have already partly fitted the scrim, tacked on at the bottom in the form of a 'pocket', to give yourself room to wield the hammer before the springs were put into place. Take handfuls of stuffing from your supply, tease it out to free it of lumps, and start to tuck it under the bridles. The upholsterer's term is to 'pick' the stuffing over the area. Tuck it down into the bottom of the pocket as well. Try to visualise how the seat will be when it is finished. The seat and arms will meet and press together, so put enough stuffing down in the bottom of the pocket to make a good contact with the seat later on, when it also has its stuffing in place.

For this part of the operation, use mainly fibre or sea grass. Hog's hair is rather expensive to install as the first stuffing in a chair of this size, when the second stuffing will cover it completely. Fibre beds down rather a lot, so put in plenty. When you have picked plenty of stuffing under the bridles, go over the arm again and tuck stuffing in the lines between the bridles, until you have an even covering all over.

Try to visualise how thick you want the arms to be and what shape they were on the chair originally. Keep pressing the stuffing down with the flat of your hand to give yourself an idea of how much it is likely to compress, and to check it for smoothness. Recollect your stuffed-over seat, and the amount of depression you made in the centre of it with the through-stuffing ties. You will have to add your one-third in the second stuffing after you have compressed the first stuffing with through-stuffing ties. The hair for the second stuffing will be more expensive, so go on generously until you have a good firm first stuffing as a base.

Also stuff the rear part of the arm generously, near the webbing arm 'post', as this rear arm edge will not be readily accessible later.

Draw the scrim up over the whole area and put in a line of temporary tacks, spaced well apart, on the top of the arm. Stuff both arms in the same operation, working evenly to produce the most accurate balance possible.

Now put in a pattern of through-stuffing ties. Thread a straight needle with twine, pass it through one arm near the bottom corner, thread it back, and secure it with a slip knot. Work in the usual way – along a couple of inches and through the stuffing, back half an inch on the webbing side, return the needle, then along another couple of inches. Take the stitching along and up, along and up, until you reach a line near to the underside of the arm rail. Finish with several strong knots. Put through-stuffing ties on the other arm.

Next release the temporary tacks. You now have two edges to deal with – the top of the arm and the arm front. Stuff the top of the arm first. This will ultimately be covered with a layer of top stuffing and felt, so you can use mainly the cheaper fibre stuffing here. Put a good thick layer on the arm; it will not be sprung on this size of chair. The filling should eventually be firm, though still giving a comfortable cushion effect.

When you have a good solid layer, draw the scrim over it, and tack it with a line of 10 mm improved tacks, on the outer edge of the arm, about halfway down.

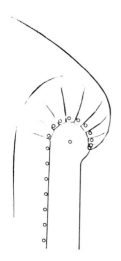

4.29 Pleat the scrim round the arm scroll and tack it down neatly.

Now test the top of the arm. Feel it. If it does not have enough stuffing, or if it is lumpy or uneven, push more stuffing in at the open ends, and work it along with your regulator. If you visualise the arm in relation to the stuffed-over seat, you will see that it is basically the same job, except that the edge, instead of going along one side then along the other, bends through 90 degrees, going first along and then down. In this case you will need a hard roll on the outer edge of the arm. So judge the quantity of stuffing, and the slackness in the scrim, to stitch in a roll about 25 mm in diameter.

Next stuff the front of the arm. If you lay the chair on its side, with the front face of the arm towards you, you will see that it also is almost the same as the edge of the stuffed-over seat, except that instead of being straight, it curves round the arm. Treat it in exactly the same way.

Start tucking the stuffing material under the fibre you already have in place. This part of the stuffing will form the outer edge of the upholstery; you will be able to feel its resilience through the cover and calico so try to use best hog's hair here. You should be able to judge how much stuffing you need from your previous experience

of building a hard edge. On each member of the chair, it should make a roll higher than the upholstery in the centre of the arm, where the through-stuffing ties are, and should overhang the edges slightly all round.

Go along the inner edge of the arm front, over the top, and down the other side of the scroll, to meet the line of tacks you have put on the outside of the arm.

Next bring the scrim over the roll of stuffing, and tack it down all round the bevelled edge of the arm front. As you start to work on the curve of the arm, you will find you have to turn a corner, and a great deal of excess material is formed. Pinch up this excess material in the form of pleats. Fold each pleat over, and tack it neatly down. Both the calico and the outer cover you put on the chair later will have to be pleated in this area, so practice on the scrim to produce a neat job. Ideally, you should arrange the pleats so that they fall pointing towards the centre of the arm scroll. Some upholsterers mark this centre with a dot to give them a target to aim for [**4.29**].

There are no strict rules governing the number of pleats. Too many will produce a series of lumps. Too few will leave ruckles in the material. The main aim is to

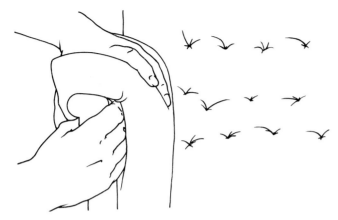

4.30   Tucking in the scrim may help the inexperienced upholsterer to form a neat roll.

keep the visible edge of each pleat following a tidy line. If you can manage it, make this outer or top edge of the fold follow the grain of the material. In pleating the scrim it is not difficult, as the weave clearly shows the grain. It can be more difficult on materials like velvets, so any practice you can get at this stage will be worthwhile. Remember to fold the pleats in opposite directions on the two arms for balance.

This entire operation – of forming a roll round a tight curve which requires pleats – is one of the most difficult in upholstery. There is a way of making it simpler. Form the roll by tucking the scrim underneath the stuffing. Tension and friction will hold it in place and you can go on pushing with your hand until the roll is the right size [4.30]. You may find the pleats tend to form themselves, but you will still have to tidy them up with the flat end of your regulator, and make sure they overlap in the right direction. When the roll is the right size, pinch out the scrim near the bevelled edge, and tack it through the double layer thus formed.

Now you need to hold all that understuffing in place, especially at the top of the arms, to prevent it falling down into the bottom edge of the roll. First sew a line of blind stitches along the top of the arm, starting your needle on the outside of the arm, in contact with the wood of the frame, and pushing it through almost horizontally. Make the usual two anti-clockwise turns of twine round the end of the needle as you pull it back, and draw the stitches tight to lock them. As you tighten the stitches, you will draw the stuffing firmly down on to the top of the arm frame.

Now carefully sew in a hard edge both round the scroll and along the top of the arm. Apply one row of blind stitches, and one or two rows of top stitches to create a roll about one inch in diameter. Regulate as you go, to avoid all bulges and dips in the edge. The hard edge will follow the gentle curve round the scroll face of the arm, and turn through the angle where the scroll meets the top outer edge of the arm. You should now have no difficulty in making your stitches follow the curve and the angle neatly. Make sure the roll does not form a narrow lip overhanging the edge. Sew the hard edge all round both arms, taking care to match them in all respects.

4.31 Sew in a hard edge about an inch thick, with blind stitches and top stitches.

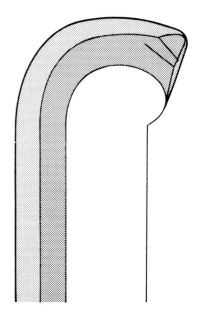

The Back. Follow roughly the same technique on the chair back. Lay the chair on its back, and start to pick your cheaper stuffing material under the bridles.

Again you will have a good opportunity to make the shape of the chair fit the most frequent user. Many modern chairs are built with little regard to variation in shape. You will be able to improve on that. Try to build up a fat padding of stuffing near the bottom of the back, working it into a gently curving hollow towards the top. The fat stuffing at the bottom is called the lumbar swell.

Also sew bridles into the hessian that covers the top rail, and put plenty of stuffing under them. The owner of a good chair should not be able to feel the wooden frame through the stuffing, especially on the top rail of the chair back.

If you have not tacked the scrim on the inside back already, push down the springs, and tack a rectangle of scrim along the back tacking rail. Cut this panel of scrim extremely generously, to take up the curves imposed by the through-stuffing ties and hard edge. Put plenty of

stuffing down into the bottom of the 'pocket', to make a good contact with the seat of the chair.

Draw the scrim over the stuffing, temporarily tack it at the sides and over the top, and put in a pattern of through-stuffing ties. The shape you achieve at this stage should give you a clear idea of whether your efforts to shape the upholstery are likely to be successful. If you have any doubts, don't be afraid to take out the through-ties and adjust the stuffing material. Beginners in upholstery cannot expect to get everything right first time.

Release the temporary tacks, and begin applying your best quality stuffing material all round the edge, both up the sides and along the top. Fill this area, from one arm, across the top, and round to the other, well enough to make a generous hard edge. [**4.31**] will show how the hard edge should look at the top. It should 'oversail' the back, and also overhang the sides by a small amount.

Cut the scrim to fit round the arm top rail where it meets the back upright. Between the arm top and the bottom tacking rail, you can tack into the front edge of the rear upright, folding the scrim under to give a double layer. Above the top of the arm, you will have to tack it to the bevel at the outer front edge of the upright after forming the roll. This bevel should run to the top of the arm, and round any scroll on the side of the arm. Along the top rail, tack the scrim about half way down the rear outer face.

To make the roll, adopt the same technique that you used on the arms. Tuck the scrim under the stuffing, until you achieve the size of roll you want. A 25 mm diameter roll edge all round will be adequate. Then pinch together two layers of scrim and tack through them both with 10 mm improved tacks. Regulate the stuffing well forward and down against the frame, smoothing out all irregularities as you go.

Try not to leave any temporary tacks in the scrim for too long. With its open weave, scrim tends to slip over tack heads, and they are better hammered home to secure the scrim in place as soon as possible.

At the top corners of the chair back, you will again encounter a curve and an angle coming together. Treat the problem just as you did the arm, and you should have no difficulty in sewing in a neat hard edge, with one row of blind stitches, and one row of top stitches, or two if necessary to make the roll really tight.

The Seat. Even more interesting will be the problems of stuffing the chair seat. Start by picking stuffing under all the bridles, and under the loops of twine that hold the hessian to the springs, if they are loose enough. Continue to apply stuffing until you have a good even layer all over. Be especially careful at the well. You will have to put plenty of stuffing down there, to keep the two sets of springs apart, but not so much that you stop them working independently. On the slopes at the back and sides, put in plenty of stuffing, to ensure that you have a good contact between the seat and the back and arms of the chair. And test to make sure that you cannot feel any of the springs through the layer of stuffing.

When you have a good even layer, as far forward as the

well, cut another generous rectangle of scrim, and push it through the gaps at the back and sides. Cut it into the corners where it meets the back uprights, and tack it in place along the top of the back and side tacking rails.

At the front, pack plenty of stuffing above the front edge springs, right up to the malacca cane. Tuck it under and between the bridles. Bring the scrim over to hang down a couple of inches below the front edge cane. At this point you will encounter another new tool – the skewer. Skewers are quite cheap, and a dozen will be enough to cover most upholstery jobs. They are used for holding all kinds of covers in place, where it would be inappropriate to put in temporary tacks. In this instance, use a few skewers to hold the scrim and hessian together just below the cane, along the front face of the seat. Push the skewers through the two layers of material, close under the cane, and up into the stuffing [**4.32a**].

Now sew a pattern of through-stuffing ties on to the top of the seat. You will need the longest double-ended needle you have. You will be sewing through only about 25 mm of stuffing, but you will have to handle the needle through the webbing at the bottom of the seat. So turn the seat on its back so that you can see through the webbing. Sew the twine round the top coil of any convenient spring for extra security, but make sure you

avoid snagging the twine round the lower coils, or the ties will not hold the stuffing down tight.

Some upholsterers complete the front edge before putting in the through-stuffing ties, which then draw the stuffing down tight.

Whichever order you choose, the front will have a hard edge. Aim to make it about an inch in diameter, but not more. So make sure you have enough hair in the front part of the seat, and bring it well forward with the regulator. There are two or three variations on the method of sewing the hard edge; the following is a standard system and works perfectly well. First, turn about 13 mm of the scrim under, and sew it to the hessian with twine, using a curved needle. Follow a thread, and pull out the skewers as you go. As an alternative you can secure the scrim with blanket stitches round the cane.

Check again that you have enough hair in the front part of the seat to form a firm edge. If not, or if the stuffing is not even, add more from the ends and regulate it along. When the front edge is well stuffed, close the ends. Form a small pleat at the corners of the stuffing, and sew it with fine twine to close it securely. Pull the rest of the excess down at the sides, and work it as neatly round the arm post as you can. Tack it to the rails at the front and sides, near to the arm posts.

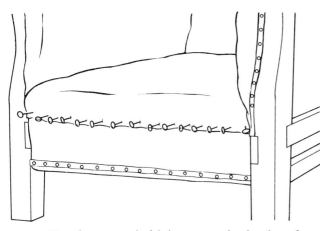

4.32a Use skewers to hold the seat scrim in place for sewing the hard edge.

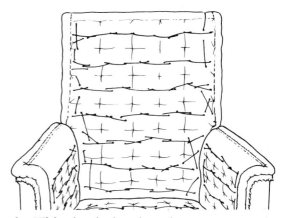

4.32b With a hard edge along the seat, arms and back, and with bridles in place, the chair is ready for final stuffing.

Now sew in a row of blind stitches. Start the needle immediately above the cane. Tuck back any stray hair to prevent it forming lumps around the cane area. Follow it with a line of top stitches. Start them near to the blind stitches, perhaps one or two threads of scrim above, and angle the needle to emerge 40 mm back from the front edge. Pull the stitches tight, and you will form a neat, even, compact roll, resting firmly on the top of the cane. The chair is now ready for second stuffing [**4.32b**].

SECOND STUFFING

Now you can proceed to the second stuffing, and for this you will need a calico cover, with which you are already familiar.

Normally, you would simply cut the calico from your supply as you needed it. But if this is the first large chair you have upholstered, you could usefully use the cutting of the calico cover as practice for cutting the cover itself. So if you are unfamiliar with the procedure, refer to the section on planning and cutting a cover, and base the cutting of your calico on it. You can make your mistakes on this relatively cheap material, and improve your work before you start cutting the more expensive top cover fabric.

The Arms. Start by working on the arms. Measure and cut enough calico to run the length of the arm at its longest, from the inside of the webbing post at the back, to the front of the arm, with three inches at each end for working. Measure the width from the bottom rail of the arm, round the curve, to the underside of the top rail, with a generous allowance for the fullness of the arm. Cut the material square to the weave.

With the chair lying on its side, apply your best quality hair to the inner sides of the arm. Sew in any bridles you may need. On top of the hair, apply a layer of felt wadding, to prevent strands of hair working through the calico.

The main difference from putting second stuffing on the stuffed-over seat is that you have plenty of latitude for making the arms the shape you want them. Generally, on this type of chair, the shape should be virtually straight from top to bottom, with a fairly tight roll on the top of the arm. You will have to add or remove hair, pulling the calico over it to compress it, until you achieve the correct effect.

Carry on compressing the stuffing and smoothing out the calico with the palm of your hand, as you knock in temporary tacks with the other hand. Use 10 mm fine tacks for calico, tacked on the underside of the arm rail.

At the back, pull the calico through the gap between the webbing strand and the back upright. For the time being, you can temporarily tack the calico to the back upright, while you work on getting the arm correctly shaped. When you are ready, release the tacks, and sew the calico to the doubled strand of webbing, just as you did the hessian and scrim. This will leave open the gap between the arm and the back upright through which the top cover will fit.

When the arm top and the inner arm are neatly stuffed and form fairly straight lines, fix the front permanently.

There are two main methods of dealing with the calico at the front scroll. You can pleat it as you turn it over the hard edge or you can gather it on a draw-thread.

If you choose to pleat it, use skewers to hold the calico in place. Pleat it exactly as you pleated the scrim, following the grain of the material and folding the pleats down tidily to point towards the centre of the circle of the scroll. Make sure no strands of hair work their way between the calico and the hard edge at that point, or they may cause lumps and irritating hard lines under the final cover.

You can tack the calico to the facing of the scroll, just inside the tacking line of the scrim. Alternatively, you can sew it to the inner curve of the hard edge. Sew it with a row of blind stitches. Use either a straight double-ended needle and twine, or a small curved needle. Make the usual two turns round the emerging point of the needle before you pull it tight.

The other method of finishing the calico is to sew a couple of 'draw strings' into the scroll. [4.33] shows the technique.

Take an ordinary sewing needle and a length of strong thread. Pull the calico down over the scroll facing, and start a line of sewing an inch in from the hard edge, and about an inch below the point where the edge starts to curve to form the scroll.

Sew through the calico with a running stitch about 2 mm long, following exactly the curve of the scroll. When you have gone right round the scroll, put a knot in the thread. Repeat the line of sewing about 2 mm away from the first line, and knot off that thread.

Now take up the two free ends, and draw them through the calico. If you work the calico against the

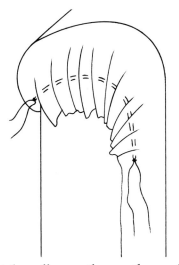

4.33 **Pleat the calico neatly over the scroll at the front, and tack or sew it in place.**

pull of the thread, it will form into a series of small gathers, folding the calico evenly over the scroll.

Knot off the two threads together at the free ends, put a couple of tacks in the centre of the scroll, and trim off the excess to give a neat finish.

Lastly, hammer home all temporary tacks.

The Back. The back is relatively straightforward. Lay the chair on its back, sew in bridles to stop the hair falling down inside the chair in use, both within the back panel and on the top. This is your last opportunity to adjust the shape of the back. If your through-stuffing ties flattened the lumbar swell you created during the first stuffing, use a good thickness of hair in that area to build it out again. When the hair is smooth, well shaped, and firmly secured by the bridles, cover it with a layer of cotton wadding, then calico. Lay the calico over it, and temporarily tack at the top and bottom. The tension in the calico should be mostly from side to side. Too much tension in the top to bottom direction will tend to pull the curved lumbar swell out of shape.

Draw the calico carefully to the sides, and tack it down. At the sides tack it to the outer face of the side uprights. At the bottom, turn it round the bottom rail, and tack it on the outside back. At the top, take the calico right over and tack it on the rear face of the top rail fairly close up under the roll.

At the arms and bottom rail, you will have to cut into the corners. The correct way of cutting at points like this is with a 'Y' cut. Make a straight cut to within about 25 mm of the corner, then two oblique cuts right up to the corners so that the material will lie snug. Push the calico through the gaps between the areas of stuffing, and fold the excess under. Work it with the flat end of your regulator if necessary, and tack it down as securely as you can.

The Seat. The method of dealing with the seat varies according to the style of the chair. If you are planning to use a cushion on the seat, you will not want to waste expensive material on the area underneath the cushion which nobody will ever see. In fact, it can be a disadvantage to use the best material on the top of the seat, because the cushion can often slide on the shiny surface

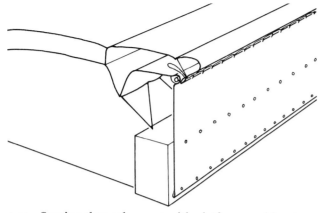

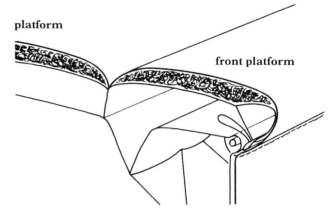

4.34 Section through a seat with platform and front platform at first stuffing stage. The springs are omitted.

4.35 The same seat at second stuffing stage.

of good materials, especially hide or imitation leather.

The top part of the seat is therefore made up in two parts, the platform and the front platform [**4.34**, **4.35**]. When no cushion is planned or on a small chair, it would be superfluous to divide the seat into these two parts.

There are also several possible treatments for the front of the chair, which is called the border. On a big chair it is customary to divide the material here into two. On smaller chairs one piece is acceptable. It may be finished with a fringe or some other decorative flourish.

The chair illustrated has a seat cover made in three parts: a platform, front platform, and a single border. If you want to make a chair with a single-piece platform, simply omit all work relating to the sewing and fixing of the seam between the platform and front platform.

In the arrangement illustrated, start by drawing a chalk or crayon line 180–200 mm in from the front edge of the seat, across the width of the chair. This is the line at which the platforms will join.

Now measure the calico pieces for cutting. Measure from side to side on the seat rails, and from the top of the rear seat rail over to the line you have drawn. Add about 100 mm for the curve of the top stuffing and for general handling, in each direction. The front platform runs

from the chalk line to the underside of the front roll edge. And the border runs from the underside of the front edge down to the underside of the front lower frame, where it will be tacked. Allow a margin of 100 mm in each case for general working. When you come to cut the top cover itself, you will be able to measure and cut to far greater accuracy.

When you measure the front border for width, add 300 mm to the measurement across the chair. The calico will have to turn round the front springs, and disappear into the recess between the front springs and the chair arms.

Start by machine-sewing the two pieces of calico for the top of the seat together and to a piece of tape long enough to run across the width of the chair. Clearly, cutting the calico in two pieces is only necessary if you are practising for later work on the top cover, where a pattern is involved. You can simply make this seam by folding the calico and sewing the tape to the fold.

Now lay the two pieces on top of the seat, and turn the platform piece over towards yourself, to expose the seam flange. Position the seam on the chalk line you have drawn 180–200 mm in from the front edge. Working from the centre to the sides, pin it in place with your skewers. Now with a 250 mm double-pointed needle and twine, sew through the calico seam flange, and through the scrim, first stuffing, and hessian. Pick up the top coil of a spring whenever you encounter one and sew round it for extra strength, but take care not to snag any of the lower coils of the spring.

Do not pull these stitches down too tight. The aim is to secure the calico in place on the seat, not to compress the stuffing. Stitch through the calico seam flange only as far as the outer edges of the springs. Do not sew down the sides of the seat. Instead, pull the tapes out at the sides, and temporarily tack them to the top of the side seat rails. Now put a thin layer of best hog's hair over the seat as a second stuffing, under and between bridles. Cover it with felt or wadding to prevent the hair emerging through the calico lining.

Push back the panel of calico that will cover the main platform, and smooth it out over the seat. Push it down through the recess between the seat and back, and start temporarily tacking along the seat rail, first at the back, then at the sides.

The process is almost the same as you have followed on simpler drop-in and stuffed-over seats. Smooth out the calico to get the tension right, then put in a tack.

Watch the weave of the calico to make sure that it goes on straight, and when you have every part well smoothed out, free of bumps, and nicely taut, hammer home the tacks.

Now turn the front platform calico back over the main platform, to expose the scrim in that area. Again, apply a thin layer of hair to form the top stuffing, bringing it up to the crest of the hard edge, but not over it, or it will form unsightly and uncomfortable bumps under the final cover. One method of applying the calico now is to bring it right down and tack it on the underside of the front frame member, with no break. On most chairs, it enhances the chair's appearance if there is a break just under the lip of the hard edge.

This break is incorporated by sewing a 'banding' in the calico. Make a fold in the calico about 25 mm high, and turn the fold up. Adjust it if necessary, and pin it so that the end of the fold butts up neatly against the underside of the hard edge.

Now sew the top of the banding in place, using a small curved needle and strong white thread.

The front border is the one part of the chair where there is no first stuffing. So you must put in a few fairly tight stuffing ties, to make a thin even layer on the chair

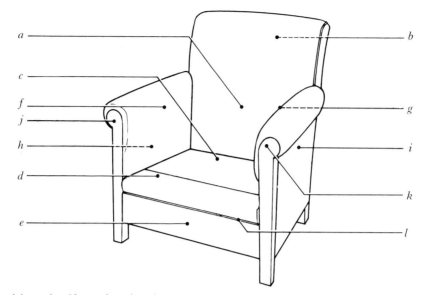

front. You will find it easier if you lay the chair on its back to deal with this part. Cover the hair with the customary layer of cotton wadding to stop the hair working through the calico. Alternatively, you can apply two or even three layers of wadding to the front of the chair, omitting the hair. This part of the chair will not be sat on, so the main aim is to produce soft-looking lines to the appearance of the chair front, and wadding will do the job well. Smooth out the calico of the front border, and tack it on the underside of the frame, working as usual from the centre to the sides.

At the sides of the front springing, tuck the calico into the recess as you did the scrim and hessian. Pull it through behind the arms, between the two rails, and tack it to the top of the rail just behind the arm.

THE COVER

With the calico in place, and well smoothed down, the most difficult part of the upholstery is done. Fitting the cover is largely a repeat of the calico covering, as it was on the stuffed-over seat. The main difference is that as covering fabric is so expensive you will have to cut it with extreme accuracy to avoid wastage.

First write out a cutting list, and make up a plot of the seat by drawing a rough outline of each component [4.36]. Then measure, on the calico covered chair, the width and length of each piece. For the chair illustrated, the list will read:

a. inside back
b. outside back
c. seat platform
d. seat front platform
e. seat border
f. inside arm
g. inside arm
h. outside arm
i. outside arm
j. front scroll
k. front scroll
l. piping

Now begin measuring. There is an old saying in the upholstery trade: 'Measure twice and cut once'. Bear

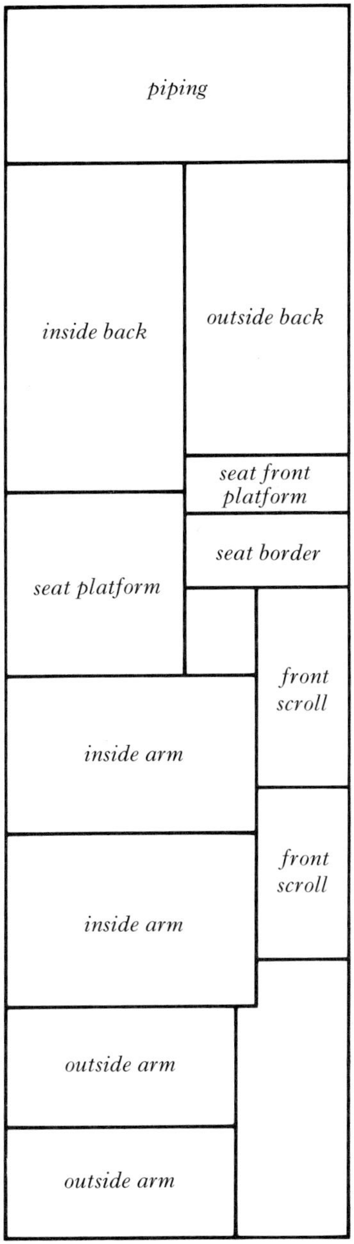
piping
inside back
outside back
seat front platform
seat border
seat platform
front scroll
inside arm
front scroll
inside arm
outside arm
outside arm

4.36 Measure for all the items on the cutting list and draw up a plot.

it in mind. It could save you some costly mistakes. Measure all lengths with a flexible tape measure round the curve of the chair, without compressing the calico and stuffing. Measure between the relevant tacking rails. Add 13 mm at each side for seams, turnings, and general working. Here are the details.

Inside back: measure the length from the outside of the top rail of the back, over the back, down through the gap between the back and the seat, and round to the rear of the lower back tacking rail. Measure the width across the chair at its widest point, round to the rear faces of the back uprights.

Outside back: measure the width to the outside edges of the frame. Measure the length from under the top rail to underside of the seat tacking rail.

Inside arm: measure length from the bottom tacking rail over the calico, without compressing it, to the underside of the arm rail. Measure width from the front of the scroll, through the recess between arm and back, to the outer edge of the back upright.

Outside arm: measure length from the underside of the arm rail, to the underside of the bottom seat tacking rail. Measure width from the front outer edge of the arm post to the rear edge of the back upright.

Seat platform: measure width from the top of one side tacking rail to the top of the opposite tacking rail, at the widest point of the seat. Measure length from the top of the rear seat tacking rail to the seam you made on the calico cover 180–200 mm in from the front edge of the seat.

Front platform: measure width as on the calico. Measure length from the seam to the underside of the hard edge, in the position where you built the banding into the calico cover.

Front border: measure width as on the calico. Measure length from the underside of the hard edge to the underside of the front lower seat frame member.

Lastly, calculate the dimensions of the scroll facings on the fronts of the two arms.

On any chair on which these parts are curved, you may find it difficult to produce accurate measurements. If so make a paper template. Lay a piece of stiff paper, large enough to cover the surface and adjust to all the curved areas. Rub round its edge with a soft pencil, keeping the paper firmly in place without it slipping. Skewers will help. Draw a second line outside the first to give a 50 mm margin all round. Before you start cutting the material, cut round the outer line, and test the template on the chair. On arms, use that template to produce a matching one for the opposite side.

Now transcribe all your measurements on to a paper plot. This is the stage at which you must take into account any pattern your material incorporates. First make sure you plot all the pieces the right way up. The right way up for a pattern is obvious on the upright parts of the chair. On the seat, consider the back as the top, and the front as the bottom. In other words the pattern should be the right way up as you stand facing the chair and look down on the seat from above.

On any material which has a nap, such as velvet, the nap should run down the chair from top to bottom, to avoid trapping dust and dirt. It will then run from the back to the front of the seat.

On any material with a simple small design, all you need do is make sure that you cut the pieces the right way up, and that the pattern runs vertically true.

If the pattern is large, you will have to work far more carefully, to make sure that any large motif falls in the middle of the inside back. If it lies to one side it can ruin the appearance of the chair. Equally, if the top of a motif disappears off the top of the chair, and reappears at the bottom, it can ruin the work you have put into the chair.

4.37 If the fabric is short or expensive, attach flies to concealed parts of the chair. For example the seat.

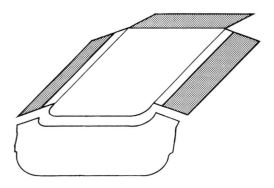

To make sure the pattern falls in the right place, measure the repeat, and measure the distance in of the motif from the selvedge. Then make a scale drawing. If you cut out the pattern pieces from your cover layout to scale in tracing paper, and lay them over the scale drawing, you will be able to check that your motif falls in the right place.

Start with the important inside back, and make sure that any motif falls in the centre laterally, and just above half-way up. Next position the seat platform, assuming that you are having no cushions. If you are, work out the cushion covers first. Again make sure that the motif falls in the centre. Also, see what you can do to ensure that the pattern 'follows through'. In other words, try to arrange the cutting so that the motif on the seat and on the back are the same relative distance apart as they are on the original material. The chair will then display throughout the same pattern that the designer of the material intended. Of course, you will not be able to do this by cutting the inside back and the seat platform next to each other, or you would have no material to fall down between the two. You will have to achieve this by clever calculation, 'losing' one repeat down out of sight between the back and seat.

Now bear in mind the possibilities of saving material

by attaching 'flies' to certain parts of the material [**4.37**]. A fly consists of a piece of hessian, or an offcut of material, either from the piece you are using on the chair, or from some other piece altogether. There is no point in having expensive covering material occupying parts of the seat that will never be seen. These are down at the bottom of the inside back, at the rear of the seat platform, and at the bottom of the two inside arms. It is perfectly acceptable to sew a fly on to any of these parts. Do not be afraid to use them, either to make your material go further, or to achieve a more attractive layout of the material you have.

When you have laid out the two main parts, plot the remaining pieces. It is important that the inside arms should display the same pattern, or you will upset the balance of the chair. The scroll facing at the front of the arms should also be a perfect match.

Try also to get the outside arms to match. The outside back may not be critical, depending on where the chair is likely to be situated, but if there is any chance of it being seen, it would be attractive to have the motif centrally placed.

Piping. Now consider the piping, which fits at the junctions of the various cover parts all round. You have a

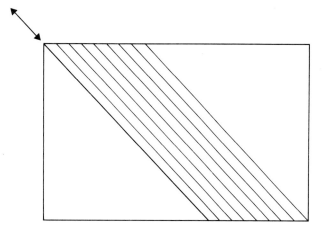

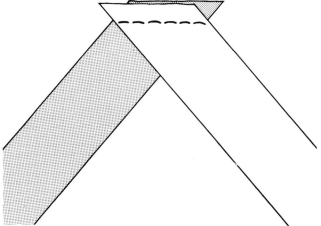

4.38a Cut the piping on the bias if you have enough spare fabric.

b. Sew it right side to right side in a V arrangement.

choice between making your own pipings, or fitting ruche in a matching colour. The piping itself is normally made in the same material as the rest of the chair covering, but if you are confident in your ability to choose well, you can make it in a compatible or contrasting colour.

Lay out several strips on your cutting pattern for making up piping. They should be set on the bias, which means diagonally to the weave, to produce the most workable piping. The material has more stretch and more flexibility when it is cut on the bias than when it is cut square to the weave. On the other hand, unless you can fit the oblique lengths of piping material into the pattern, there will be some waste at the two sides of the cuttings.

To make the piping, mark out a line with tailor's chalk across a conveniently wide and long area of the material. Draw other lines parallel to it, 40 mm away. Cut the strips at the same time as the rest of the material.

To produce the piping, first sew the lengths together. If you have been forced to cut them square to the weave, simply sew the ends together on a sewing machine, and turn the seams over. Press them with an iron and damp cloth to give a smooth finish. If you have cut them on the bias, lay them together to form a 90 degree V-shape, right side to right side, and sew them together [4.38]. Then turn the top one over on itself, and you will produce a continuous length. Trim off the untidy ends, and iron down the folds to smooth out the material. Roll it up carefully until you need it.

To sew the piping, you will need a ball of piping cord, and a piping foot on your sewing machine. Fold the piping cord into the piping material as you go, and sew the fold as close to the piping cord as you can. On any material with a loose weave, sew a double or treble seam at the junctions between the cut strips to prevent it unravelling.

CUTTING THE COVER

When you are absolutely sure that you have measured up the pieces accurately, draw them out on your material. Use tailor's chalk, with a sharp edge, and mark on the right side of the material. Draw the outline lightly. Then cut along the outline through the centre of the chalk mark. Do not worry if the material appears to warp

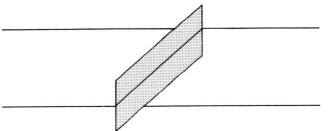

c. Open out the fabric and iron the seam flat.

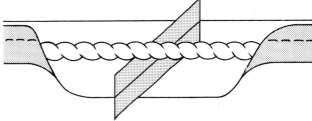

d. Sew in the piping cord, preferably on a machine with a piping foot.

out of shape as you cut. Follow your chalk mark, and the material will work back into shape when you have finished cutting. Fold each piece carefully as you cut it, sides to the centre, and lay it safely aside.

COVERING THE SEAT

Start by laying in place, on the seat of the chair, the piece of material cut for the platform. You will recall that it can be either your best material, or, if there is to be a cushion, a piece of lining material.

Take the piece for the front platform, and try it in place. The process is virtually identical to fitting the calico cover. The only difference is that calico is normally (if you have not followed the procedure recommended for beginners) cut generously and trimmed on the chair. The top cover material will be cut far more accurately and you will have to work it into place carefully. When you have it in place, measure in from the sides, and cut a small notch to mark the exact centre of each of the two pieces of material. Follow these centralising notches throughout the covering operation.

Now lift the front platform piece over and lay it upside down on the seat, so that the two flanges lie together. Pin the two pieces of material together, then take them away and sew along the seam, at the same time sewing a length of tape to the seam, both to give it strength, and to enable you to draw the seam taut across the seat.

Return the platform and front platform to the seat, and lay them in place, but upside down. Draw the front platform over the front edge of the seat, and smooth it down over the front and sides.

There will be a fold of excess material at the sides. Draw the excess up into a pleat, and pin it at each side, as close as possible to the calico lining. Then take the material back to the machine, and sew up the pleats on the inside, with several lines of stitches. Trim off the excess, and try the cover on the seat the right way up. If you have made both sides accurately, it should be a perfect fit, with the two pleats transposed.

At the sides, the material will now lie comfortably down the sides of the seat. If you try the front border in place, you will be able to push that also round the sides of the seat. Clearly, the double layer of material is unnecessary, so you will have to sew in another join. To make it as unobtrusive as possible, it should be formed

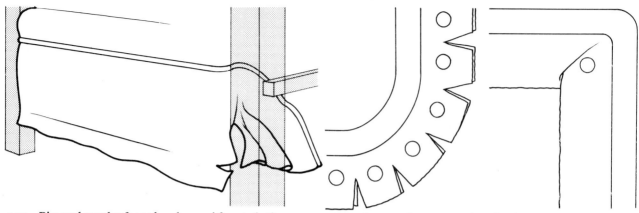

4.39 Pin and try the front border and front platform on the chair until you achieve a good fit.

4.40 Cut notches or overlap the flange when turning a corner.

as a curved seam, starting at the bottom of the front platform pleat, and running down in a curve to the bottom tacking rail. It is almost impossible to cut this curve in situ, so the answer is to cut as far back as you can on the front platform piece with a small pair of scissors, then remove the front platform piece and continue the cut freehand. Now fit the front border to it, at the angle the chair will form. Pin them together, and try them in place, changing the pinning as many times as necessary to achieve a snug fit without any strain or gaping. Then cut the front border piece to meet the curve on the front platform piece, with an overlap of about 20 mm [**4.39**].

Now sew the join between these two pieces, across the front and down the side seams, but this time you will be adding a length of your recently finished piping, to give the seam a professional finish.

Check the pieces again to see that they fit well on the chair. Then take them away again, and turn them inside-out to expose the flanges of the pinned seam.

Working a few inches at a time, remove the pins, slide the flanges of the piping between the flanges of the front platform and border pieces, and re-pin them. Then take the whole assembly to your sewing machine and sew the four flanges together, with the sewing hard up against the roll of the piping.

To end the piping, peel back the last 13 mm at each end, cut the piping cord, and sew across the end to close it.

At various points in the sewing of the cover, you will find you have to work the piping round an awkward curve, in either the inner or the outer direction.

To turn a corner inwards, snip the flanges of the piping at enough points to allow the piping to turn without stress [**4.40**].

To turn a corner outwards, fold the flange over on itself as you go. To reduce any possible lumpiness, hammer the folds flat. If that does not work, iron them under a damp cloth. If the material is still too thick, cut out the bulky material.

The seat cover is now ready for fitting.

Lay it in place, starting with the platform. Fold the front platform and the border back over the seat, to expose the seam between the platform and the front platform.

This should now be located over the seam you sewed into the calico cover. Take your 250 mm long doubled-ended needle, and once more sew with twine right through the seam flanges, and through all the layers of stuffing, to secure the cover to the seat. Be careful not to snag the twine round lower coils of the springs. Sew across the top of the seat, but not down the sides, and do not pull the stitches too tight or you will compress the top stuffing and form a well. At the sides, tack the tape to the top edge of the bottom tacking rail.

Now smooth out the seat platform, and make sure that the motif in the pattern, if there is one, falls accurately in the centre of the seat. If you have done all the cutting and sewing correctly, you should have no problems. Tack the material at the side and at the back to the tops of the respective tacking rails.

Next pull the front platform piece forward, and smooth it snugly over the corners of the front edge springs. If you lift the front border piece, you will expose the flanges of the seam that lies just under the lip of the front edge of the seat, where you folded the banding into the calico. This is the stage at which you should begin to check the position of the piping, relative to the front seat rail. It should be at precisely the same height all across the width of the chair. At this stage the piping will be covered by one layer of material, but if you feel for it, and check with a ruler as you go along that it is at the same height from the bottom of the front rail throughout, you will avoid one of the most unsightly faults in upholstery. As you check the position, secure the material with skewers. Then sew the flange to the upholstery

beneath it. You will not be able to use a double-ended needle in this location, so use a curved needle.

You can now pull down the front border material, and tack it to the underside of the frame. Start at the centre, and smooth it out towards the sides, working with temporary tacks until you are sure you have the material on neatly. Tuck the material away between the front edge springs and the arm. Here you may have to do some careful pleating, in inaccessible places, or even cut into the material to get it to lie smooth.

Draw the excess through behind the arm post and tack it to the side tacking rail.

COVERING THE INSIDE BACK

Covering the inside back should present no real problem. If you have done your planning and cutting correctly, the pattern should look right, either following through with the seat itself, or having the main motif falling centrally and slightly above half-way up the back. Remember, the back is the most visible part of the chair, and the greatest care taken in fitting the inside back cover will be greatly rewarded.

Start by tucking the bottom of the cover down behind the seat, and pulling it through to tack the central part temporarily on the top of the lower back tacking rail.

Now smooth it upwards. The tension in the back is particularly important. It is subjected to continual downward pressure from people sitting in the chair, and if not correctly fitted the back will soon show ruckles from this pressure, and the ruckles will soon turn into permanent folds that gather the dirt and show as unsightly ridges.

On the other hand, you cannot afford to put too much tension in the back cover in a vertical direction, or you will cancel out the elegant and comfortable curve that you have carefully built into the upholstery.

The way to deal with this problem is to tack the material on temporarily with fairly firm vertical tension, but not so much as to stretch it out of shape or distort the pattern.

Then stretch it across the back with slightly greater tension, though again taking care not to pull the pattern out of true. Finally re-tack at the top. The sideways tension should then be enough to prevent any creasing.

You will have to cut the material to fit round the arm rails and the tacking rails where they meet the back uprights of the chair. Here extremely careful cutting is called for. If you cut too short, the material will not lie comfortably round the joints in the wood. If you cut too long, you will produce gaping and looseness.

Above the arms, you will be able to fit the cover exactly as you did on the simpler stuffed-over seat.

Deal with the pleats at the top corners as you dealt with the stuffed-over seat. Smooth the material over the corner, pull the two folds together, and sew them with a slip stitch. Alternatively, make one pleat from the crest to the corner, tucking the material away down the sides. Sew up the gap.

COVERING THE ARMS

Finally fit the arm covers. It is vital to get the cover material on the arms in the right direction, and without either creasing or looseness. Fit it from back to front first. Work each stage of the two arms alternately. First lay the covering over the calico, and tuck it through the

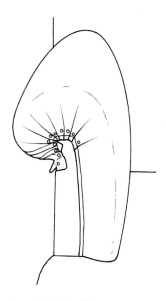

4.41 Pleat the edge of the inside arm cover and tack it round the front scroll.

gap where the arm meets the seat back. Smooth it forwards, and secure it to the calico and stuffing with a run of skewers, close to the hard edge round the scroll front. Temporarily tack it at the back, on the outside of the back upright. Pull it through the gap at the bottom, and tack it in on the outside of the bottom seat tacking rail. At the top, bring the cover over and tack it on the underside of the arm rail.

Now adjust the cover in any direction where it is necessary to even out any creases, or give the pattern a better set. If one arm is vastly different from the other, it is not too late to lay the covering material aside, open up the calico, and apply a bit more stuffing, with wadding to prevent it working through the covering material.

You will see, as you apply the cover, that it is fixed in several places to different tacking rails from the calico that lies beneath it. The calico is fixed to leave gaps between the various parts of the chair. But the two parts of the final cover are fixed to the same part of the frame specifically to close this gap to prevent objects falling in and being lost.

When you are satisfied with the lie of the covering material, start to cut into the corners. You will need to cut it where the bottom tacking rail meets the back upright, and where the top arm rail meets the back upright. Tuck the excess material away with the flat end of your regulator. At the front, pleat the material round the scroll, in the way you have already practised on the scrim and calico. This time, tack the cover material in place all round the scroll and down the front of the arm, about half an inch in from the bevelled edge. Leave the raw edge of the material exposed [**4.41**].

The only work that now remains on this seat is to cover the outside back and two outside arms, apply the facings for the scroll fronts of the two arms, and fit a black lining layer to the underside of the seat.

FITTING THE OUTSIDE COVERS

As it is the outside back which puts the final seal on the visible part of the chair, you will have to install it last. Therefore install the outside arms first, so that the back

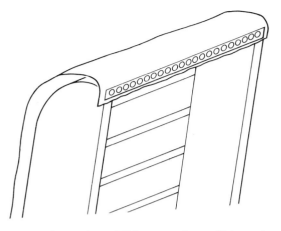

can cover their edges. This operation will introduce a new skill – back tacking. It is designed to give a straight edge to a junction between two materials.

Turn the chair on its side, protecting the new coverings from damage or soiling on the floor or bench, so that you can work on one of the arms. Position your outside arm material on the area it will cover. Then, keeping its upper edge in place, fold it back over the arm.

Now take a strip of buckram, 13 mm or 20 mm wide, and as long as the underside of the chair arm. Lay it over the two layers of material, with the outer edge of the buckram lying accurately on the line where you want the join to be. Tack through it with 13 mm improved tacks fixing the material in place under it. Now, when you fold the outer arm covering down into place, the buckram inside the join will give a neat straight edge [**4.42**].

On large seats, you may find it useful to reinforce the outer coverings with a layer of strong hessian, to protect it from behind from the damage it is likely to receive in use. If so, tack the hessian under the buckram at the upper edge. You may also find that a layer of thin nylon wadding gives a soft and well-cushioned look to these outside parts of the chair.

Fold the cover material down and tack it, with the hessian and the wadding, on the underside of the bottom tacking rail.

Fold the layers round the front of the arm scroll, and temporarily tack them, leaving the cover fabric with a raw edge. You may need to open up this edge later to fit the scroll facings. Cut the fabric to work round the chair leg at the front, and round the back upright at the back. You should now be familiar and perfectly confident with the techniques of cutting the cloth to meet the wood. Trim off all unnecessary material as you go, and tuck the folds under with the flat end of the regulator to give a neat finish.

Tack the rear edge of the cover, near the inner edge of the rear outer face of the back upright.

FITTING THE OUTSIDE BACK

On this kind of chair, the outside back is straightforward. Add a panel of hessian and perhaps thin wadding for protection and to soften the appearance, and with a length of buckram to fit across the width of the chair, back-tack the top of the panel. Then begin stitching down the two sides. Use a small curved needle, and thread which matches the colour of the upholstery as closely as possible, and use a slip stitch or ladder stitch which will lie concealed under the seam. At the bottom, go right under the bottom tacking rail and tack the outside back cover in place.

4.43 The slip stitch or ladder stitch forms a neat seam with almost invisible sewing.

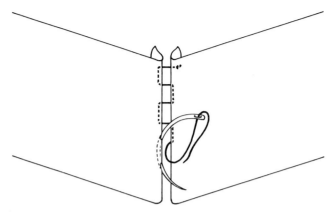

HOW TO SLIP STITCH

Whenever you have to join two pieces of cover material on the chair itself, and the join will be visible, you will have to sew them with a slip stitch. This gives a neat finish, in which the two edges of material butt closely together, and the thread is concealed behind the material itself. It is also called a ladder stitch, because the stitches between the two pieces of material resemble a ladder. American upholsterers call it a blind stitch, but do not confuse it with the blind stitch used to make hard edges in upholstery.

The technique of slip stitching is the same whether you decorate the seam with piping or not. If you are having piping, sew through the flanges of the piping cord cover, to link with the other material underneath it.

If you are sewing two panels together, proceed as follows.

Thread a fine curved needle with thread to match the cover material. Knot the end. At the beginning of the seam, fold one of the fabrics under. Start the needle behind the fold to emerge on its crest. This will bury the knotted end of the thread [**4.43**].

Now take the point of the needle across the gap to the other material. Count back two threads. Push the needle into the material at that point and bring it out half an inch down the seam. Cross back to the first material. Count back two threads, push in the needle on the crest of the fold, and bring it out half an inch along the seam. After you have sewn three or four stitches, draw the thread tight, and rub the seam lightly with your finger.

You will see that the thread completely disappears, running in and out behind the two pieces of material in turn. The reason for going back two threads is to pull the material down tight over the links in the thread, and prevent the stitches showing.

When you come to the end of the seam, if it ends on an accessible part of the frame, knock in a tack half way, make a couple of half-hitches in the thread round the tack while keeping the thread pulled tight, and hammer the tack home.

If you have to end the seam on a visible part of the chair, carry the stitching back for two or three inches, pull the thread tight, and cut it off close to the material. Rub the seam lightly with a finger and the thread will disappear.

MAKING THE FRONT SCROLLS

At the fronts of the two arms, you are left with a facing of wood, surrounded by the raw edge of the fabric used to cover the inside and outside arms. If you have stuffed the arms properly, they will be a pleasant scroll shape. You must now fill this facing with fabric.

There are several ways of preparing the front scroll facings.

The most reliable method is to use plywood. It will be covered with fabric material, and surrounded with piping to give a neat finish to the join.

On smaller chairs cardboard may be sufficient. Sometimes fabric with two or three layers of wadding to soften it gives a pleasing finish. First the plywood technique.

The problem lies in fixing the plywood to the front of the chair arm, when the material is covering it.

One method is to nail through the fabric with a small-headed nail. If you are careful, you can part the threads of the covering fabric, knock in the nail, and rub your finger over the head of the nail to work the threads together and close up the hole in the fabric. This method is not suitable for delicate fabrics like silks, nor for hide or leathercloth.

An improvement on this method is to hammer flat-headed nails through the plywood first, then cover it with material, and protect the material from the hammer with a large piece of softwood as you hammer home the facing.

Neither of these solutions is as elegant or effective as the double plywood method. The only disadvantage is that a double layer of plywood might produce too bulky a facing if you have made your arms with very thin stuffing.

First make a template of the facing panel. Hold a piece of paper against the face of the scroll and draw carefully and closely round the line where the face meets the hard edge.

Cut out the template and check it, and trim or remake it if necessary. Also check it against the other arm. The scroll facings should be the same size and shape to ensure an even appearance to the front of the chair, so if your two sides are different, try to work out whether adding to one and forcing the roll edge out, or leaving a slight gap, will produce the more evenly balanced compromise.

Using the template as a guide, cut out four panels of thin plywood, two to fit on each side.

Now obtain six one-inch flat-headed round-section nails. Find a drill bit with a diameter identical to or slightly smaller than the nail shank.

Offer up a single piece of plywood to the arm facing, and drill through it into the arm, 25 mm deep in three evenly spaced places.

Push three nails through the holes in the plywood, and glue the second piece of plywood over the first, to cover the heads of the nails. You may produce a better job if you countersink the nail holes to lower the heads to level with or just below the surface of the plywood. Bevel the outer edges of the plywood shapes to remove sharpness.

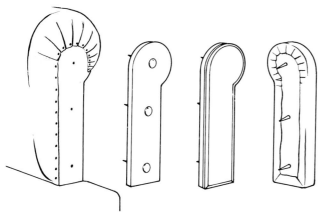

Now cut your facing material, to give a 25 mm margin all round the edge of the plywood. Take the usual care to match the patterns, and if possible to have an interesting part of the pattern showing [**4.44**].

Lay the facing material face down on a clean surface, and lay the double layer of plywood on the material with the nails up. Draw over the edges of the material, cut or pleat them to accommodate the curves, and tack down the material to the plywood with 10 mm fine tacks. On a chair of the type illustrated, the scroll facing runs flush with the outer edge of the chair, because of the way the hard edge is constructed. On a chair which has a stuffed edge right down the outer side, you will be able to tack the fabric to the plywood all round the scroll facing. On the chair illustrated, tack only round the inside edge. Leave the outside edge open.

Next prepare some piping, long enough to go round the facing, either all round, or as far as the join between the arm roll edge and the outer arm cover. You may want to fit piping all round the facing. Or you can choose to finish the join between the facing and the outer arm cover with a simple slip stitch. To finish the piping, peel back the cover, cut the cord, and sew the cover closed.

Now offer up the completed facing to the arm, and push it firmly home. The nails should match the holes exactly, and should hold the facings in place with a tight push fit. There should be no need to hammer the

material, but if there is, protect it with cloth and a large piece of softwood.

Where the outer edge of the facing remains open, tuck it behind the outer arm cover, and sew up the join with a concealed slip stitch.

SEWING ON SCROLL FACINGS

An alternative method of attaching scroll facings, especially in more modern and softer lines of furnishing, is to sew them on without any plywood or cardboard support. They can be decorated with cord, piping, or ruche, or left without any of these to give the chair the cleanest possible line.

First fit the outside arm, temporarily tacking it at the junction with the scroll face. Then, with the chair on its back, cover the scroll face with a thin layer of stuffing covered by wadding. A modern material like foam, normally frowned on by purist upholsterers, is ideal here, as ordinary stuffing tends to sink to the bottom of the scroll.

Trim the fabric for the scroll half an inch over-size to give an underturn, and cut V-shaped notches where necessary to avoid lumpy folds. Do not cut too close to the visible face of the fabric.

Sew the facing fabric in place with a slip stitch all round. If the facing meets the outside arm cover at the outer front edge, release the temporary tacks and fold

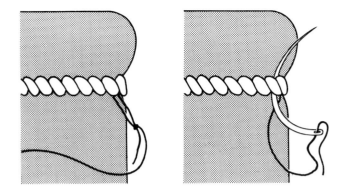
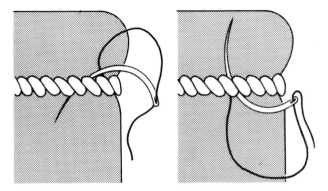

4.45 Chair cord can be sewn over exposed seams as an alternative to piping.

the fabric of the scroll front under the arm cover. Next fold the outer edge of the outside arm back to give a ½-inch underturn. If the underturn is greater than half an inch, you will risk unwanted folds appearing in it, which will show through the cover itself. Any less than half an inch will risk the material fraying so that the seam comes apart, especially in a loosely woven material. Slip stitch the two together. If you are using piping or ruche, fit it in place as you go, and take the needle through the flange of the piping or ruche and into the fabric of the inside or outside arm cover.

CHAIR CORD

An alternative method of concealing or decorating a seam is to use chair cord, a decorative twisted cord that gives a luxurious finish to a chair and saves you the bother of making up piping. Of course, you have to be able to obtain it in a colour that will harmonise with your covering fabric, and it can be unsuitable for use with some patterned fabrics. Also it is difficult to use it where it comes to an exposed end. But where the cord disappears out of sight beneath the frame, or where it comes to a T-junction with another length of cord, it is ideal. It will have to be sewn on with a thread of matching colour.

Firstly secure the seam; with either tacks, or back-tacking, or with the invisible slip stitch where it cannot be tacked.

Secondly pin the cord in place to cover the seam. You will remove these pins gradually as you sew. Start sewing with a slip knot underneath the end of the cord, buried in the slip stitching below [4.45]. Then sew directly through the cord. Next insert the needle into the fabric below, underneath the point where the thread emerges from the cord, and make a stitch of about 10 mm. At that point, sew back through the centre of the cord, and begin another stitch. Draw the stitching taut every couple of inches, and the cord will lie quite flat and conceal the seam.

You can use chair cord at any point where you might otherwise choose piping – round the facing scroll, round the front border, and along the top of the chair back, or right round the outside back.

LINING

The final task is to add the cover of black lining underneath the chair, to keep it free of dust. Install it shiny side out, cutting it carefully to fit round the legs.

VARIATIONS

Chairs and settees are so variously designed that it is

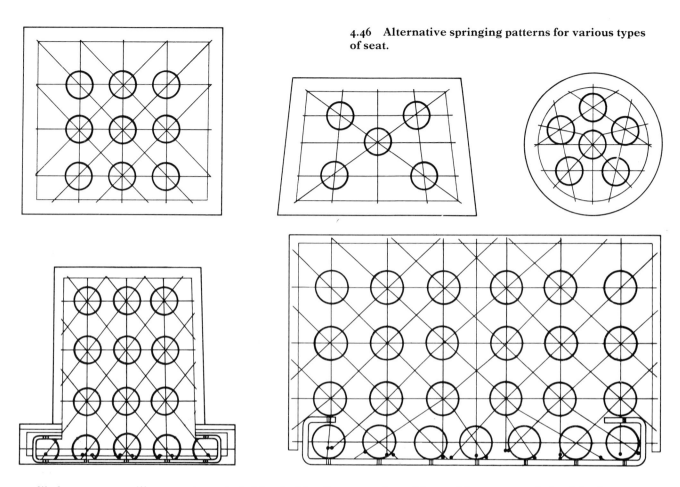

unlikely an owner will encounter a chair identical in all respects to the basic design described in the preceding chapter.

Nor can any single book give an account of every problem you are likely to encounter. Individual craftsmanship is called for, and any upholsterer must make several decisions about the most suitable method of working on any given chair.

However, there are a number of common variations, which are considered below, and reference to them and to the basic techniques previously outlined should offer a good working guide to most of the jobs home upholsterers are likely to undertake.

SPRINGING PATTERNS

The layout of springs in a seat depends largely on shape and size. The chair described above narrows slightly towards the back, making a simple 3–3–2 pattern suitable.

Other shapes of seat are shown in [4.46] with suitable spring layouts. Bear in mind that the side and rear

4.47 Build a rear wing 'post' of webbing to take the hessian.

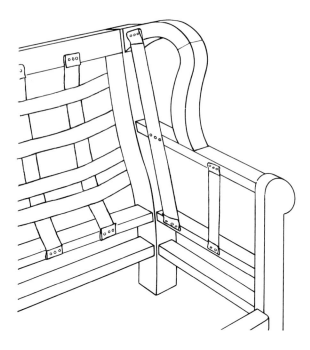

springs should not be placed too close to upholstered arms and backs, where the effect of the spring may be lost under the overhang of the upholstery.

Springs should be placed where possible in straight lines, to make lashing them with laid cord easier and more effective.

WING CHAIRS

Wing chairs are similar in most respects to the basic sprung chair. Working through the basic chair, you learnt to think of the chair as four separate surfaces, three of them unsprung. You only have to think of the wings as a fifth and sixth surface to be upholstered.

First check on the type of frame on which you will be building the wing. All wings will have a wing rail at the top and a wing post at the front. They should be well curved to merge together. But these alone are not enough to carry the upholstery. You will need a third

and fourth sides to form a frame on which to tack or sew the various layers that make up the upholstery. More elaborately manufactured chairs will have a wooden slat running from top to bottom near the back of the wing. This forms an open gap through which will pass the covers to be tacked on to the rear and outer surfaces of the frame.

If yours does not have such a slat, you will have to make one with webbing. It is simplest if you run the webbing that forms the back post of the arm right up to the top of the wing, more or less parallel with the back upright [**4.47**].

If the wing is large enough, you can usefully add a strand of webbing in each direction, tacked to the inside of the frame, to support the upholstery. The wing does not have to carry any appreciable weight, but webbing will give it a more solid and durable feel. Then apply a layer of hessian, tacked on at the top of the frame and round the front curve, and sewn to the upright webbing 'post' you have fitted yourself. At the bottom, leave a gap of about an inch above the arm rail. Simply underturn the hessian at this point, and for neatness, sew up the underturn.

There are several methods of upholstering the wings, depending on the style of the chair and the time and patience available to the upholsterer. The method which will produce the most professional job is well within the capabilities of anyone who has completed the basic work so far described in this book.

First make sure that the outside edge of the curved part of the frame has a bevel cut on it. This is to take a roll or hard edge sewn into it, exactly as other parts of the chair have roll edges.

Producing that roll is slightly different from building an ordinary seat roll. First, with a piece of chalk, lightly mark the hessian round the curve of the wing, about 75 mm in from the outer edge.

Cut a length of scrim, 200 mm wide, and long enough to reach generously from the arm rail to the top rail of the chair back. Underturn the scrim one inch, and sew it to the hessian round the chalk mark, pleating it as you go. [4.48] shows the building of this type of roll.

Now fix some bridles to the curved wooden frame of the wing. Fix a few tacks round the inner face of the frame, about 13 mm in, and loop some twine between them. Pick some stuffing under these loops, and also down between the loops and the sewing line of the scrim. Draw the scrim over the stuffing, so that it forms a long curving tube, conforming to the curve of the wing. Adjust the scrim, and add as much stuffing as necessary, so that you can turn the scrim under the stuffing, ready to sew in a hard edge. Add enough stuffing to produce a hard edge about one-inch in diameter. When you have it taut and well filled, tack the scrim down to the bevelled edge of the frame. You will have to do some skilful pleating as you work round these tight curves.

4.48a Tack bridles on the wing outer edge, and draw a chalk line on the hessian.

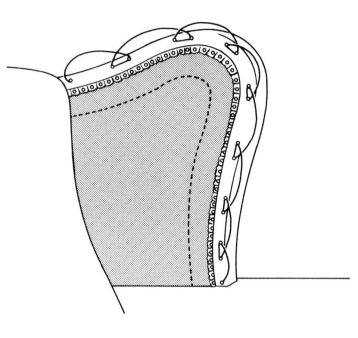

Work on both sides to ensure a good balance. Also, do your best to achieve good continuity between this roll and the roll across the top of the chair back, and try to produce a good firm junction with the upholstery of the arm. At the top corners of the wings, you can either turn the end of the tube under or sew the scrim to the hard edge of the chair back.

Regulate the stuffing inside the tube, taking care to avoid snagging the bridles, to eliminate all bumps and bulges, and to give a slight overhang all round the wing frame. Then sew in the one-inch roll with a row of blind stitches and a row of top stitches.

A simpler arrangement, which is acceptable on wings without pronounced curves, is to treat the wing as one area, omit the separate tube, and upholster it with webbing and hessian, bridles all over, first stuffing, scrim and through-stuffing ties. Regulate the stuffing to the edge of the frame, and sew in the hard edge.

STUFFING

It is usual to take the arms and back as far as the calico stage before adding the second stuffing and calico to the wings.

When you come to the wing second stuffing, sew some bridles on to the hessian in the area not covered by the stuffing in the 'tube', and pick some hair under them. Add hair all over, to form an elegantly curved shape meeting the crest of the roll edge all round the wing. Cover it with wadding to prevent the hair working through the covers, and start applying your calico. You will have to make several cuts in this small piece of material to meet the many tight curves and frame joints, so do not be dismayed if you have to have more than one go at it on your first wing-chair. Start by cutting your calico fairly generously. Make cuts in the bottom of the panel to allow it to go through the gap between the

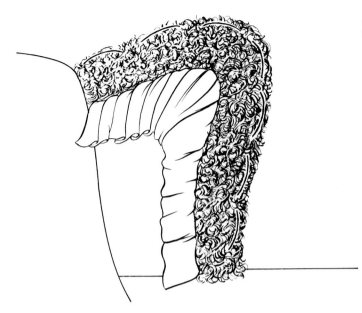

4.48b Sew a band of scrim round the chalk line, add stuffing and tack down the scrim to form a roll.

underturned edge of the hessian and the top of the arm. Temporarily tack the calico to the top of the arm.

Now take the calico over the top of the wing, and temporarily tack it there. Pull the calico through the gap at the back so that you can temporarily tack it to the back upright. And pull it round the front curve of the wing, to tack it to the outer rail. Be prepared to adjust these tacks several times, as you smooth out and compress the calico with the flat of your hand. Pleat the calico on the convex part of the wing curve, and make several small cuts into the edge so that it follows the concave part of the curve. At the top back, tuck in the calico with the flat end of your regulator to give a good junction with the chair back, and to seal in the stuffing and wadding.

Keep all hair and wadding away from the crest of the hard edge, where it would cause unsightly and uncomfortable lumps. Finally, release the temporary tacks at the rear of the calico panel. Turn the rear edge and sew it

to the webbing, to re-open the gap between the wing and back upright [**4.49**].

The method of dealing with the bottom edge of the calico depends on the style of the final cover. In most chairs, the wings are upholstered separately from the arms, to give a seam, either plain or piped. This treatment is elegant, and allows you to build interesting shapes into the wings. If you plan to use this method, release the temporary tacks at the bottom of the wing panel of calico, and turn the calico up so that you can sew it to the hessian, to open up the gap between the arm and the wing, ready to apply the top cover. At the same time make sure you have a good supply of stuffing in the bottom of the wing to ensure that no gaps appear between it and the arm.

Less elaborate styles of chair often have the wing and the arm upholstered in the one piece. If you plan this treatment, loosen the calico of both the arm and the

4.49 Sew a hard edge all round the wing, add second stuffing and wadding, and cover with calico.

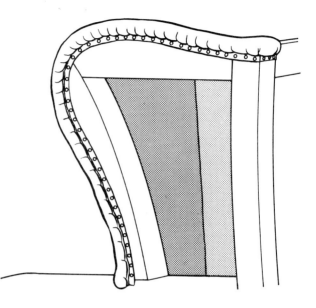

bottom of the wing panel. Add stuffing in the opening to give a smooth surface where the two meet. Underturn the arm calico, and draw the wing calico down over it. Underturn the wing calico also, and sew the two together with a slip stitch.

COVERING THE INSIDE WINGS

If you are treating the wings as separate from the arms, it is normal to cover both the inside back and inside arms first. The cover for the wings is then tacked down over them, to the same tacking rails.

First cut the covers for the two wings, ensuring that the pattern is balanced. If there is a pronounced motif to the cover design, make sure that it sits well on the face of the inside wings. There are at least two ways of treating the wings at the point where the wing cover meets the inside back cover at the top of the chair. One method is to fold both covers under and slip stitch them together to form a mitred joint.

The alternative is to overlap the two covers. Cut the inside back cover in such a way as to leave a 'tab' of material a few inches long, running along the wing and tacked neatly in place. Do not turn the material under or over, as the double thickness will cause an ugly bulge. Then fold the material of the wing under, and slip stitch the two together.

Of course, if you choose to cover the wing before the inside back, you should leave the tab on the wing, and fold the material of the inside back cover over it.

Fitting the cover is then more or less the same as fitting the calico. Smooth the material over the wing, and tack it down firstly with temporary tacks, at the bottom, then at the sides. The main difference is in the tacking rail. Just as the seat and inside arm cover are tacked down together to the same rail to give a smooth run to the material and prevent gaps forming, so the inside arm and wing covers are tacked together, on the outer side of the back upright. Also the cover material at the bottom is drawn through the aperture, and tacked down on the outer side of the arm rail, giving an almost continuous run with the arm cover itself.

You will have to work the material carefully over the curving roll edge, pleating it and cutting notches into it to accommodate to the curves.

When it is tacked all round, with all the folds and creases smoothed out, add the piping. Generally a wing chair looks best if the piping sits just outside the line of the crest of the roll edge. You will be able to tack it in position, covering the tacking of the inside wing cover itself. The piping will normally run from the junction of the wing with one arm, round the curve of the wing, across the chair back, and down the other wing to meet the opposite arm.

OUTSIDE WING COVER

It is usual to finish the outside wing covers before the outside back and arm covers. The top of the outside arm cover then overlaps the bottom of the wing cover. The outside back cover will go on last, overlapping the covers of both the outside wing and outside arm, where they are pulled round the back upright.

If the wing cavity is a large one, it is advisable to fill it with stuffing – the cheapest type will do the job – to prevent the cover being forced in, stretched and ultimately made slack during use. Fill the cavity with stuffing, then tack hessian over the frame.

If the wing itself has a pronounced shape – and some of the most elegant and expensive chairs have generous curves on the outside wings, you will have to add bridles to the hessian, then stuffing, then scrim, and finally a layer of wadding and calico. On this type of chair the frame will probably be built to incorporate these curves, in which case one or two strands of webbing across the wing frame underneath the hessian may help in building up and holding the shape.

If the back upright is to have piping, install it at this stage, tacking it so that the roll of the piping lies exactly on the crest of the corner.

Finally, lay the outside cover in place, and slip stitch it to the flanges of the piping all round, snugly up with the cord inside the piping. When you come to the bottom of the wing you can pull the cover down flat, and tack it to the arm rail, leaving a raw edge to be covered by the outside arm cover.

Once the wing is completed, add the outside arm cover as on the basic chair, back-tacking the top edge with a length of buckram. Slip stitch the cover to the vertical piping at the front and back of the arms, and turn it under the bottom seat rail for tacking. Install thin padding or wadding to give a softer look under these outside covers.

Follow with the outside back cover. Back-tack this to the chair if you can work buckram close up to the piping along the top edge, then slip-stitch it vertically down the sides. Alternatively, slip-stitch it all round, and turn it under at the bottom for tacking. Finally, cover the underside of the chair in a black lining.

DEEP BUTTONING

Deep buttoning is one of the more difficult operations in upholstery. However, deep-buttoned chairs and settees are popular, and on the right furniture this treatment gives one of the most elegant finishes – occasionally the only appropriate one. It is well worth trying.

The main difficulty lies in getting the right quantity of stuffing in the 'bun' between the buttons – too much and the pleats between the buttons strain and develop an unsightly gape; too little and the upholstery looks flimsy, and lacks the character of a well-crafted luxury article. The worst possible combination is to have uneven amounts of stuffing and covering fabric between buttons, with the result that the job looks irregular and lopsided.

However, the operation itself is perfectly simple. Any mistakes can only arise from incorrect judgement, and if you have taken the trouble to build up experience on simpler seats and basic sprung chairs, you may feel you have the confidence to tackle deep buttoning with a fair chance of success.

The first task is to plan the buttoning. Make a sketch of the parts of the chair which will feature deep buttoning. It will normally be the back, sometimes the seat and arms as well. Then mark out your buttoning points on the plan.

The shape between the buttons usually takes the form of a diamond. The exact dimensions of the individual diamonds are not critical, but they are generally longer vertically than horizontally. 200–300 mm is generally an acceptable height, depending on the size of the chair.

First consider some typical shapes for the backs of medium-sized chairs.

If the back is almost square, start by drawing a straight horizontal line near the bottom. A good guide to the height of this line above the seat is to take the height of the diamond you plan to use, halve it, and add 50 mm. The bottom row of buttons will lie on this line, and the lowest row of diamonds will then sit comfortably rather less than a diamond's height above the chair seat.

Now draw a second horizontal line 100–150 mm above that (half the height of your diamond), then another, and so on until you reach the same height from the top as your first line is from the bottom.

Now strike a vertical line down the dead-centre of the plan. Follow it with other vertical lines, to the right and left, at a distance that will give well-proportioned diamonds when the intersecting points (where the buttons will be) are joined up.

Illustration **a** of [**4.50**] shows a simple arrangement.

However, such an arrangement is only suitable for regular rectangular seats. Many seat backs are wider at the top than at the bottom, and may also have a slight barrel shape. So you can improve on the basic shape by drawing all the lines with a greater artistic flair than mere straight and parallel lines.

If the chair back is slightly barrel-shaped, the horizontal lines should curve downwards slightly from the centre towards the ends. And the top lines will curve

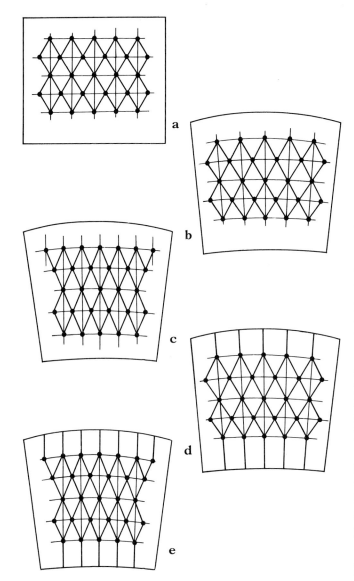

4.50 Deep buttoning patterns suitable for (a) a square back; (b) a curved back; and (c) a curved and tapered back. Curved (d) and tapering curved (e) backs incorporating vertical channels at top and bottom. Side pleats can also be added.

down more than the bottom ones. Start by drawing the bottom line almost horizontal. Draw a vertical centre line and mark off the measurements up it. Then draw the top line parallel with the curve of the top of the chair back. Curve the lines in between them slightly less as they go from top to bottom.

You can also vary the vertical lines. On a chair back which flares outwards towards the top, you can either draw the vertical lines to fan out slightly, or you can have more buttons at the top, or both. [**4.50b,c**] shows these effects.

To get the buttoning points right, first mark the intersection of the bottom horizontal line with the centre vertical line. Then mark the points out along the bottom line in each direction. Mark the next-but-one line up at similar points. And, if you have enough lines, the next-but-one line above that – first, third, fifth lines, etc. Mark the alternating points on the second and fourth lines, and draw in the diamonds to link these points. You will produce a pattern of diamond shapes between the buttoning points.

Be careful how far you extend the points towards the sides. The distance from the visible side of the buttoned panel to the nearest vertical line with a button on it should be approximately the same as the distance between buttons on the nearest horizontal line. Do not button too close to the sides.

On large surfaces, the top and bottom of the buttoning panel often carry vertical pleats, which sink down into channels just as the buttons sink down into recesses. If the chair back flares towards the top, it is usual to have one more channel at the top than at the bottom. These patterns are shown in [**4.50d, e**].

MEASURING THE COVER

Consider first the process of deep-buttoning a chair back without springs. First install the webbing, hessian, first stuffing, and scrim.

Put in some through-stuffing ties, then add some

4.51a Use a regulator and another similar tool to form a smooth pleat between buttoning points.

4.51b When the buttons are fixed, form the channels to the top, bottom, and sides of the frame.

bridles to hold the second stuffing in place. The buttoning itself will do most of the work of keeping the stuffing in place. In fact, the original reason for inventing deep-buttoning was to hold stuffing on chair backs in place without it slipping. But stuffing can easily be dislodged during the actual process of buttoning, so the bridles will help maintain the regular shape.

'Pick' some best quality stuffing under the bridles, then between them, until you have the required thickness. In general, a thickness of 40 mm–50 mm, when the stuffing is compressed, is about right. But the thickness depends to a large extent on the style of the article, and on the firmness or softness required. Thicker stuffing is usually softer, thinner stuffing generally more firm. You will have to use your judgement, compressing by hand and trying to imagine how the finished article will look and feel.

Now cover the stuffing with a layer of cotton wadding, ready for installing the calico cover. This will give excellent practice for working on the final cover.

Refer to your buttoning plan, and mark the buttoning positions on the back of the chair. Push skewers through from the back at these positions. From the front of the chair, carefully feel with your fingers for the points of the skewers to determine the position of the buttons.

Now tear a neat hole in the wadding, and push away the stuffing behind it with your regulator or your fingers, to make a recess in the stuffing running right back to the scrim cover.

Next you will have to determine the measurements for the calico and outer covers. They will be different from the original button plan, to accommodate the curves of the 'buns' between the buttons. And, of course, on any given seat the measurements for all the buttons may not be the same. They will vary slightly if you have incorporated curves in your original lines. And they will vary according to the pattern of curve in the chair surface – less for a concave surface like the barrel back of the chair, considerably more for the convex curve of something like a Chesterfield. That is one source of difficulty in deep-buttoning.

The easiest answer is to work with a second paper plan. Start with a sheet of calico big enough to cover the chair back and to take up all the curves of all the buns, with a generous margin for error. Draw the bottom horizontal line of the button plan on it, following a thread if the line is straight. Now, on the chair, measure from that line to the bottom tacking rail on which the calico will be fixed. Take all measurements for this stage with a flexible steel tape measure. Push it down into the

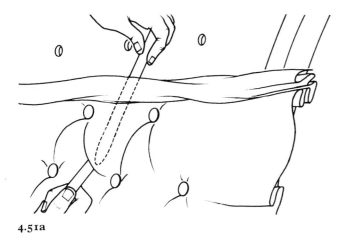

4.51a

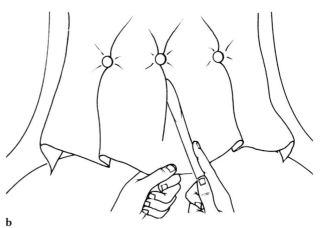

b

button hole as far as the scrim, and bend it to follow the curve of the stuffing, when the stuffing is compressed. Transfer that measurement to the second paper plan. It will give you the bottom tacking line. Take the measurements to the next button line, and the next, working up the centre of the chair. Then work towards the outsides. Accommodate all the curving lines as you go.

Go on taking the measurements until the cover plan is finished. Make small holes in the paper, and mark through them on to the calico. Keep your plan to mark the final cover.

Now lay the calico over the wadding. Tuck it into the recesses in the stuffing along the bottom two rows of buttoning points. At the buttoning points on these two lines, sew the calico to the base through the scrim, first stuffing, and hessian, using either strong thread or fine upholsterer's twine. Tie it at the back with a slip knot.

The reason for sewing only two rows at first is that you will need access to the insides of each diamond for adjusting the stuffing, and for setting the pleats.

So first adjust the stuffing if necessary, to ensure that you have the right degree of fullness, as far as you can judge it. Put more in or take some out, but try not to disturb the wadding. Then put in the pleats, between the buttoning points you have so far sewn down. You

will need the flat end of your regulator, and some other similar instrument. Another regulator is ideal. Failing that, an old kitchen knife or the handle of a spoon will do. Push one flat blade under the calico, to ease out the fold of the top of the pleat. Push the other blade into the pleat from the top of the calico. Hold the two blades lightly pushed against each other, and draw them along the pleat between the buttoning points. This will take up any slack, and leave you with a well-formed flat pleat [**4.51a**].

Remember that all pleats on a deep buttoned surface must face downwards, to prevent the open side of the pleat from forming a dust trap. Arrange the pleats in the calico to fall the same way.

Go on to the next row, and sew the calico to the base at the buttoning points. Check the stuffing, and ease out the pleats. Go on and finish all subsequent rows.

With the calico well fixed all over the central part of the panel by these buttoning points, you can deal with the sides. Their treatment largely depends on the design of chair. Refer again to your first buttoning plan. Did you incorporate channels running from the top and bottom rows of buttons to the top and bottom rails. If so, make the channels exactly as you made the pleats between buttons [**4.51b**].

Catch about 20 mm of the calico, and turn it to form a pleat. Temporarily tack it on the relevant rail.

Finish the channels all round, and when you have eased out all the creases and wrinkles in the calico, tack it down with 10 mm fine tacks, leaving a raw edge.

Now take up the cover itself. Recall the way the calico went on, and make any necessary adjustments in the measurements between buttoning point, and the measurements from the sides, top, and bottom of the frame. Lay the fabric face-down on a clean surface, and lay the second paper pattern over it, amended as necessary. Carefully push a regulator point or sharp skewer through the pattern at the buttoning points, and right through the material to leave a small hole that will show on the face of the fabric. Where the pleats or channels meet the sides, top, and bottom of the frame, cut a small notch. You are now committed to fitting your buttons in the positions marked.

THE BUTTONS

What of the buttons themselves? The only way to produce buttons of the quality needed to complement the work you are doing is to buy button bases, and cover them yourself, in the material you are using to cover the chair. Button bases come in two parts, with various types of fixings. You need the looped variety.

To make up the buttons, you will need a button making tool. This will cut a small circle of material for you, and in a simple quick operation install it on the button base, and press the parts of the base together to complete the button.

It might be worth buying one if you are planning to do a great deal of this kind of upholstery. Or you might be able to contact friends who would form a group to buy and share one. Alternatively, you might be able to find a professional upholsterer who would be prepared to make up a few buttons from your own material quite

4.52 Insert a toggle of tough fabric under each twine, to prevent the twine cutting into the upholstery base.

cheaply. Upholstery departments in some major stores will make up buttons for the home upholsterer.

FITTING THE COVER

As always, once you have the second stuffing and calico installed, the remainder of the operation is relatively simple.

Take up your cover, buttons, a medium length double-pointed needle, and a length of medium twine one metre long for each button.

Start at the centre of the bottom row. Drape the material over the chair so that the holes coincide roughly with the buttoning points. Then fold the right half of the material to the left just enough to reveal the bottom-centre buttoning hole on the reverse side of the material.

From the back of the chair, sew the twine through the stuffing 10 mm away from the centre of the buttoning point. Pull the twine through half its length. Pass the needle through the correct hole in the top cover, and turn the folded part of the cover to face out again. Thread the needle and twine through the loop of a button, back through the hole in the material, and then out through the stuffing, 10 mm on the opposite side of the centre of the buttoning point.

Tie the upholsterer's slip knot in the twine at the back of the chair. Now cut a 50 mm square of any heavy material that you have to hand. Leather or leathercloth are ideal. Failing that you can use strong hessian, or any robust waste fabric. Roll up one square to form a small toggle, and place it under the loop you have formed in the twine. Its purpose is to stop the twine cutting through the upholstery [**4.52**].

Draw the slip knot taut, just enough to hold the toggle in place. Do not tighten it fully home yet.

Go along the bottom row, working from the centre towards the two sides in turn, threading on the buttons, with the two strands of twine passing through and back

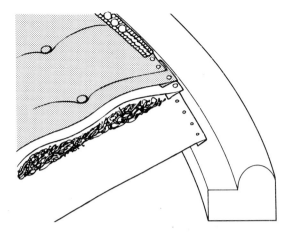

4.53 Typical stuffing sequence for a show-wood chair comprises hessian, hair, calico, top cover and gimp, all tacked on to the same rebate.

through the upholstery 20 mm apart, and the toggles held underneath them at the back of the panel. When you have two rows in place, lay the seat on its back and carefully arrange the pleats to be tidy, flat, and facing downwards. Follow the same procedure, using the flat of the regulator and another similar blade that you employed on the calico.

Then go on to complete the succeeding rows up the buttoned panel, arranging the pleats as you sew on each row in turn.

When you have drawn up all the twines moderately taut, with the buttons held in place on the front and the toggles on the back, stand the chair upright and start drawing them tight. Do this gradually, working from the centre and round the panel, pulling each button twine slightly tighter each time. This will help to prevent any buttons pulling the stuffing out of shape. When you have them all quite tight, lock the slip knots with a couple of half-hitches on top, and cut off the spare twine 50 mm from the knot.

FIXING THE EDGES

Now deal with the material round the edges of the buttoned area.

You may find it a simple matter to fold the pleats over exactly as you did on the calico and tack the cover in place along the relevant tacking rail. On some chairs there will be no pleats at the sides, and the material is simply drawn over the stuffing, smoothed into place, and tacked down. Use temporary tacks all round until you are satisfied with the set of the material, then tack home. Remember to use 'fine' tacks of the smallest useable length, for final coverings.

When working on some styles of chair, for example a Victorian deep-buttoned spoonback, you will need to finish your material in a rebated channel. First finish your calico neatly just short of the rebate corner. On this style of chair you can afford to underturn the calico edge, to ensure that no stray threads creep out to spoil the appearance of the finished article.

Bring the cover over the upholstery edge, turn it under, and hold it in place with skewers. Go all round the chair skewering the material until you have a perfect fit. On surfaces that are more or less straight and square, you will have no difficulty in determining where the pleats should lie. But on this kind of Victorian furniture the shapes can be extremely irregular. Generally pleats will look best if they meet the nearest part of the frame at an approximate right angle. But you might find the material falls into more comfortable pleats at different angles in some places. Use your judgement.

When you have positioned the pleats and flattened them out with the two-regulator system, tack them down all round. Push the material well into the corner of the rebate with your regulator. Tack home well between the pleats. Take great care when tacking, to ensure that you do not hammer the surrounding frame. This is 'show' wood, and it will be extremely difficult to repair any damage once the upholstery is in position. Using a small-headed 'cabriole' hammer will help.

On show-wood chairs, you will have to apply a decorative trim to cover the exposed edges of the material. You can use either gimp or braid, in a suitable matching colour. Glue it in place with white adhesive, then stitch it for complete safety. Be careful with the adhesive. The slightest bit spilled at this stage will be difficult to remove and may wreck the entire operation. Alternatively you can fix it with gimp pins, which are small tacks painted to match most colours of fabrics, so they cannot be seen [4.53].

Because of the danger of spilling adhesive, most professional upholsterers prefer to finish all the work on the back of the chair before they begin to cover the seat.

CLOSE-NAILED FINISH

Instead of braid, an attractive finish for the edges of most types of seat can be achieved with decorative nails, knocked in to form a row all round the length of the rebate. It is possible to buy studs covered in fabric or leather, and you may be able to find one that matches your covering material. Usually, however, upholsterers use brass dome-headed nails. They are available in three finishes – polished brass, light antique, and dark antique. Buy nails with solid brass heads and steel shanks. Brass plated studs soon loose their finish.

It takes great patience, a skilled hand, and a good eye to space a row of nails perfectly all round a rebate, each one sitting snugly against the shoulder of the show-wood and against its two neighbours. Experienced upholsterers can work successfully by eye, but the beginner might usefully make up a device for indicating the position where the point should be started. A pair of dividers makes a good tool. Also, it can help if you make a pilot hole, half the length of the shank of the nail, with a fine awl or even a fine drill. This will help you hammer the nails in perpendicularly in the right place, and will help prevent splitting the wood with the neat line of perforations which close-nailing produces.

SPRUNG SURFACES

If you are buttoning the seat of a sprung chair, or the sprung back of a Chesterfield, you will not have the ready access to the reverse side of the upholstery base that you need. Important parts of the work will therefore have to be done from the face side of the article.

You will not, for example, be able to work the slip knot tight behind the surface. You need room to work with your hands for that. Instead take the upholstering up to the calico stage as on a webbing base. Then instead of threading the needle and twine through from the rear to the front, stitch through from front to rear, then back. If you can skewer a toggle on to another long needle, you should be able to poke it in from the back, through the webbing and among the springs, and slip it under the loop of twine. Then you can pull the twine taut from the front, trap the toggle, and withdraw your needle.

Now, at the front of the buttoned panel, pass the two ends of twine through the hole in the covering material and one of them through the loop in the button. Tie a slip knot, and draw the twines taut enough to hold the button in place while you go on to the other buttoning points and pleats, as before. Carry out the final tightening from the front, by easing the slip knot down into the button recess, with the button following it. Knot the two ends of the twine together against the slip knot.

Now you can either cut off the ends of the twine close to the knot, and tuck them away under the button, or you can make a better job by threading the ends in turn on to a long double-pointed needle, and taking them down through the cover close to the button. Pull and push the needle right through the base and out at the webbing side. The twine will pull out of the eye of the needle inside the upholstery base, and lie out of the way among the springs.

APPLYING THE CALICO LOOSE

The second main variation lies in the second stuffing process.

Some upholsterers prefer to start fitting the calico, and apply the second stuffing with the calico in place. Proceed as far as the scrim, and mark out the buttoning points on it, using skewers from the rear, according to your first paper plan.

Now, take a steel tape measure, and form it into the shape the final stuffing will take between two buttoning points. Transfer the measurement to your second paper

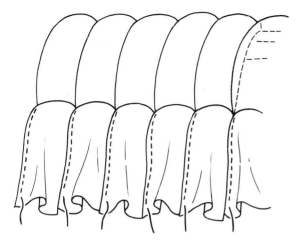

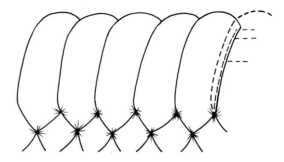

4.54 Sew a length of twine into a pleat as an aid to ensure that the pleat lies flat.

plan. It is well worthwhile building a small sample area of deep buttoning to these measurements, to check that they are exactly what you want. Alter them if necessary, and go on to complete the paper plan for the entire surface. Cut small holes in the paper at the buttoning points, and transfer them on to the calico by marking through the holes.

Now sew the calico to the seat, at all the buttoning points along the bottom two rows.

This will form a row of loosely hanging half pockets, open at the top and bottom alternately.

Take small wads of stuffing, tease it out, and stuff it into these half pockets, pushing it well into the corners, and building up the curving shape of a half-bun. When the pockets are well filled, you can pleat the calico along the zig-zag line between the two rows of buttons.

Now sew the third row of buttoning points, and begin stuffing the new set of half diamonds you have formed. Work first on the alternating pockets that will complete the first row of diamonds, or they will shortly be inaccessible. Follow by working stuffing into the new half-set. Pleat between points and sew on the new rows as you go, to complete the area.

Of course you will have now to apply the protective

wadding between the calico and top cover. This is perfectly acceptable, and is in fact the procedure adopted by many upholsterers as normal practice.

SEWN CHANNELS

In some cases simply pleating the channels at the side and edges of a panel of deep-buttoning is not enough to hold them firmly in place. This applies especially where the stuffing between the channels runs over the edge of a surface, and where it is bulbous. Also, when upholsterers use foam under the deep-buttoning, the pleats tend not to be bed into the stuffing well enough to hold. The answer is to saw the pleats invisibly.

Cut a half-metre length of twine, and secure one end at the buttoning point, either by knotting the end and sewing it through from the reverse side, or knotting it round the shank of the last button before the channel.

Arrange the material into the channel, pleat it temporarily, and mark the exact bottom of the pleat with a notch. Fold the material back over the buttoning points. Now fold up the pleat again, so that the material lies right-side to right-side, and so that the pleat runs exactly to the mark you have made. Pull the twine up into this

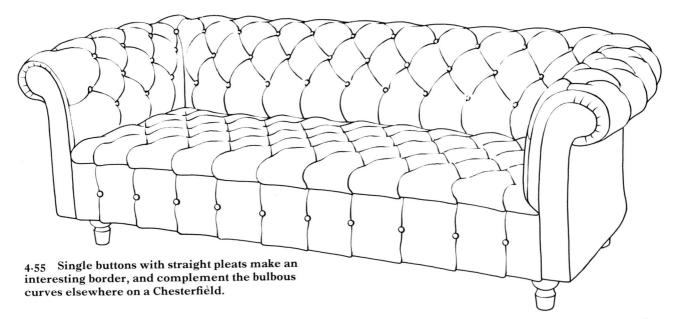

4.55 Single buttons with straight pleats make an interesting border, and complement the bulbous curves elsewhere on a Chesterfield.

pleat, and sew a line of neat stitches into the pleat, half an inch below the twine [**4.54**].

Pull the material back over the stuffed area, and distribute the material along the twine to take up the shape of the crowns between the channels. Tear out the stitches as far back up the channel as the edge of the frame. Cut a small hole in the covering material so that you can pass the twine through it to the outside of the cover, and knot the twine round a tack to keep it taut.

ALTERNATIVE BUTTONING PATTERNS

Bear in mind that not all deep-buttoning patterns involve diamond shapes. The sturdy Chesterfield has a front border decorated with straight pleats with a button at the centre [**4.55**].

This style can also be used to advantage on the arms of show-wood chairs, like the arm of drawing room chair. The pleats go across the arm and are tacked down into a rebate. Fixing the buttons in place is slightly complicated by the wood of the arm. You can deal with it either by drawing the twine to the sides and trying it out of sight round two tacks. Or you can use a different kind of button, made with a nail-type shank instead of a loop. Hammer it into the wood when you are ready to tighten down the buttoning points. Protect the material from the hard face of the hammer with waste cloth.

OMITTING THE CALICO

Having got to this point, and produced a good job of deep-buttoning, it may be dismaying to learn that most professionals do not work like this at all. Normally, they do not bother with a calico cover, but fit the top cover material on to the top stuffing, with just a layer of wadding over it to stop the hair coming through. You may prefer to do this, but you will still find that the calico makes the whole job easier. You have some opportunity to correct your mistakes before working with the expensive top cover and you do not have to handle the cover material so much.

Many experienced upholsterers will also use a layer of 10 mm thick foam instead of the felt. Foam will keep the hair from penetrating the cover, just as wadding does. In addition, it gives a smooth finish, especially when used underneath hide or leathercloth.

To accommodate the buttons, cut a clear 25 mm diameter hole in the foam at each buttoning point. And be careful to keep the foam in position as you draw each of the twines taut. The foam tends to grip the covering material, and is easily pulled out of place.

OTHER KINDS OF UPHOLSTERED CHAIR

Anybody who develops an interest in upholstery will soon realise that chairs and settes cover an almost infinite variety of designs, and that only rarely can any two examples be upholstered exactly alike.

However, there are only a limited number of basic processes, and these can be learned to a level which will cover most kinds of seat. After that the upholsterer's own individual skill comes into play, to enable him or her to amend and adapt the basic processes to fit any seat he or she is working on.

Apart from restoring existing chairs to their original specifications, the experienced and confident upholsterer can enjoy the even more rewarding activity of building upholstered furniture to his own design, producing a completely custom-made article. Even if you do not feel competent to design your own upholstery from the bare frame, you will nevertheless have the skill and technical knowledge to build your own chairs and settees to designs taken from elsewhere. You can study existing designs, in museums, furniture showrooms, books and catalogues, and if you have followed through the basic processes, you will be able to reproduce them, or develop and amend them to meet your individual tastes.

SPRUNG BACKS

Sprung backs present no more problems than the sprung seat, but you must build them carefully, because any lumps and ridges in the stuffing can cause great discomfort. If the top stuffing is made smooth, using best quality hair, then the springing can produce a pleasant and luxurious support for the sitter.

Installing the springing is almost the same process as on the seat. First you must plan where the springs should fit, and what gauge you plan to use.

Back springs do not carry any direct weight, so they can be softer than seat springs. But the back should give a relatively firm support, as softness can itself produce discomfort.

On a typical high-backed chair such as a wing chair, four rows of three make a suitable pattern. Start the bottom row three inches from the top of the seat, or seven inches up if you are planning to use a seat cushion. The top row can curve gently in line with the top of the chair back about two inches below the rail. Position the other rows evenly in between, using your experience on the seat as a guide to achieve a good layout.

Install the webbing to suit the spring pattern. In a sprung back, the webbing is fitted to the rear edges of the back posts, just as the seat webbing was fitted on the underside. The structure will be stronger if you arrange the points where the webbing strands cross so that they fall directly under individual springs.

Sew on the springs with triangular patterns of twine, then lash them with laid cord. Cover with a layer of hessian, and tack it down all round, just as on the seat.

You can now proceed through the standard upholstery steps for a sprung surface.

Secure the hessian to the springs, put in some bridles, and apply the first stuffing. Put on a scrim cover, and secure the first stuffing with through-stuffing ties. Work from the back of the chair with a long needle, and make sure that you do not snag any lower rungs of the springs.

Stuff and regulate the edges, then sew in any hard edges to give the shape you want. Sew a pattern of bridles into the scrim, and apply the second stuffing, followed by wadding, and calico.

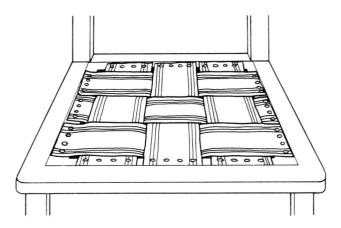

4.56 On a rebated seat frame, install the dust lining directly beneath the webbing, and tack the two together.

SPRUNG ARMS

Sprung arms are quite straightforward. They are appropriate on large balloon type armchairs and settees, on which the top rail of the arm is in the form of a board or platform.

Four four inch springs are generally enough, stapled to the board or tacked down under a strand of webbing as the front seat springs were.

The top coils of the springs are fixed in place by another strip of webbing, with the springs pulled down and sewn to it. Cover this with hessian, and tie the springs to it with the usual triangles sewn on with twine.

Add through stuffing ties, hair, wadding, and calico. There is no second stuffing, because in chairs of these type there is no need for a hard edge.

SMALL CHAIR WITH SEAT FITTING IN REBATED FRAME

A common type of chair has a padded seat fitted into a rebate in the top of the frame [4.56]. It is generally delicate, and experience on more robust upholstery is advisable before you start work on this type of chair.

You will need, in addition to the normal tools, the cabriole hammer, with its small head designed for fixing tacks with less risk of damaging the show-wood of the frame.

All layers of upholstery must fit into the rebate. So cut and fold a square of black lining to meet exactly the shoulder of the rebate. Lay it in place, and fit the webbing over it, with the webbing tacks holding the black lining.

Add hessian, and sew bridles into the hessian with a curved needle, taking care not to pick up the black lining in the stitches. Add stuffing, felt, calico and the cover. The cover can be left with a raw edge. Cut and fold it at the corners to give the smoothest possible fit. When you have tacked off the cover all round, finish the job with matching braid or gimp, glued and sewn all round in the rebate.

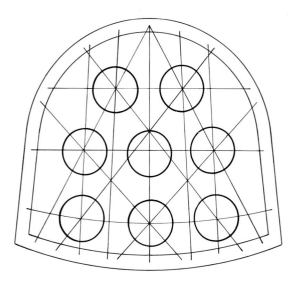

4.57 The spring and lashing pattern for a wide range of Victorian and other show-wood chairs.

SMALL SPRUNG CHAIR

The combination of a sprung seat in show-wood frame occurs in many different styles and sizes of chair. A wide range of Victorian chairs need this treatment.

Because the bottom of the front frame member follows a pronounced curve in several directions, it is difficult to fit the webbing on the underside of the frame, as you normally would do to carry springing.

Instead, fix the webbing on the top side of the frame, and install a small spring. A 75 mm or 100 mm spring of light gauge would be suitable, depending on the height of the seat you are finally looking for. A pattern of eight springs, set as in [**4.57**], would be appropriate, but you will have to use your judgement depending on the exact shape of the seat frame.

Fit the springs, sewing them to the webbing, and lash them with laid cord. Cover them with hessian, and sew them in. Add bridles and the first stuffing. Cover with scrim, and sew a pattern of through-stuffing ties. Cut the scrim to fit all back posts exactly as you did on the stuffed-over seat.

Now sew in a roll edge about three inches high. It will take at least one row of blind stitches and two rows of top stitches.

This combination – springs in the centre and a hard edge sitting directly on the frame – occurs widely. It differs from work previously described in this book in that there is no complicated sprung front edge to deal with, as illustrated in the basic sprung chair described in this chapter.

Add bridles for a second stuffing, then wadding, calico and cover.

Bring the cover down to fit into the shoulder of the rebate at the front of the frame, smoothing it out and cutting it off to shape.

The normal trimming in a chair of this type, would be gimp, glued and sewn in place. Useful alternatives are a line of close-nailing, which is especially appropriate with hide, leathercloth or velvet, and piping or double piping.

If you plan to trim with piping, fit the piping first, using a strip of cardboard tacked in place to keep the piping securely against the show-wood. Bring the cover

4.58 Install the outside back cover first, followed by a double layer of hessian, on this type of show-wood back.

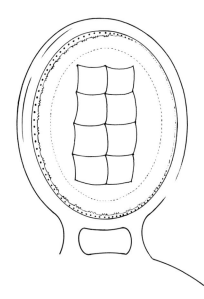

down to it, turn it under, and fasten it to the piping all round with a slip stitch.

FRENCH-BACK CHAIRS

Chairs falling into this category include several styles of spoon-back and medallion-back articles. The back consists of a circular or oval open frame, with a rebate round the front. Upholstering this type of chair back involves installing the cover fabric to both the outside and inside faces of the chair back.

This chair back, like the small rebated seat which in many ways it resembles, is a delicate piece of furniture, and not recommended as a first project for the inexperienced upholsterer. The rebate may not be all that robust, and if it is not treated carefully it can be split by tacks, and involve a major repair job before the upholstery can be completed. Use a small cabriole hammer, and work with the smallest possible number of tacks, of the smallest possible size consistent with a secure finish.

The outside back must be fitted first, as it is tacked to the rebate.

Temporarily tack the cover in place, right side facing outwards. Check that any pattern, or the 'grain' in plain material, is upright. Start the tacking at the bottom, and pull the material to the top. It is important to get the right tension in this piece of cover. Too tight, and it will run the risk of tearing under the pressure of handling in use. Too loose, and it will sag and look unattractive. A good guide is to try to pinch it between a thumb and finger. If you can pinch it up between opposite tacks, it is too loose. Smooth it out and tack at points between the top and sides, and then between the bottom and sides, and lastly at the sides.

Next install padding, to give a softening effect to the outside back. A layer of thin nylon wadding is ideal. Follow it with two layers of hessian, cut to fit inside the rebate. This kind of chair is not suitable for webbing; there is no space for it in the inside back, and it is difficult to stretch it over the frame. A double layer of hessian is enough to hold the stuffing in place for the inside back [**4.58**].

Tack the hessian in place in the rebate, and sew in a pattern of horizontal bridles to prevent the stuffing falling down when the chair is in use. Stuff it carefully. Next comes the operation which is often omitted, and betrays the difference between quality upholstering and production-line work. The inside back should be built up proud of the wood of the frame. This gives the chair comfort, as the sitter's back need not come into contact with the wood. Recall the first edge sewn on the stuffed-over seat. Upholstering this chair back uses the same techniques.

Start by picking stuffing on to the hessian, and between the lines of bridles, until you have a smooth surface. Add a cover of scrim, cut generously, and sew in through-stuffing ties with a curved needle, taking care not to let your needle catch the fabric of the outside back. Lift the edge of the scrim all round, and tuck in best quality hair, sufficient to make a firm roll. You should have just enough room to tuck the scrim under the hair, to give a good estimate of when you have enough stuffing in place to complete the roll.

When you are ready, tack the scrim down all round the rebate. Now sew the hard edge, with a row of blind stitches, followed by two rows of top stitches. You will not be able to get your double-pointed needle into the

roll because the frame itself will cause an obstruction. Instead use a curved needle. If it is not sharp enough at both ends to sew blind stitches, sew top stitches only.

Follow with a second stuffing, of best quality hair. Add more bridles if the through-stuffing ties are too tight. Then add wadding, and the customary calico cover. Finally, fit the top cover, again ensuring that any pattern or grain is exactly vertical.

By this stage you will appreciate the reason for care, and skill, and a little experience. Installing the upholstery has taken a separate circle of tacks for the outside back cover, hessian, scrim, calico and inside back cover, all in the same line in the same thin rebate. It would be easy to force a split in the wood by careless handling.

Because there is a roll edge sewn in the back, there should now be a pronounced valley between the upholstery and the frame, showing a row of tacks and the raw edge of the top cover material. Finish this edge with braid or gimp. It should be possible to glue it on, carefully avoiding spillage. But it may be difficult to sew it in place in this inaccessible location. Fortunately, because the trim is out of the way and protected by the hard edge and the frame, it does not get the buffetting that can tear

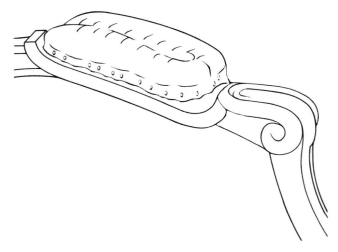

4.59 **Build up the padded arms on show-wood chairs with a hard edge. The sequence is the same as on any other upholstered surface in miniature.**

braid off more exposed parts of chairs. The extra security of sewing the braid or gimp in place is therefore not so important.

BUILDING ARMS ON A SHOW-WOOD CHAIR

The small padded arms on Victorian and French-style chairs [4.59] do not require any unfamiliar techniques, but they can be difficult to match to each other. Because they are small, any irregularities show up all too clearly.

The upholstery process is similar to that on the stuffed-over seat, so start by chiselling a small bevel round the edge of the top surface, on which to tack the scrim.

Put a couple of bridles along the top of the arm, held in place with tacks, and tuck some stuffing under them. Cut a cover of scrim 100 mm over length and 75 mm over width to allow for handling, and for the extra surface of a rolled edge.

Underturn the scrim, and adjust the scrim and stuffing to give a firm roll about 20 mm thick when finished. Tack it all round into the bevelled edge.

To sew the roll you will probably have to use a medium size curved needle. The wood of the arms at the ends of the pad will prevent you using the double-ended needle.

Put in one row of blind stitches, and a row of top stitches, and you should produce a firm dished platform overhanging the show-wood by a small margin all round. Trim off the excess scrim.

Add a layer of top stuffing and wadding to give a slightly crowned finish, and cover it with calico, tacked down round the rebate where the pad area meets the show-wood of the frame. Most professional upholsterers prefer to complete these small items up to calico covering stage early in the process. Installing the cover is virtually the same as installing the calico. If there is a pattern, make sure it runs accurately front to back, and cut both arm covers at the same time to be sure of a perfect pattern match. Finish by trimming with gimp, close-nailing, or piping according to the rest of the chair.

VICTORIAN BALLOON BACK CHAIR

Chairs of this type, variously called Victorian balloon

4.60 A deep-buttoned chaise-longue with sprung seat will call for a full range of skills from the most advanced upholsterer.

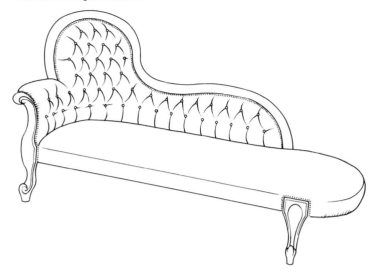

back lady's or gentleman's chairs, spoonback chairs, or nursing chairs, may well present the most interesting challenge to your upholstery skills, drawing together most of the techniques learned on simpler articles. But they must be done correctly. Like medallion and spoonback upright chairs, often sold as antiques, the commercial product is rarely made to the best standards, and consists in many cases of a few layers of padding and foam, stapled into place. The home upholsterer with plenty of time and skill can match the highest grades of hand-crafted quality from the periods when these styles originated.

As in the upright chair, the main difference from factory products lies in the treatment of the edge of the upholstery, where it meets the frame on the inside back.

The basic steps for this type of chair are: sprung seat with hard edge; padded back with hard edge all round as on the medallion chair, produced from a scrim 'tube' as on the winged chair; installation of a 'lumbar swell';

deep buttoning, and trim; possibly padded arms.

Work on the seat as on any sprung seat with a hard edge. It may be stuffed-over at the sides, and have show-wood left at the front. On larger 'gentleman's' chairs the seat cover will require cutting round wooden arm uprights at the front. Work on the seat is, however, best left to last; the back is the interesting part. The frame will probably have an upright at the centre of the back. If so, tack three or four horizontal strands of webbing across the inside back, tacking to the centre upright at the same time to preserve the curve. Add a layer of hessian, pulled tight and tacked into the rebate all round. You will have to cut notches out of the overturn in the hessian to accommodate all the curves of this type of back.

Now recall the upholstery procedure for the wing of an arm chair. It involved sewing a strip of scrim on to the hessian to form a roll edge. This chair back is similar. Cut a strip of hessian 180 mm to 200 mm wide, long enough to fit right round the curves of the chair back.

Draw a line accurately 75 mm in from the rebate all round, with either tailor's fine chalk or a soft pencil.

Sew a row of bridles into the hessian all round the back, between the rebate and the line on the hessian. Sew the scrim, with a 13 mm underturn for strength, to the chalk line all round the chair. Gather it into pleats as it goes round the curves at the top, and tack it to the bottom tacking rail where it meets the bottom at each side.

Pick stuffing hair under the bridles, and then arrange the scrim to form the 'tube'. Continue to fill it, and tack it down temporarily round the rebate. Regulate the hair to produce the size, shape, and firmness of stuffing that you require.

Here, more than ever before, you will have to use your own judgement to determine how much stuffing to put into this part of the chair. But if you have worked progressively towards this job, you should have no particular difficulty. The key is to have a clear picture in your mind of what you are aiming for.

The idea is to build up, by stitching, a hard roll standing out about 50 mm proud of the rebate, so that the upholstery clears the frame by a generous margin. Also, the edge will be at right angles to the frame, leaving a clear, well defined channel all round the upholstery. To work in this channel you will of course need to use your fine cabriole hammer, and you will have to take great care not to damage the show-wood of the frame.

Also, you will have some difficulty in sewing the blind and top stitches that make the roll, because of the problems of access. A straight needle will be useless; a curved needle will do the job, but they are not easy to obtain with both ends pointed, which you will need for the blind stitching. You could take one and put a sharp end on it yourself for this particular operation. Otherwise, try penetrating the stuffing and scrim with the threaded end of the needle as it is. You may manage it.

Now another complication – the 'lumbar swell'. This covers the area of the back from the arm tops to the seat, in a gentle curve. It is formed from the roll edge stitched into the 'tube' but will have to stand away from the frame by several inches more than the rest of the scroll, to give the kind of shape you are looking for in a chair of this quality and style.

So, put much more hair in the roll from the arm tops to the bottom rail. Regulate it, and insert an extra row of blind stitches and an extra row of top stitches to form a really pronounced hard edge, as much as five or six inches high.

In the centre of the lumbar swell, sew a panel of scrim across the hessian, between the two rolls. Fill it with a well-shaped first stuffing, and tack the scrim to the bottom rail. Then put in a pattern of through-stuffing ties to prevent the stuffing falling.

You should now have the base for a well-shaped Victorian chair. And you can go on to finish the back with deep-buttoning.

The technique for deep-buttoning is standard except for two points. In the centre of the back is a vertical rail.

Run the twines on each side of it, and do not bother with a toggle.

The other special consideration is to decide what pattern of buttons would suit the chair and what direction to arrange the pleats between the outer buttons and the frame.

Finish all the edges with matching gimp or close-nailing.

BUILDING CUSHIONS

Although you will have fixed the general design of your cushions even before you began upholstering a chair, so that you can build your seat accordingly, you should leave making the cushions until last. Then you can make them an exact fit to the chair, with the pattern exactly corresponding with the chair cover.

However, keep your eye on the production of the cushion as you work on the rest of the chair. When you come to cutting the covers, check that the area of cover-

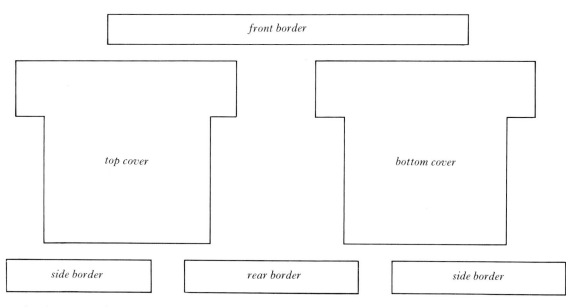

4.61   Parts for the cover of a typical T-shaped cushion.

ing fabric earmarked for the cushion will make a good cushion cover, on the top at least. Remember also that the cover will last longer if you can turn it over periodically, so it is useful to have the bottom matching, as well as the top. If neither of these looks possible, check the outside back and outside arms. It may be that you can get a better match by interchanging one of these with the cushion cover. And as a last resort, if the pattern arranged for the top cushion panel makes a thoroughly bad match with the rest of the chair, try switching the outside back to the cushion top, and using a different – but compatible – fabric on the outside back. Most chairs are seen more from the front than from the back.

FILLING

The details of how you treat the cushion depends to a great extent on your choice of filling. All good cushions should have an inner and an outer case. The case will be made of down-proof ticking for a down filling; hair-proof ticking for hair filling; ticking of any kind, or calico, for kapok; and you can dispense with an inner casing if you are filling with a synthetic cotton.

When planning the cushion take account of the problem of venting. Casings made in close-weave materials can make a loud noise when somebody sits on them, or can be uncomfortably hard, or both. Install a breather-vent to let the air out freely. Small vents are available for sewing into the material. Alternatively, include a panel of some open-weave material like denim, in an unobtrusive part of the cushion such as the rear border.

The best way to cut the cover is to make a paper template of the chair seat. Lay a piece of brown paper (not newspaper – the ink is liable to rub off on to your cover) on the seat itself. Hold a soft pencil or blue crayon vertically against the sides and back, and scribe a mark along the line where the sides and back join the seat. If the sides and back have been upholstered correctly, they should be vertical at these points, to give support to the cushion.

At the front of the chair, lay a heavy book on the seat so that it lines up with the front edge, and fold the paper up against the edge of the book. Rub the pencil or chalk along the angle to indicate the front of the cushion on the template. It will leave a rough line. Smooth out the line, and push skewers through it to show on the top side of the template. Join up the holes, and cut round the line with a 50 mm margin to complete the template.

Fold the template down the middle. The two sides should match. If they do not (and this is more often the case than not) then trim one or mark the other for over-cutting, to achieve a compromise. If the disparity is too great, you may not be able to eliminate it, and you will have to accept that the cushion will fit only one way up.

When you are ready to cut the top and bottom of the cushion cover, lay the template on the fabric. Make sure it is square to the weave and the pattern, and that the design falls just where you want it. Mark round the template, allowing 20 mm excess all round for sewing. Lay the top cover over the other fabric wrong side to wrong side, and use it as a template to cut the bottom panel.

Finally cut the borders of the cover. The width should be equal to the depth of cushion you require. The length is the distance round the cushion, cut in three pieces, to be joined at the sides and back. Also make sure you have enough piping made up to go round the top and bottom of the cushion.

First sew the piping to the top and bottom covers all round, using a sewing machine. Cut a notch into the corners so that the piping can turn the corner cleanly. Where the piping joins, take the material from the machine, and peel back the piping cover. Cut the cord to form a butt joint end to end. Underturn one end of the fabric, slot the other under it, and sew a neat obliquely angled join as flat as possible.

Take up the pieces for the border, and check to make sure that any design falls correctly in the centre of the front border, and that it corresponds as well as possible with the design on the top cushion panel. Sew the border pieces end to end. There should not be a seam on the front of the cushion.

Before you sew the border to the top and bottom, plan to incorporate the opening through which you will insert the filling when the cover is completed. The traditional method is to close the cover finally with a slip stitch. Modern practice is to close it with a zip. The zip gives access to the filling at a later date for any adjustments.

It is not intended to let you take out the filling to wash the cover. Washing or cleaning the cover of the cushion cover is not advisable. It will never again match the rest of the chair cover, which you cannot wash.

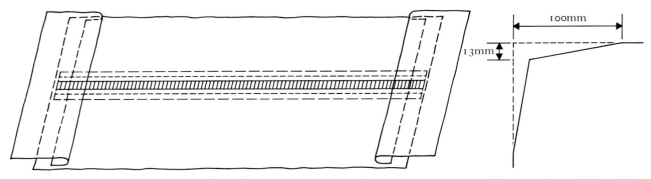

4.62a Sew the zip into separate half widths of the border. Then sew the zipped section into the rest of the border.

b. Trim the corners to avoid long points which might overhang the seat.

If you want to close the cushion with a zip, buy one specially made for upholstery. Zips made for dressmaking or men's suits are not strong enough. Arrange the zip to fit in the centre of the rear border.

Cut the panel into two lengthways to accommodate the zip, and sew one part of the zip to each side. Sew the ends to the border.

Before you start assembling the cover, trim it at the corners. Cut a small triangle off each side of each corner, 100 mm × 13 mm. This allows for the 'crown' of the cushion, and gives the corners a neatly rounded look. If this trim were not made, the cushions would develop a slightly acute angle at the corners and form a weak point [**4.62**].

Sew the border to the top cover. Align the pattern exactly, and pin the seam allowance on each part together. Start sewing at the centre, and sew towards each corner, then along the sides. Go all round the top cover.

The difficulty starts when you come to the bottom cover. If it is not applied accurately, the top panel and bottom panel will not correspond, and the entire cushion will warp and wrinkle. Start by marking the centre of the bottom panel front edge with a pin or a small notch. On fabric covers, you can follow a thread across the border fabric to give you the exact centre of that. Pin the two centres together for sewing.

On the non-fabric material, such as hide or leather-cloth, there will be no thread to follow. Instead, fold the border material in half lengthwise, and align the two edges. Mark the bottom centre to correspond with the top centre, and unfold the border. Do the same at the corners to make sure they align accurately, following a thread on fabric or folding it edge to edge on other materials. Continue sewing the bottom cover to the border, until you have just enough left to fit the filling into the casing comfortably.

On a down-filled or kapok-filled cushion, leave a gap of about ten inches to be sewn after filling. If you are inserting a slab of foam rubber, sew it only a couple of inches beyond the front corners, leaving almost three complete sides open to work the cover on to the foam. Of course on a cover with a zip, there will be no opening for later sewing.

To stop the ends of all the flanges of these seams from fraying, sew them all round with one or two lines of small stitches or with a zig-zag stitch if your machine can produce one.

THE INNER CASING

Most types of filling require an inner casing for the cushion, to stop the filling penetrating the cover. Down-

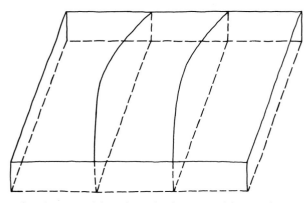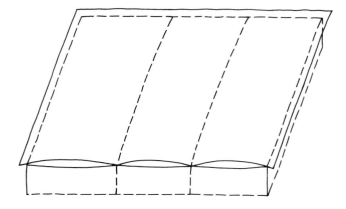

**4.63   Sew partitions into the inner cushion casing,
then sew on the top cover, leaving gaps for the filling.**

filling can penetrate ordinary material, and needs a specially coated ticking. Do not crease down-proof ticking or the coating may be broken and the filling may penetrate.

Make the inner casing 25 mm bigger than the outer cover, in its length and width. This will make it fill the cushion completely, and help to preserve a good firm shape.

Large cushions, and cushions for the back of a seat (generally called pillows) should have partitions built into them to prevent the filling moving backwards or downwards.

Cut out the top and bottom, and the border, of the inner casings, using the same template as for the cover, but with the 25 mm overlap.

Measure and cut the partitions. They should be between 150 mm and 225 mm apart, so the length of the cushion will determine how many you have. They are shaped to preserve the fullness of the cushion, rising to a crown. Make them the same height as the border at the ends, rising to twice the height of the border 150 mm in from the cushion sides. The plan for cushions and their partitions is illustrated in [**4.63**].

Sew the border to one cover all round. You can leave the seam allowance on the inside. Do not attempt to turn a down-proof ticking casing inside out or you will crack the coating. Sew in the partitions along the bottom of the 'box' you have formed, and at the sides. Sew the top to the partitions and to the border, except along one side of the cushion. This will leave an opening for filling each compartment.

Start filling the cushion. If you are lucky enough to have a top quality filling begin taking it up carefully by the handful and push one handful into the back corner of each partition, working in rotation to keep them balanced. When the cushion is almost full, add more to the centre pocket or pockets because they are cut fuller than the end ones.

Be extremely careful in handling the filling material. Not only is it too expensive to waste, but any form of feather filling is easily blown about a room and is extremely difficult to clean up.

Finally, sew the gaps in the ticking to close the pockets completely. Give the casing a good pummeling with your fists to distribute the feathers evenly.

Now all you have to do is insert the filled inner casing into the outer cover. The seams of the inner cushion will remain on the outside, but not cause any problems. You can close the outer cover, either by drawing the zip, or sewing up the gap you have left with a slip stitch close up against the piping.

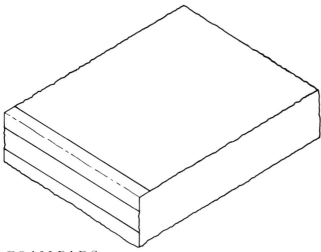

FOAM PADS

There is less objection to using foam rubber as the filling for a cushion to using it in the upholstery of the chair itself.

Any deterioration it might suffer will matter less. It is a simple operation to unfasten the cover of a cushion and insert a new piece after a few years, whereas it would be highly inconvenient to have to re-upholster the chair itself.

Foam, generally a form of polyurethane foam, can be hard to sit on and flat to look at when used by itself. It is also liable to compress in use and not return to its original shape. The answer is to use a pad of wadding or linter's felt on the top of the cushion, or on both sides if the cushion is intended to be reversible.

There are no strict rules for producing polyfoam and foam rubber upholstery. The techniques are too new for any rigid rules to have been established, and you can take advantage of the ample opportunities to work out your own system and practices.

If you are using wadding round the foam, you might find it useful to encase the wadding in a pocket of calico, to reproduce the feeling of traditional upholstery on the other areas of the chair. You should sew the calico-encased pad to the polyfoam, to prevent it from moving in use.

First prepare the foam for sewing, or the stitches will pull right through it. Cut strips of calico about three inches wide, to fit along the edges of the polyfoam block. Apply an impact adhesive to both the calico and the foam, and when the adhesive is dry, smooth the calico firmly into the foam. You can then sew the calico pad to the calico edge on the foam.

Use this technique when fitting the cover to a foam pad. It helps to preserve the shape of the cushion if the cover is not able to slide on the foam. A cover should turn inside out for fitting, like a sock. Before you roll it on, sew the front edge to a calico strip along the front edge of the pad, using small stitches close to the piping [**4.64**]. Adjust the flanges of the piping seams to lie vertically down the sides of the foam, rather than horizontally along the faces, to encourage the piping to stand up sharp.

You can also adjust the shape of a polyfoam pad. It is sold in various thicknesses, and you can build up exactly the thickness you want by bonding two or more slabs together. You can also cut the foam to shape, using a light saw with short rapid strokes. A bread saw works well.

You can produce rounded edges, by drawing together

the two outer edges of a square shaped slab, and bonding them with an impact adhesive.

When you have completed the foam filling, with the calico strips glued to it, the calico-encased pad sewn to that, and the front border of the cover also sewn to the calico strip, roll on the cover and zip up or sew the opening.

Your upholstered article is then finished.

CANE COVERED SEATS

Caning may look like one of the most impenetrable mysteries in all restoration work, but is in fact relatively simple. Apart from the cane itself, you will need hardly any special materials or tools.

Make up half a dozen small tapered pegs, known as 'doublers', to hold the cane in the holes while you work. Two-inch lengths of thin dowel, golf tees, or fibre wall plugs do this job well.

First carry out all the necessary structural repairs to your chair. Cut away all the old cane, and clear out the caning holes with a bradawl or drill bit of the same diameter as the holes. Drill out any stubborn pegs completely.

Stain and polish the chair to the required finish. Caning is the last operation on a chair.

There are several complicated patterns that might interest advanced chair caners with unusually shaped chair frames, but the traditional standard pattern known as the seven-step or seven-stage pattern will suit most chairs.

To seat the average chair, you will need about two ounces of cane. The cane used in seating is a split strand with one hard glossy surface, which comes in six sizes. The finest is No 1, and is used only on delicate small chairs. For the average household chair, try to obtain approximately equal supplies of Nos 2 and 4. If you are caning only one or two chairs, this might mean buying a lot of surplus cane, so compromise with one gauge only, No. 3.

As you work, soften the cane by running it quickly through a bowl of hot water, or moisten your finger and rub it along the flat underside of the cane only. Soaking the cane in hot water will discolour it.

Stage 1. The first strand of cane runs from front to back. You can start at a corner and work directly across the seat, or at the centre and work outwards. Starting at the centre helps if the chair is not exactly rectangular. When you reach the sides you can thread the cane into any hole that keeps the strands parallel. Measure to establish the centre at the back and front, and start your first strand either at the centre hole, or if there is no centre hole, then at the hole immediately to the left of centre. If you are working directly across the seat, start at the hole nearest to the corner that will allow the cane to lie clear of the frame.

Thread one end of the length of cane down through the hole to protrude by about four inches. Put in a doubler to peg that end of the cane in place, then bring the other end across the seat to the corresponding hole.

Thread it down through that hole, along to the next hole, back up through the frame, and across the seat again.

As you pass the cane through the holes and along the frame, turn it to make sure that the glossy surface remains on top throughout. Do not twist the cane.

Peg the cane where it comes up through each hole, to hold the strands in place without stretching or slackening. Except where you need to peg the end of a length, move the pegs along as you go, holding the cane in the most recently threaded hole.

Make the cane for this stage tense but not over-taut. The later stages will pull it tighter.

When you come to the end of a length of cane, start the new length beneath the frame. Secure it by looping it twice round the preceding strand at a point where it lies firmly stretched between two holes. The tension in the loop will be enough to hold the new length in place [**4.65**].

Continue working the cane back and forth along the seat until the frame is covered [**4.66**].

Stage 2 is a similar process. Work a single strand across the chair from side to side, so that the cane lies over the strands laid in stage 1.

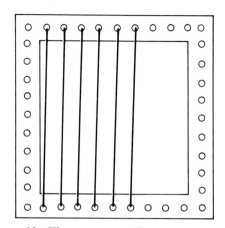

4.65 A neat taut twist will hold two lengths of cane firmly together on the underside of the frame.

4.66 The sequence of seven strands of cane across the frame produces an attractive and reliable seat.

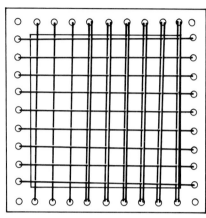

4.67

Stage 3 is also straightforward. Go back to the same holes as in stage 1, and work a second strand from front to back. These should lie over the strands in stage 2, and neatly to the sides of those in stage 1. Arrange your starting point so that the cane underneath the frame occupies the spaces left vacant in stage 1 [**4.67**].

Stage 4 is the first stage that involves any 'weaving'. The strands for this will run from side to side, and viewed from above should lie neatly to the side of those in stage 2. But they must run under all the strands in stage 1, and over all the strands in stage 3. They will lie in opposition to the strands next to them, and thereby produce a taut woven effect [**4.68**].

You can work the cane for stage 4 through the pattern with your fingers, but it is much simpler if you have a tool of some kind. The right tool for the job is a 'spoon bodkin'. Thread it through the work to pick up about four of the strands under which the 'weaver' will pass. Then grip the end of the cane in the spoon with your thumb, and pull it through. If the proper tool is not available, make a substitute with a length of wire bent into a hook at the end.

Stage 5 is the first of the diagonal strands. It should be made with the thicker of your two gauges.

Start at the rear left hand corner of the seat, and thread the cane through the corner hole. Peg it there. You may find that these corner holes are 'blind' and do not go right through the frame. If so, double the end of the cane over before inserting it into the hole, and make up a wooden peg big enough to jam the cane in. Later, trim off the peg flush with the frame.

Start weaving the free end of the cane diagonally across the chair, passing it under the vertical pairs of strands, and over the horizontal pairs. Pass the end down the hole where it meets the frame on the opposite side. On a square chair it will be the corner hole.

You will find that you have to use the corner holes for two adjacent strands. Continue working across the chair until you have completed that set of diagonals [**4.69**].

Stage 6 consists of the opposite set of diagonals. Start at the rear right hand corner hole, and thread the cane under the horizontals and over the verticals. You will

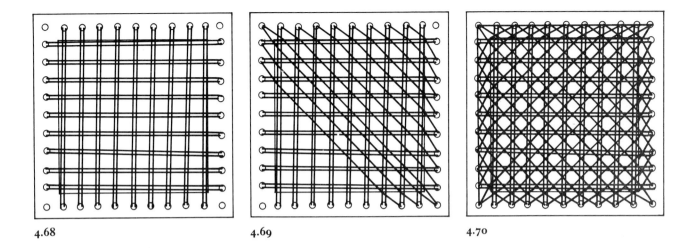

4.68   4.69   4.70

also be going under and over the preceding set of diagonal strands. Keep checking the pattern as you go. If it has gone wrong, the only way to correct it is to unweave all the incorrectly placed strands [**4.70**].

The pattern should now form a firm even structure, held in place by several pegs. Turn the chair over and secure all the ends, if you did not do so during the earlier stages. To do this, first trim the end of each strand to a point with a sharp knife. Moisten the cane to make it flexible, then loop it two or three times under a secure part of the cane. The bodkin or wire will also help with this awkward job. Finally hammer the twist flat, and trim the ends off close. Remove the pegs.

Stage 7 consists of laying a length of cane to form a beading that will cover the holes. It is not essential, but it gives the chair a neatly finished appearance.

If you are prepared to buy another gauge of cane, the correct type is No 6 beading cane. You will then need some No 2 to 'couch' it with. If the holes are very narrow or close together, or if you wish to economise, use No 4 cane for both parts of the beading operation.

Trim the beading cane to a point, and insert it into a corner hole. Bend it over and lay it along the line of holes in the frame. Trim some of the thinner cane to a point, and pass it down through the frame one hole along from the corner. Secure it on the underside of the frame. Pass the other end over the beading cane, and back down through the same hole.

Take the thinner cane along the underside of the frame to the next hole. Pass it up through the frame, over the beading cane, and down through the same hole. Stop at the hole next to the corner hole. Thread the beading cane itself down through the corner hole, and secure it under the frame.

Pass another length of beading cane down through that same corner hole, and bend it along the next side of the chair. Secure the end of the thinner cane below the second hole, and pass it over the beading cane and back down through the hole.

Continue working, beading each side of the frame separately. Finally turn over the frame, and check that all the ends are neatly trimmed and hammered flat.

MATERIALS AND SUPPLIES

Finding a good source of supply for the materials used in furniture restoration is one of the first problems that the amateur restorer must solve. Standard d-i-y stores stock only a limited range of polishes: most timber merchants stock only softwoods: old-fashioned corner-shop ironmongers, where the men who made the furniture that is now antique bought their supplies, have all but disappeared. Even woodworking and hobbyist shops are now comparatively rare and locating reliable supplies of these materials requires ingenuity.

WOOD

The hardwoods used in cabinet making are expensive, and only a limited number of specialist timber merchants now stock them. To find a wood supplier in your area may need a little research in the Yellow Pages and a few telephone calls.

The magazine *Woodworker*, and other craft and hobby magazines, might carry the name of a conveniently placed supplier in their small-ad columns.

In time, you will be able to solve the problem by building up your own stocks. It is vital, of course, never to throw away any hardwood offcut, however small, nor any scrap of veneer. Store it, and one day it will almost certainly prove just the right size and type for some repair.

Personal contact is always useful, and if you should encounter other amateur restorers who have built up similar collections of offcuts, you can arrange a swopping system from each other's stock.

In recent years, one of the best sources has proved to be the auction rooms. While antique dealers have concentrated on bidding for small items in good condition that would appeal to the collector, the restoration enthusiast has been able to pick up quite cheaply big uninteresting articles like wardrobes and beds. The result has been a marvellous supply of seasoned mahogany, oak, beech walnut and other woods, and a few items have formed the basic stock for many a restorer's needs for several years.

Unfortunately, that supply has tended to dry up. The number of people collecting antiques has multiplied, and the supply of genuine antique items has dwindled, as much of the stock has gone abroad. Antique dealers have therefore had to widen their range, and items that were once bought for the value of their wood alone have become collectable.

At the same time more people have recognised the value of restoration work, and the number of customers competing for a diminishing supply of materials has risen. The results have been a reduction in the supply, and inflation in the cost. It is still worth bearing this source in mind, but it is no longer realistic to regard it as a major solution to the problem.

Today, the most reliable way of ensuring the supply of wood you need is to buy your own and build up a stock of offcuts.

SUNDRIES

For glues, polishes, glasspaper, metal fittings, and other sundries, a combination of local knowledge and ingenuity still provides the best leads.

Some parts of the country, London especially, are well covered by specialist suppliers. Elsewhere you may have to rely on your local d-i-y shop. But talk to the manager. He might, through his own trade contacts, be able to help you to get the materials you want. Most retailers are pleased to help an enthusiast.

Those who live in the right areas will find it useful and instructive to visit some of the suppliers on the following list. Most suppliers will send out catalogues, and will post ordered supplies to customers for the usual postage and packing charges.

The list is not exhaustive, and the amateur will soon be able to add his own contacts.

Upholstery materials are generally more easily obtained. Many towns now have shops dealing in the tacks, needles, trim, and stuffing that the upholsterer uses in his work, and many large department stores also stock these items. Readers who still have difficulty finding the tools should contact the tools suppliers listed.

Polish manufacturers

Gedge and Company
(Clerkenwell) Ltd,
88 John Street,
London EC1M 4EJ
01–253 6057/8

W S Jenkins & Co Ltd,
Jeco Works,
Tariff Road,
London N17 OEN
01–808 2336

Fiddes & Son,
Trade Street,
Cardiff

Henry Flack Ltd,
Borough Works,
Croydon Road,
Elmers End,
Beckenham,
Kent

John Myland Ltd,
80 Norwood High Street,
London SE27 9NW
01–670 9161

Rustins Limited,
Waterloo Road,
Cricklewood,
London NW2 7TX
01–450 4666

Leather table linings and skivers

J Crisp & Sons Ltd,
Crispin Works,
Hawley Street,
London NW1
01–485 8566

Victor Allen Leathers,
68 Goldstone Villas,
Hove,
Sussex
0273 733482

Messrs Woolnough Ltd,
23 Phipp Street,
London EC2
01–739 6603

Veneers, stringing, and banding

J Crispin & Sons,
92–90 Curtain Road,
London EC2A 3AA
01–739 4875

Art Veneer Co Ltd,
Industrial Estate,
Mildenhall,
Suffolk
IP28 7AY

Danum Venners Ltd,
243A Wheatley Lane,
Doncaster

Elliott Bros Veneers,
PO Box No 6,
Glossop,
Derbyshire

Leather and Hides

J Hewit & Son Ltd,
89 St John Street,
London EC1

Connolly Brothers (curriers) Ltd,
Chalton Street,
Euston Road,
London NW1 1JE
01–387 1661

Glue and gluepots

J Hewit & Sons Ltd,
89 St John Street,
London EC1
01–253 6082

Ed Gorton Ltd,
Paddington,
Warrington,
Cheshire

R Oldfield,
143 Cotefield Drive,
Leighton Buzzard,
South Bedfordshire
LU7 8DN
0525 373976

Brass fittings

J & D Beardmore & Co Ltd,
3–5 Percy Street,
Tottenham Court Road,
London W1
01–637 7041

J Shiner & Sons Ltd,
8 Windmill Street,
London W1P 1HF
01–636 0740

John Harwood & Company,
13 Elmwood Grove,
Bolton,
Lancs
0204 53089

Woodfit,
Whittle Low Mill,
Chorley,
Lancashire
PRG6 7HB
02–572 2478

Hardwoods (A small selection of suppliers)

C & S Agate,
Hardwood Suppliers,
Horsham,
Sussex

S J Atkins & Cripps Ltd,
Southmill,
95 London Road,
Bishop's Stortford,
Herts
CM23 3DU

Chantler & Anderson,
Winchills Mill,
Near Crewe,
Cheshire

Fitchett and Wollacott Ltd,
Popham Street,
Nottingham
NG1 7JE

Joseph Gardener (Hardwoods) Ltd,
Peel Road,
Bootle,
Liverpool
L20 4JZ

Moss & Co (Hammersmith) Ltd,
104 King Street,
London W6
01–748 8251

North Heigham Saw Mills,
Paddock Street,
Norwich
NOR 52K
0606 22978

Joseph Thompson & Co Ltd,
Hendon Lodge,
Sunderland,
Tyne and Wear
SR1 ZPA

Harry Venables Ltd,
Doxey Road,
Stafford
ST16 ZEN

W Mallinson & Sons,
130 Hackney Road,
London
E2 7QR
01–739 7654

Cane suppliers

Dryad Ltd,
Handicrafts Shop,
178 Kensington High Street,
London W8
01–937 5370

Smith & Co Ltd,
99 Walnut Tree Close,
Guildford,
Surrey
0483 33113

Brass and other metals suppliers

J Smith & Sons (Clerkenwell) Ltd,
50 St John's Square,
London EC1
01–253 1277

Frank Romany Ltd,
252 Camden High Street,
London NW1
01–387 2579

Mouldings

Winther Browne & Co Ltd,
119 Downhills Way,
London N22
01–889 0971

Highfield Tiomer & Mouldings Ltd,
Hall Road,
Heybridge,
Maldon, Essex

General Woodwork Supplies Ltd,
76 Stoke Newington High Street,
London N16
01–254 4543

Specialist tools suppliers

Buck & Ryan Ltd,
101 Tottenham Court Road,
London W1
01–636 7475

C D Monninger Ltd,
Overbury Road,
London N15
01–800 5435

Parry & Sons (Tools) Ltd,
329 Old Street,
London EC1
01–739 9422

Cecil W Tyzack Ltd,
79 Kingsland Road,
London E2
01–739 2630

S Tysack & Son Ltd,
341 Old Street,
London EC1
01–739 8301

Buck & Hickman Ltd,
Bank House,
100 Queen Street,
Sheffield S7 2DW

Robert Sorby & Sons Ltd,
817 Chesterfield Road,
Sheffield S8 0SR